# The Neighborhood in the Internet

Today, "community" seems to be everywhere. At home, at work, and online, the vague but comforting idea of the community pervades every area of life. But have we lost the ability truly to understand what it means? *The Neighborhood in the Internet* investigates social and civic effects of community networks on local community and how community network designs are appropriated and extended by community members.

Carroll uses his conceptual model of "community" to re-examine the Blacksburg Electronic Village – the first Web-based community network – applying it to attempts to sustain and enrich contemporary communities through information technology. The book provides an analysis of the role of community in contemporary paradigms for work and other activity mediated by the Internet. It brings to the fore a series of design experiments investigating new approaches to community networking and addresses the future trajectory and importance of community networks.

This book will be of interest to students of sociology, community psychology, human–computer interaction, information science, and computer-supported collaborative work.

**John M. Carroll** is Edward Frymoyer Professor of Information Sciences and Technology at the Pennsylvania State University. His research is in methods and theory in human–computer interaction, particularly as applied to networking tools for collaborative learning and problem-solving and to the design of interactive information systems. His books include *Rationale-Based Software Engineering* (Springer, 2008, with J. Burge, R. McCall and I. Mistrik) and *Learning in Communities* (Springer, 2009).

# Routledge Advances in Sociology

# The Neighborhood in the Internet

Design research projects in community informatics

**John M. Carroll**

LONDON AND NEW YORK

First published 2012
by Routledge
2 Park Square, Milton Park, Abingdon, Oxon OX14 4RN

Simultaneously published in the USA and Canada
by Routledge
711 Third Avenue, New York, NY 10017

*Routledge is an imprint of the Taylor & Francis Group, an informa business*

First issued in paperback 2014

*British Library Cataloguing in Publication Data*
A catalogue record for this book is available from the British Library

*Library of Congress Cataloging in Publication Data*
Carroll, John M. (John Millar), 1950–
The Neighborhood in the internet: design research projects in community
informatics / John M. Carroll.
p. cm.—(Routledge advances in sociology ; 59)
Includes bibliographical references and index.
1. Community life—Technological innovations. 2. Computer networks—Social
aspects. 3. Blacksburg Electronic Village. 4. Electronic villages (Computer
networks) 5. Information society. I. Title.
HM761.C37 2011
004.67—dc23
2011037037

ISBN 978-0-415-78308-8 (hbk)
ISBN 978-1-138-02005-4 (pbk)
ISBN 978-0-203-09357-3 (ebk)

Typeset in Times New Roman
by Book Now Ltd, London

# Contents

# Illustrations

**Boxes**

# Preface and acknowledgments

I moved to Blacksburg, Virginia, a university town in the southern Appalachian Mountains, in January 1994, as head of the Computer Science Department at Virginia Tech (aka Virginia Polytechnic Institute and State University) and as a professor in computer science, education, and psychology. For more than two decades prior to that move, I had lived in the New York City metropolitan area – four years in upper Manhattan as a graduate student at Columbia University, and eighteen years in Westchester County as a scientist in IBM's Thomas J. Watson Research Center. At IBM, I worked in a new area of computer science that eventually became known as human–computer interaction (HCI). I investigated the professional work practices of software designers and other computing professionals in the 1970s. As computing expanded outwards toward office workers and other non-computing professionals, my research shifted toward the difficult processes of learning and appropriation that new users faced in the 1980s.

This was a wonderful time to be a young scientist in HCI at IBM. Everything in computing and computer science was changing at once. I was drinking from a fire hose of research opportunities. I developed the *minimalist information model* to address the paradox that system documentation and user instructional materials provided huge volumes of information that did not effectively address the actual concerns of users (Carroll 1990). I developed *scenario-based design* showing how systems, applications, and services could be created from stories about how people wanted to use them (Carroll 1995). I developed an approach to integrating disparate sources of science and theory in HCI through design rationales (Carroll 2000). But all of my research work was focused on computer-based systems for work activity, primarily software development work and office work.

When I arrived in Blacksburg, the town and the campus were abuzz with excitement about the Blacksburg Electronic Village (BEV) project. The concept for the BEV was to use the emerging World-Wide Web platform to create a new sort of community network, an open-ended set of resources and services for people considered more broadly than merely as workers. The BEV was to be for parents, children, and elders coordinating family, extended family, and community life. It was to facilitate participation in civic life, to include more voices in the discussion of local issues. It was to help teachers teach. It was to help community groups be more visible and serve the community better. It was to help a wider range of people tell a wider range of stories about Blacksburg and southwestern Virginia. It was to better integrate the town, the local schools, the university, and other institutions. It was to engage the whole community in planning, learning, and innovating.

I could not *not* have been drawn into the BEV. My work with information technology and people at IBM had vividly taught me that computer-based systems are never the panacea they often seem at first, but that it is possible to make progress in designing and engineering those systems if one stays close to the users and listens carefully. As a new department head in computer science, I felt it was a strategic opportunity for the department and for the discipline to dive into this project, to investigate, to discover, and help to define a new arena for computer systems, services, and applications (Carroll 2001). Finally, the BEV appealed to me as a new direction in my own research. Community networking is a kind of computer science research, and a kind of HCI that I could not have pursued as an IBM scientist. I wanted to challenge myself with new kinds of possibilities and problems.

I agreed to serve as chair of the BEV Research Advisory Group, to help stimulate and coordinate Virginia Tech faculty initiatives in the BEV. However, a more important role, to me, was as a participant and observer. As for many of my neighbors, the BEV project was an opportunity for me to learn and to try things out. I am fortunate also to be able to collect and make sense of my reminiscences as part of my professional work.

In early spring of 1994, I received a telephone call from a local man who owned a gas station. He had heard that someone had made a complaint about him "in the BEV" and wanted to know how he could see it and answer it. He had a PC, but not an Internet connection. Calling me made some sense from the standpoint of telephone book listings; there was a listing for "Department Head, Computer Science." But the man clearly did not know how useless academic administrators are in solving real problems. In talking to him, I was impressed at how little he knew about the Internet or the BEV, but also how constructive he was about what must have been a frustrating and upsetting circumstance. He was not complaining to me about the BEV; he wanted to better understand what it was, to join in, and to participate. It struck me that there was a lot to do to make the BEV work, but that, with people like this to work with, a lot was possible.

In this book I have attempted to integrate across a series of projects and to convey the main flow of ideas, events, and outcomes. I have tried to focus on higher-level themes, lessons, and contributions, rather than on the technical details of the projects. Each of the individual efforts described here has also been more extensively reported in one or more research papers. Even so, I have had to omit several important initiatives that would have made the book too long. A sequel is planned.

I am grateful to many colleagues and neighbors for drawing me into research interests concerning the Blacksburg Electronic Village and for helping to define and carry out the projects described in this book. Mary Beth Rosson, my wife and universal research collaborator, was a partner in all of this work. She led the CommunitySims and Web Storybase projects, described in chapter 6. Philip Isenhour was the primary software architect behind the Virtual School, MOOsburg 2, CORK (Content Object Replication Kit) and BRIDGE (Basic Resources for Integrated Distributed Group Environments), described in chapters 5 and 7.

My version of the BEV project, in chapter 3, owes much to interactions with Andrew Cohill, Andrea Kavanaugh, Mary Beth Rosson, and Murali Venkatesh, as well as with Jongwon Park, Jock Schorger, and Carmen Sears, around their excellent and provocative Virginia Tech thesis and dissertation projects. I am also grateful to members of the BEV staff who helped in many ways, especially Cortney Martin and Luke Ward. The large empirical project described in chapter 4 was initially planned with Mary Beth Rosson. Andrea Kavanaugh and Jennifer Pretti played enormous parts in implementing that project. Anne Bishop and Robert Kraut served as provocative and really helpful outside advisors. I am grateful to all the other members of the project team, including Dan Dunlap, Philip Isenhour, Debbie Denise Reese, Wendy Schafer-Colvin, Jason Snook, and Lucinda Willis.

The participatory design effort described in chapter 5 and subsequently was initially developed with Stuart Laughton in his Virginia Tech PhD project. Our participatory concepts and methods were developed further and refined through a long-term collaboration with Montgomery County Public Schools; George Chin, through his PhD project, was a major contributor to this. I am grateful to the members of the LiNC (Learning in a Networked Community) project team: Marc Abrams, Larry Arrington, Kathy Bunn, John Burton, Laura Byrd, Peggy Davie, Dan Dunlap, Jim Eales, Mark Freeman, Craig Ganoe, Alison Goforth, Jürgen Koenemann, Shannon Gibson, Philip Isenhour, Stuart Laughton, Suzan Mauney, Dennis Neale, Fred Rencsok, Mary Beth Rosson, and Cliff Shaffer.

Connie Anderson, Andrew Cohill, Gary Downey, Edward Fox, Keith Furr, John Kelso, Neill Kipp, Dave Messner, Joe Reiss, Mary Beth Rosson, K. William Schmidt, and the BEV Seniors contributed to the concept and development of Blacksburg Nostalgia and our related archiving and discussion projects, A Web Storybase and the BEV HistoryBase. Erik Dooley, Justin Gortner, Tracy Lewis, Mary Beth Rosson, Cheryl Seals, and Jason Snook contributed to organizing the software and workshops for the CommunitySims project. The MOOsburg project was initiated by Jonathan Kies, Brian Amento, Michael Mellott, and Craig Struble as a course project. I am grateful to Cara Cocking, Dan Dunlap, Umer Farooq, Craig Ganoe, Philip Isenhour, Dennis Neale, Con Rodi, Mary Beth Rosson, Wendy Schafer-Colvin, Craig Struble, and Lu Xiao for a wide variety of contributions over a number of years.

I am also grateful to my collaborators on community informatics projects subsequent to those described here. They have helped me to find additional meaning in this work even as we push onward with its continuations. I thank Honglu Du, Umer Farooq, Craig Ganoe, Blaine Hoffman, Michael Horning, Sue Kase, Roderick Lee, Cecelia Merkel, Harold Robinson, Mary Beth Rosson, Lu Xiao, Jamika Burge, Louise Campbell, and Yang Zhang.

My research on community networking has been supported by several agencies, foundations, and institutions. I am grateful to the Hitachi Foundation and the Knight Foundation and to Intel Corporation and Apple Computer. The US Department of Education's Eisenhower Program, administered through the State Council of Higher Education of Virginia, supported our technology support program for teachers. The US Office of Naval Research (ONR) supported the software technology research for MOOsburg and BRIDGE under award N00014-00-1-0549. The National Science Foundation supported a series of BEV-related projects, including development and study of the BEV HistoryBase, the Virtual School, and CommunitySims, investigation of activity awareness in MOOsburg, support for collaborative infrastructures for teachers and investigation of their knowledge-sharing practices, and study of sustainable learning and innovation practices in community nonprofit groups under the following awards: CDA-9424506, REC-9554206, EIA-0081102, IIS-0080864, IIS-0113264, REC-0106552, IIS-0342547. Several graduate students who contributed to these projects were supported by an NSF Graduate Research Traineeship program (DGE-9553458). My research on community informatics was supported from 1994 to 2003 by Virginia Tech and from 2003 by Pennsylvania State University.

Preparation of this book was supported by the Edward M. Frymoyer Chair endowment at Penn State, the Shaw Professorship in the Department of Information Systems at the National University of Singapore in the fall of 2009, and the Cátedra de Excelencia (Chair of Excellence) at the Department of Computer Science and the Institute of Culture and Technology at Universidad Carlos III de Madrid in Spain during the first eight months of 2010. I am grateful to Craig Ganoe, Philip Isenhour, Hao Jiang, and Mary Beth Rosson for comments on parts of the manuscript and help in refinding old screen shots.

Finally, I thank my wife and daughter, Mary Beth Rosson and Erin Marissa Carroll. I think it was essential to this work for me to be an engaged member of the Blacksburg community. Being a family in a friendly community, with a child moving through the local school system, was a most pleasant facet of this research.

# 1 Introduction

## Community lost, community regained

In contemporary times, the clamor of "community" is so pervasive that one can miss it. If two people attend the same university, they are said to be members of the same university community. If they work for the same corporation, they are members of the same corporate community. And if they do similar work, they are members of the same professional community. If they shop at the same store or use the same service, they are members of the same customer community. If they support the same sports team, they are fellow members of a community of supporters. If they visit the same website or participate in the same online activity, they are members of the same virtual community.

Communities can be both large and vague. In an American television advertisement a celebrity looks into the camera, and says "Public broadcasting is my source for intelligent connections to my community." The implication is that a community is comprised of everyone – or at least celebrities – who watches American public television. Social networking sites with hundreds of millions of members also call themselves communities, as in Facebook community. But why stop there? One hears references to the "Internet community," which would include everyone with any sort of computing device. And, indeed, these recent expansions of community are dwarfed by the Catholic Church characterizing social justice as "participation in the life of the human community" (US Catholic Bishops 1986).

Molière's character Monsieur Jourdain in *Le Bourgeois Gentilhomme* (The Middle-Class Gentleman) was surprised and proud to learn that he had been speaking prose all his life without even knowing it! Perhaps we should all be proud to know that we are embedded in a vast variety of communities, with all the warmth and intimacy that may imply. Better yet, all of us are members of the *same* communities – the Internet community, the human community. Molière was having fun at the expense of Monsieur Jourdain, whose pretensions were exposed by his ignorance of the word *prose*. But are we being Jourdains in labeling every possible grouping of humans as a community?

Perhaps this overuse tells us something about our times, about contemporary society, or even something fundamental about human beings. Perhaps it reflects an abiding aspiration to create and participate in rich, supportive, and intimate social systems connoted by *community*. Ironically, though, when terms are used too disparately and too frequently, they can be drained of meaning (Osgood 1980: 25). Thus, *community* has to some extent been rendered a vague euphemism. When a group is referred to as a community, one is invited to ascribe unspecified social goodness to that group – intimacy, sharing, warmth, autonomy, social support, democratic ideals, to name a few. Community is actually more interesting and more complicated than that.

## Searching for Camelot

Members of ancient hunter-gatherer communities benefited directly and obviously from strength in numbers: They were able to hunt more effectively, and they were able to attack and defend against competitors more effectively. Membership in ancestral communities was for the most part involuntary, exclusive, and comprehensive: A person was born into a band and grew to adulthood, parenthood, and old age within the band. All life activity was communal and inscribed in the group. But, as far as we know, Paleolithic band communities were relatively egalitarian, relying on consensus for group decisions. A hunter-gatherer group is a collection of individuals with more or less identical skills that carries everything it needs and draws resources directly from the immediate environment. Hence, leaving the group is just a matter of walking in a different direction – setting aside complications of being unable to successfully hunt large game alone, of being overwhelmed by a hostile group, and so forth. Trading relations originated in the middle Paleolithic, providing opportunities for dissatisfied members to encounter, and perhaps to realign with, other groups. But these would have been momentous, risky, and life-changing decisions (see Lee and Daly 2002).

Membership in Paleolithic band communities had many specific and weighty indirect consequences. For example, the continual and highly lethal inter-group violence among bands has been identified as a key factor in the emergence of altruistic behavior, a significant, if primitive, social glue. This connection was originally suggested by Darwin ([1871] 1983), and was recently supported by simulation modeling and ethnographic and historical data (Bowles 2009). Game theoretically, the altruist benefits, even at a mortal cost, by ensuring the survival of the group's shared genes. Other simulation modeling work suggests that groups in the upper Paleolithic were able socially to maintain and develop early modern skills, such as symbols, hunting and trapping tools (such as bows, nets, barbed harpoon points), musical instruments (such as bone pipes), and personal ornaments (such as threaded shells, ochre pigments, and tattoos) *only if* the group population exceeded thresholds (Henrich 2004). For relatively isolated bands, 50 – a large band – is a point of inflection for skill accumulation (Powell, Shennan, and Thomas 2009). Thus, maintaining what we might call group cohesion and critical mass – sheer population – was very likely critical to maintaining Paleolithic bands *at all*.

The advent of agriculture, and the Neolithic period, starting about 10,000 years ago, entailed diverse and fundamental changes in human society.

Agriculture and the domestication of animals vastly increased the predictable availability of basic resources. It transformed human communities by tying them to fixed places. This arrangement added many collective activities and roles to the fabric of human community. Members cooperated to plant, tend, and harvest crops, to care for children and elderly, to build and maintain permanent residential structures, and to develop infrastructure for drinking water, sanitation, irrigation, food storage, and domesticated animals.

Neolithic communities replaced the egalitarianism of Paleolithic communities with a variety of administrative and craft divisions of labor and political and economic hierarchies. Membership in such communities became more involuntary. Leaving a place-based agricultural community meant leaving one's fields, pens, house, and other infrastructure, as well as one's clients, coworkers, and collaborators, and perhaps having to move a family including many small children (fertility rates were at least three times higher among more sedentary Neolithic people than among Paleolithic people, who had to carry their young children everywhere). Moreover, increased interdependence and specialization of labor roles in agricultural communities made individuals less viable outside the community, and increased the potential cost to the community of losing members (see Miller *et al.* 2006).

The gross functional parameters of Paleolithic and Neolithic communities help to emphasize several points: Collective living was a key adaptation for personal and cultural survival and development. Thus, maintaining community critical mass has been an abiding priority concern. The salience of collective outcomes impelled identification with and commitment to the group – including the emergence of altruism. Nevertheless, living collectively has tended to make individuals increasingly specialized with respect to societal roles, and decreasingly autonomous in directing their own lives. It tended eventually to tie people, and their progeny, to a place. Paleolithic and Neolithic patterns of community interaction describe more than 99 percent of human history. They suggest why analysts, and people generally, continue to return to a somewhat romanticized picture of the band or the village as a touchstone of human organization.

For more than a century, discussions of community have started from the distinction between *Gemeinschaft* and *Gesellschaft* originally drawn by Tönnies ([1887] 2002) in the 1880s. Tönnies's concept of *Gemeinschaft* emphasized bonds of kinship, friendship, and place that were typical in rural European villages, the culmination of the Neolithic pattern. As described by Tönnies, bonds of *Gemeinschaft* derive from personal identification with the community, from seeing other members of the community as whole people (e.g., rather than with respect to specific instrumental goals) and from embracing shared emotions, traditions, and attachment to the "soil" – the common place in which community members lived and worked. *Gesellschaft* was pretty much just the polar opposite of *Gemeinschaft*: rational, individual, solitary, affectively neutral, non-identified with groups or places and with viewing other people instrumentally.

Tönnies conceived of *Gemeinschaft* and *Gesellschaft* as pure types anchoring the poles of a spectrum of possibilities against which actual social arrangements could be classified. Nevertheless, drawing typological distinctions by emphasizing extreme points can entrain caricature. Tönnies's distinction tends to romanticize *Gemeinschaft* as a picture of what human life was like in a better time, a sort of social Camelot. Conversely, his distinction tends to oversimplify *Gesellschaft* as a picture of what life is or is becoming in a dark time of isolation and foreboding. The romanticizing of rural village communities resonated both in Europe and in America. Early European sociological analyses, notably by Durkheim ([1897] 1952) and Weber ([1921] 1968), cast *society* as a historical development caused by capitalism, urbanization, and/or industrialization, supplanting the community of the medieval agricultural village. Tönnies's distinction provided a simple articulation for many concerns arising from the Industrial Revolution and continuing into contemporary times. *Gesellschaft* became the label for these concerns.

The ideal of *Gemeinschaft* preoccupied American sociology for 60 years, serving as its defining problem. American society had been famously studied by the French political scientist Tocqueville in the 1830s. Tocqueville's ([1835] 2003) study is still an archetype of revelatory empirical detail and sharp insights; for example, his analysis of the dilemmas and trajectories of slavery proved to be prophetic. His overall characterization of American society emphasized the self-assurance and grassroots pride, which he attributed to Jacksonian enfranchisement of non-landowner citizens (albeit limited to white males), balanced by collective activity and concern for others in every facet of public and private life, which he associated with exigencies of frontier life and with religious "habits of the heart." Tocqueville contrasted the energy of American society with the social stasis of still feudal Europe. He understood this contrast as deriving from Americans' relating to their society through strong and direct participation in local community life.

Many of the touchstone empirical and theoretical works in American sociology are community studies. For example, there is an extensive genre of community ethnographies throughout the first half of the twentieth century, the most well known of which is *Middletown* (Lynd and Lynd 1929), a detailed study of pre-Depression Muncie, Indiana. Community ethnographies provide a rich and grounded picture of small-town life, connecting the ideal of *Gemeinschaft* to contemporary realities of scale and social complexity (for example, Muncie had a population of nearly 40,000 in 1929 – hardly a medieval village). This picture also validated early *Gemeinschaft* skeptics, such as Simmel (in Wolff 1964), who had written about the "pettiness and prejudices" of small-town life. Interestingly, one of the characteristic themes of these community studies is the concern – of the investigators and, apparently, of their study participants – that the community-based fabric of American democracy was threatened and eroding. Thus Lynd and Lynd (1929) report that technologies like radio were isolating people and weakening personal ties – an interesting echo of the original *Gemeinschaft/Gesellschaft* concerns from 50 years before.

It was not until the late 1950s that community sociology was supplanted by studies and analyses of mass society as the paradigmatic issue of American sociology. In the decade after World War II, Americans had flocked to suburbs, emptying many rural communities and making suburban settings the modal social arrangement. And community studies themselves had come to focus increasingly on breakdown phenomena. For example, Coleman (1957) created a stage model of community conflict, detailing how isolated disagreements regarding specific issues can successively escalate into more general and more personal antagonisms, increasingly isolating individuals and their groups within the community, and ultimately creating community-wide antagonisms between different groups. Most dismally, but rather emblematically, Coleman was unable to suggest remediation for such community conflict. His study concluded that these conflicts tend to be self-fulfilling after the very early stages and run to their awful conclusion. The best one can do, Coleman suggested, is to recognize and settle conflicts in their earliest stages.

The guidance of Tönnies's pure types has been very significant in the development of sociology. It is the foundation for all subsequent sociological analysis. One might have expected that the utility of the *Gemeinschaft/Gesellschaft* pure types would have run its course after 130 years. But curiously, although community studies is no longer the dominant problem for American sociology, Tönnies's distinction seems no less appealing now than it was to early sociologists, and the reciprocal tendencies to romanticize community and despair about modern society are alive and well in contemporary analysis. Nonetheless, the opposition of *Gemeinschaft* and *Gesellschaft* can distract from the obvious fact that, in the modern era, our concern must be with community as an aspect of mass society, embedded in mass society, and not as an alternative paradigm to mass society.

Studies of community in society returned to the spotlight in American sociology in the late 1960s as a consequence of race riots in American cities. One line of analysis of cause and possible mitigation for this crisis focused on enhancing community identity, development, and power. This shaped the modern era of community studies, which has focused on the articulation of identity, development, and power between local communities and mass society. To some extent, this is still *Gemeinschaft/Gesellschaft*: The emphasis is not on the opposition of pure type alternatives, but rather on the relationship and articulation between two coexisting levels of social structure that inherently conflict. A thread of the romantic still persists, however, in the fact that communities are dwarfed by the influence of mass society. There is an inherent structural conflict, but not a fair fight.

Contemporary analysis of community embedded in mass society has primarily been framed system theoretically – that is, as a functional analysis of social systems, and systems of such systems. The seminal work is Warren's (1978) system theoretic analysis of macrosystem dominance and the contrast between vertical and horizontal integration. Macrosystem dominance is Warren's term for the contemporary lopsided relationship between community and society. It is comprised of seven, largely co-occurring societal transitions. These are:

1   finer division/specialization of labor entailing greater diversity and reduced solidarity throughout society;

2 more differentiation of interests and associations entailing greater mutual isolation;
3 increasing relations to mass society spanning personal ties, dependence for services, etc.;
4 more bureaucratization and impersonalization in social interactions;
5 transfer of functions from families and friends to business and government;
6 urbanization and suburbanization as modal social contexts;
7 value shift from work ethic to pursuit of consumption and enjoyment.

Warren refers to these transitions in aggregate as the "great change" in contemporary relationships between society and community. He observes that in modern society the causes for community phenomena and many of the solutions for community problems must be found at higher levels. Thus, community members may want to control school operation, water systems, sanitation, regulations for local business, location of highways, public transit systems, etc. But many of these systems are merely local regions in systems of the larger society, such as the regional watershed systems, interstate highway and railroad systems, state educational systems, and so forth. It is not desirable, indeed not even coherent, to have total local control of such systems. On the other hand, the absence of *any* local initiative or responsibility entails a society in which communities are blandly self-similar nodes in the one-size-fits-all societal system.

In Warren's (1978) analysis the strength of a modern community is reflected in a balance of horizontal integration versus its vertical integration. Macrosystem dominance is reflected in vertical integration: Local businesses are franchises directed substantially at the national or global level, local schools are directed by state standards and state boards of education, municipal governments implement state mandates and initiatives, local churches and service organizations are directed by national coordinating bodies, and so forth. Local initiative and responsibility are reflected in horizontal integration: Local businesses are integrated through local chambers of commerce, local schools are directed through the community boards of education, municipal governments are managed through town councils or boards, and community groups are coordinated through local councils. In essence, horizontal integration is the extent to which actors and their activity are locally planned, implemented, and evaluated. Sutton and Kolaja (1960) described this quality as "communityness."

The concept of horizontal integration raises questions about how members of contemporary communities can coordinate effectively. The *Gemeinschaft* conception of community is one in which each member is connected to every other member through strong social ties. This is plausible for Paleolithic bands of 50 people and perhaps, barely, for Neolithic villages of 150, but it is just not plausible that such ties could be established or maintained between every pair of residents in a town the size of Muncie when the Lynds carried out their Middletown ethnography – nearly 40,000. Indeed, Durkheim ([1893] 1947) and Simmel ([1908] 1972) had identified the potential benefits of *Gesellschaft* ties with respect to integrating society through facilitating more complex patterns of interdependence among members. More recently, Granovetter (1973) showed that acquaintances – people one knows, but not well, people one knows only through others – can be crucial to interactions like gaining employment. Granovetter called these "weak ties" and emphasized their importance in contemporary communities both in the diffusion and adoption of new ideas and in providing individual members with better access to resources and information.

The shift from describing ideal community to analyzing facets of horizontal integration or communityness is very significant. It helps to clarify the role community can possibly have in contemporary mass society. Warren (1978) defined community as the locality of linkages in interpersonal and inter-organizational networks for distributing resources, information, and support. That is to say, if we conceptualize society as a network of links among people and organizations, representing exchanges of resources, information, and social support, a community is a relatively densely linked region in the overall social network. Conceiving of community as relatively dense regions of interpersonal linkage also helps to resolve the seeming contradiction in what Rubin (1969) called nonterritorial communities, such as religious groups, professions, and ethnic identifications.

## The darkening darkness

Contemporary discussions of community are often pursued against a backdrop of concerns about civic and social decline. Community, in the sense of *Gemeinschaft*, may already be lost, but now, it is suggested, we are losing communityness as well. A range of evidence suggests that a pattern of solitary individualism has broadly diminished collective identity and participation in many contemporary societies (Bell and Newby 1971; Frankenberg 1966; Wellman 1988). Bellah *et al.* (1986) and Putnam (2000) are two widely cited studies focusing on American society.

Bellah and his colleagues interviewed over 200 Americans about their values, experiences, and relations to others, including the relation between public and private life. These interviews suggested that American individualism (circa 1980) had become distortedly utilitarian. Bellah describes his interviewees as lost and confused, obsessed with work and career, and inclined to see all human relationships as mere contracts. They perceived their own society as something other than them. Even participation in civic associations was frequently conceived of in largely personal terms – for example, as self-discovery. Bellah *et al.* also report a pervasive angst about these attitudes and behaviors – that is, their informants characterized their individualism as an obstacle to their own satisfaction.

Bellah *et al.* contrasted this picture of contemporary American society with Tocqueville's account of that during the 1830s in *Democracy in America*. Tocqueville was famously impressed by the number and variety of voluntary associations in which Americans participated, and took this as a validation of the Jeffersonian ideal of citizen participation in democracy. However, Tocqueville's enthusiasm was not unqualified. He described a tension between *expressive individualism*, which seeks connection, fulfillment, and growth through relating with other people, and *utilitarian individualism*, which is focused narrowly on satisfying, protecting, and isolating the self. Tocqueville was skeptical that the two tendencies of individualism could be integrated. Bellah *et al.* were troubled by their interviews, and with justification, but their programmatic remedy is a return to the values and mores that underpinned early American society.

Putnam (2000) drew upon large-scale survey data, focusing on various trends in reported behavior. Between the 1960s and the 1990s, participation rates in a variety of civic activities declined in America: Red Cross volunteering declined by 60 percent; participation in parent–teacher organizations declined by nearly half; membership in the League of Women Voters and in the Jaycees both declined by 40 percent; the number of people reporting that they attended a public meeting on town or school affairs in the past year had declined by more than a third; volunteering of Boy Scout troop leaders declined by a quarter; voter turnout in national elections declined by nearly a quarter; churchgoing and church-related activities declined by a sixth; the proportion of Americans who socialize with neighbors more than once a year declined by nearly a sixth. Putnam's touchstone for this broad trend is the decline in bowling leagues. Although the total number of bowlers in America increased by 10 percent between 1980 and 1993 (to nearly 80 million people), league bowling *decreased* by 40 percent. As Putnam put it in titling his book, Americans are bowling alone.

Putnam investigated various possible causes for these trends – the pressures of modern life, economic hard times, residential mobility, suburbanization, two-career family stresses, the weakening of marriage and family ties, the rise of franchising and the service sector, disillusion and cultural conflicts of the 1960s/1970s, the growth of the welfare state, the civil rights revolution, and television and other technological developments. Putnam ultimately favored a generational cohort account, arguing that civic behaviors such as voting and membership in community groups, and the belief that most people can be trusted, began to decline for people born after 1930. For example, people born in the 1920s are twice as likely to vote, belong to twice as many civic groups, and are twice as likely to trust other people as are people born in the 1960s.

Putnam considered in detail the shared experiences of what he terms the "civic generation," people born between 1910 and 1940. He focuses special attention on the cohort born between 1925 and 1930. These individuals grew up during the Great Depression, coming of age during World War II. Thus, they shared the sustained terror of significant crises in their youth and the singular triumph of saving the world from fascism as young adults. These experiences may have established both sociality and optimism, particularly when the civic generation is compared with successive generations who grew up in the ambiguities of the Korean War, the Cold War, and the Vietnam War, and the turmoil surrounding civil rights and women's rights.

In an early version of this work, Putnam (1996) emphasized the role of technology – television in particular – in fostering decline in civic life. Indeed, the civic generation was the last American generation to grow up without the experience of television. Television viewing has increased in each successive generation since its introduction in the 1950s, and correlates negatively with participation in all other social and media activities (Neuman 1991). Among children aged nine to fourteen, television consumes as much time as all other discretionary activities combined – an average of 40 hours per week. Television has increasingly displaced other activities. People who watch less television and read more newspapers than average belong to 76 percent more civic organizations and are 55 percent more trusting than people who watch more television and read fewer newspapers than average. People who report being happy when engaged in social interaction report being bored and unhappy when watching television (Kubey and Csikszentmihalyi 1990). Television watching has been linked to reduced physical activity and poorer physical and mental health (Anderson *et al.* 1998; Sidney *et al.* 1998).

The theme of social and civic decline, and the association of this decline with technology, has become a touchstone of modern times. This can evoke a sense of darkening darkness, an endless downward spiral of human expressiveness, community engagement, and quality of life. Tönnies and the early sociologists analyzed the decline of strong emotional bonds of *Gemeinschaft* in rural villages and the rise of isolating and utilitarian individualism of *Gesellschaft*, triggered at least in part by the Industrial Revolution. Half a century later, the Lynds and other community ethnographers expressed concern that inventions, then new, such as the radio, would destroy community ties and threaten American morality and democracy. Another half century on, Bellah and Putnam observed that Americans were less engaged with one another and with civic activity. Technology again was among the culprits, this time television.

But this touchstone is a bit flimsy. Like most social concepts, *community* has referred to different things at different times and in different places. Thus, different crises of community are often crises pertaining to different social institutions and arrangements labeled as *community*. For example, the crisis of community that occurred when Paleolithic bands developed agriculture and animal domestication and established the first Neolithic villages about 10,000 years ago, or when British peasants were drawn to and then packed into the first modern cities during the 1820s, or when more Americans lived in suburbs than anywhere else in 1950, or when half a billion people were connected through Internet social networking sites in 2008 (comScore 2008), are diverse episodes in which people organized new ways to cooperate and interact as part of cultural and technological changes. And of course technology is not a monolithic influence on human activity either. Neolithic villages, the factories of Industrial Revolution, radio and television, and the Internet all had quite different and distinct affordances for human activity and had very different impacts.

Community has no doubt declined in some respects, but it is just as important to see it as changing and evolving. Neolithic villages, medieval towns, and indeed American small towns like Middletown are gone. They are defunct social paradigms. Along the way, something about community was no doubt lost, and it is worthwhile to ponder this and to try to learn from it. However, it is important to understand how community has been transformed, and how it may be transformed further and, perhaps, even improved in some respects. Consider that a paragon of strong *Gemeinschaft* bonds might also tend to be a rather closed and intolerant place. To paraphrase Putnam (2000: 350–63), in such a community, social capital can be at war with equality. Indeed, the Lynds reported this pattern in their study of Middletown (Lynd and Lynd 1929). One must concede that losing this community paradigm is, at worst, a mixed blessing.

## Articulating facets of community

Early in his book *The Community in Urban Society*, Lyon (1986: 4) remarks: "in the social sciences, there seems to be an inverse relationship between the importance of a concept and the precision with which it is defined." He goes on to consider some of the more than 100 definitions of community in the literature of sociology, noting that the vast majority enumerate three common qualities: shared place, common ties, and distinctive social interaction. These three qualities do capture critical facets of what community has meant or entails, but it is immediately evident that they are not independent qualities. As Nisbet (1976) observed, identification with place, close ties, and interaction are mutually reinforcing; the three are distinguishable, but would tend to co-occur and mutually entail one another in most circumstances. Community is perhaps more a *nexus* of these qualities than merely a summation.

In concluding his book, Lyon (1989: 240–51) returns to the definition of community in a discussion of what makes for good community, distinguishing between "bare necessities" public safety, strong economy, health care, education, clean environment, and optimum population and "subjective components" of individual liberty, equality, fraternity, responsive government, local identification, and member diversity. He makes several interesting points regarding "bare necessities." First, echoing Warren's analysis of horizontal and vertical integration, Lyon notes that even these basic needs must be addressed locally. To be effective, societal-level policies and programs must be supported, implemented, localized, and sustained by the community. But, second, Lyon recalls Maslow's (1970) hierarchy of needs, noting that, when basic needs for food and security are achieved, higher-order needs for belonging, for creative living, and for self-actualization become *just as keenly felt* by people.

Indeed, most of Lyon's discussion of good community focuses on subjective components, which he concedes are more difficult to define and measure, but which he reckons are also more significant. The subjective components are in addition more nuanced and more complex in that they inescapably entrain social tradeoffs. For example, individual liberty has always been a central value in American communities, but it inherently conflicts with the values of equality and fraternity. Individuals, free to do as they please, may treat others unequally or impersonally. But, to give liberty its due, a community in which everyone was treated equally, no matter what he or she actually contributed, and in which everyone was expected to be closely involved with everyone else, would be a small and stifling place. Perhaps it would be the *Gemeinschaft* ideal that Tönnies nostalgically described. But it would not be an attractive place to modern people. In this vein, it is notable that Lyon enumerates heterogeneity or diversity as one of the six subjective components of community. Diversity plays no role in Tönnies's *Gemeinschaft* concept; it is all but antithetical to *Gemeinschaft*.

Lyon's subjective components underscore some of the ways a modern construction of community differs from *Gemeinschaft*. In a modern community there can be, and indeed Lyon suggests there should, there must be, a dynamic balancing of liberty, equality, fraternity, and diversity. This analysis of community allows more articulated characterizations of the observations of Bellah and Putnam. Bellah was concerned about the rebalancing that favored liberty over equality. Putnam characterized a generational rebalancing favoring diversity over fraternity. This is not to say that merely labeling these analyses dissolves the problematic. It is just to say that deconstructing community allows us to be more specific about various crises and developments in contemporary communities. In contemporary communities, balancing a variety of higher-order needs that inherently conflict is essential and requires social mechanisms for community monitoring and self-regulation.

Lyon's remaining two subjective components, responsive government and local identification, emphasize his interest in place-based communities, towns, and neighborhoods. He says that the community should matter to its members, that they "should define themselves in terms of the community" (Lyon 1989: 248). His notion of responsive government entails broad community involvement, and the general understanding among community members that they can easily have impact on local government. Place-based identity and community collective efficacy beliefs are central to Tönnies's conception of *Gemeinschaft*. Modern people are less intimately, singularly, and irrevocably tied to place that our Neolithic forebears, but it is still easy to appreciate the importance of place when one ponders its counterfactual: Imagine that we felt nothing more for our own towns and neighborhoods than we do for a motel on the side of a highway where we stop to sleep while traveling. Yet it also seems that other totems may be able play the role of common place as an anchoring community identity, as illustrated by Rubin's (1969) nonterritorial communities – religious groups, professions, and ethnic identifications – and today the many Internet organizations often called virtual communities (Rheingold 2000).

As early as the 1960s, Webber (1963: 29) speculated that interest-based communities were replacing place-based communities in American society. This was surely a precocious observation for 1963, and sociological fieldwork has not borne it out (Guest, Lee, and Staeheli 1982; Hunter 1975). There is something special about common place. When people live near one another, social interaction and shared identity are entrained, where in a nonterritorial, interest community such social investments and commitments are deliberate decisions that are easily revoked (Komito 1998; Zablocki 1978: 108). The past decade has seen rapid expansion in virtual communities, and studies of these communities make it clear that socially deep and significant relationships emerge (Preece

2000). Perhaps a way to think about this is that a critical subjective component, in Lyon's sense, of community is shared identity, and that common place provides an obvious referent for creating such symbolic relations, but that other shared activity can also be recruited to this purpose – such as shared religious, professional, and ethnic artifacts, practices, and beliefs.

Lyon's subjective components expand the social analysis of community to encompass psychological analysis of the personal experiences and interactions of community members. Since the 1970s, the psychology of community has pursued this analysis, focusing on the construct of *sense of community* (Sarason 1974), defined as

> the perception of similarity to others, an acknowledged interdependence with others, a willingness to maintain this interdependence by giving or doing for others what one expects from them, and the feeling that one is part of a larger dependable and stable structure.
>
> (Sarason 1974: 157)

This analysis addresses the experience of community by the people who comprise that community. Thus, membership, for example, is not merely a grouping or a set of linkages among people, it is also particular feelings, beliefs, and behaviors of members. Sarason emphasized fraternity and solidarity, participation and reciprocity, and identification with a social organization through membership. Interestingly however, his notion of sense of community did not directly incorporate liberty, diversity, or common place, three of Lyon's six subjective components.

Sarason's concept was further developed in a highly influential paper by McMillan and Chavis (1986). Their definition differentiates four facets of the psychological experience of community: membership, influence, integration and fulfillment of needs, and shared emotional connection. They admit (1986: 10) that the four propositions in their definition are not independent and are circularly related – both causes and effects of community. McMillan and Chavis elaborated Sarason's conception of membership as feeling part of a stable social structure. They characterize membership as a sense of belonging, of identification, of being accepted. They say that members experience feelings of emotional and physical safety through the collective. People who have traversed membership rites of passage feel invested in the community, engaged in it, and important to it. The community defines a social boundary that signifies the social achievement of membership: Non-members are outside.

McMillan and Chavis also elaborated Sarason's notion of reciprocal influence. They say that members feel they are able to make a difference in the community, but also that they should conform to community norms. However, they go beyond this notion of reciprocal influence to emphasize integration and fulfillment of member needs, which they differentiate as a first-order facet of sense of community. In their conception, community members experience the community as integrating and fulfilling their needs through access to resources and social support.

The apparent competence of the community in meeting needs evokes commitment to action from members, which in turn helps to meet members' needs.

Sarason emphasized fraternity and solidarity in saying that members perceive similarity to others. McMillan and Chavis reconceptualized this more broadly as shared emotional connection, understood as a belief in and commitment to shared heritage, place, and experiences. This is a much richer symbolic foundation for sense of community than mere similarity. In McMillan and Chavis's concept, even if a particular member did not participate personally in the actual events, he or she can still embrace and be committed to these as symbols of the community.

McMillan and Chavis were influenced strongly by the social psychology of *cognitive dissonance* (Festinger 1957), the principle that people try to align their beliefs and their actions – that is, to minimize the dissonance between what they believe and what they do. With respect to membership, McMillan and Chavis recall how early American communities banished and murdered heretics in part to enhance cohesion and solidarity (Erikson 1966), and how college fraternities use hazing rituals to strengthen the commitment of new members. Punishing deviant members and enforcing rites of passage creates dissonance that can be reduced to the extent that members believe there is sufficient justification; for example, the community must be protected from deviants, and membership in the community is worth working for, even suffering for. With respect to influence, a community member will minimize dissonance by carefully conforming to community norms. With respect to needs, community members will come to share values and work to help meet the needs of other members because, by doing this, they reduce possible dissonance between their own values and actions and their commitment to community values and initiatives. Finally, with respect to emotional connection, identification with and belief in the symbols of one's community – including the significance of common place and history – further validates and harmonizes actions and beliefs regarding the community.

Cognitive dissonance – sometimes, invertedly, also called cognitive consistency – is a powerful concept in understanding the mutual influence between beliefs and actions. But it is not a comprehensive account. Even within social psychology, alternative theoretical accounts have been developed that explain tendencies to balance action and belief in terms of self-perception and identity management, rather than of conformity (Bem 1967). People do things for a great variety of reasons. And cognitive dissonance has obvious downsides as a source of motivation. Social pressure to change one's beliefs, and to reduce dissonance through actions compatible with group norms, can be experienced as coercive. As observed earlier, community membership in modern society is just less important than it was in the medieval villages that Tönnies idealized. No one in contemporary America loses their life, or even their livelihood, by bowling alone. That is just not the issue. Thus, it is easier to resolve cognitive dissonance aroused by community interactions simply by leaving the community; college fraternities have no doubt lost many potential members who do not want to be associated with hazing. This somewhat severe and frankly dated view of membership is the weakest element of McMillan and Chavis's analysis.

In 1996, McMillan revisited the four facets of sense of community. The facet of membership (renamed "spirit") still emphasized cognitive dissonance mechanisms, sacrifice, and humiliation enough to provoke commitment to the community but not so much as to provoke revulsion and withdrawal. However, McMillan emphasized two new themes: friendship and diversity. He described friendship bonds as critical to the overall fabric of community. He said that members must feel emotionally safe in telling their truth to other members, that part of belonging is acceptance. Influence was renamed "trust" and seems more reciprocal and more complex in this reformulation than mere conformity. Integration of needs was renamed "trade," seemingly a more austere concept. McMillan articulated bonding and bridging more sharply (he calls them similarity and diversity), saying that bonding forces seem more important especially in early stages of community development, and that they help to enable the subsequent development of bridging. Curiously, shared emotional connection was renamed as "art" and emphasized more strongly "dramatic moments."

Comparing the two papers is interesting in that it also helps to highlight some trajectories in the ideas that were *not* developed. For example, influence became trust, a more sophisticated social framework, but there is no discussion of the role that trust might play in enabling community learning and innovation. Nor is there discussion of how trust can be used to propel action – for example, to facilitate the volunteerism upon which communities depend. The analysis, in both the 1986 and the 1996 version, underemphasizes the importance of individual initiative-taking at the level of neighborhood organization. Conformity to norms is important for social cohesion, but it is inherently stultifying. Small social entities also constantly need to innovate. Communities particularly need to innovate in order to promote horizontal integration against societal forces for vertical integration. This creates a need for emergent competences, and for individual community members to eschew conformity and to invent and assume new leadership roles.

McMillan and Chavis explicitly trace their notion of shared emotional connection to Tönnies's notion of bonds based on common place. However, their concept is psychologically richer, and helps to articulate what it is about common place that could encourage and strengthen shared emotional connection. They enumerate seven features: substantial social contact, positive interactions, collective endeavors successfully completed, shared significant experiences, tangible stakeholding in community outcomes, public recognition of members' contribution, and community spirit. This list is interesting in that it places the emphasis on shared activity rather than on (mere) shared place. Community members do things together. Moreover, to McMillan and Chavis it matters that the shared activity is generally successful – that is, that the community is effective, not just supportive. And it matters that community members put their resources at risk in community endeavors; to be a community member is to be a stakeholder. Finally, McMillan and Chavis are straightforward in calling out spiritual bonds as a key to sense of community: This part of community membership is identity, a sense of who and what we are.

Hester (1993) presents an inspiring description of a community design study in which he identified what he calls the "sacred spots" of Manteo, North Carolina. In the study, Hester observed everyday friendly and informal interactions among residents. He noticed that these interactions clustered around specific locales – the post office, the town hall, a downtown diner, the docks, a gravel parking lot near the docks, a statue of Sir Walter Raleigh, a small park. He presented this "analysis" directly to the residents of Manteo, who were surprised at some of the mundane places that nevertheless ranked above churches and cemeteries; one resident called those places the "sacred structure" of the town. Hester (1993) defined sacred structure as

> places – buildings, outdoor spaces and landscapes – that exemplify, typify, reinforce and perhaps even extol everyday life patterns and special rituals of community life; places that are so essential to residents' lives through use or by symbolism that the community collectively identifies with them.

Hester's investigation and insights developed in the context of a redevelopment plan that just incidentally could have destroyed much of the town's sacred structure. He emphasizes that merely codifying the list legitimizes sacred structure. In this case study, the town was able to protect its sacred spots through what was apparently a successful redevelopment process. Hester's notions of sacred spots and sacred structure seem appropriate as an updating of Tönnies, emphasizing how place can matter to contemporary people who may no longer farm the land, who indeed may commute to work in adjacent towns and cities. (Oldenburg 1989 developed a similar concept in his discussion of "great good places.")

## Toward a conceptual model of community

Box 1.1 presents a simple conceptual model of community, based on synthesis of the ideas surveyed above (an earlier version was discussed in Carroll and Rosson 2003). In this model, the three facets of community are collective identity, local participation, and diverse support networks. As with the Lyon and McMillan/ Chavis models, the three facets are distinguishable, but not independent.

*Box 1.1*  Three facets of community: Collective identity, local participation, and diverse support networks

> • Collective identity (community attachment): Members evoke and experience the social ideal of community through sharing values, episodes and traditions, mores, folkways, and experiences of community and world events. They feel belonging, shared emotional connection and sacred structures. They experience their community membership as part of who they are. They are committed to and believe in the community's power and capacity to thrive and develop.
>
> *(Continued)*

*Box 1.1 (Continued)*

- Local participation (community engagement): Community is sustained by (at least some) members enacting shared identity, and by initiating and innovating new practices that challenge and stimulate the community. Members feel and observe that they can have an impact on community decisions and initiatives (self-efficacy) and believe that community is sustainable and effective (collective efficacy). Members are known; their conduct and contributions are visible; they feel accountable.
- Dense and diverse support network: Members provide and reciprocate social and material support through a multitude of different tie types. The community is a relatively densely interconnected subnetwork of the societal social network. Community members typically play a variety of roles, and often have multiple types of ties to the same other members. Community groups comprise a relatively densely interconnected subnetwork of the overarching societal network.

*Identity* integrates bonds of common place, as in Tönnies's classic notion of the soil, Lyon's notion of shared identification, and Hester's concept of sacred structure, with McMillan and Chavis's notion of shared emotional connection, focusing more on totemic activity. It incorporates what is sometimes called community attachment (Kasarda and Janowitz 1974). But identity also encompasses community values, as enumerated in Lyon's subjective components – individual liberty, equality, fraternity, and member diversity. Identity includes commitment to and belief in community power, the community's capacity to manage, achieve and advance; this is one aspect of what McMillan and Chavis called influence. More operationally, identity includes much of what McMillan and Chavis discuss under membership, community practices, folkways and mores, etiquette, and rituals.

Identity is listed first because it seems the most fundamental to community, at least to contemporary community. There can be no sense of membership without shared identity. Shared identity is psychologically prior to the conformity and rites of passage aspects of membership that were emphasized by McMillan and Chavis: Conformity, after all, is acquiescence to coercion *with which one identifies*. Acquiescing to externally imposed authority is not conformity, it is just submission. It is difficult to say with any authority that identity is more or less a modern characteristic of community, since it is a subjective experience. It seems plausible that a strong sense of identity might have been concomitant with the emergence of altruistic behavior in Paleolithic band communities (Darwin [1871] 1983; Bowles 2009). For contemporary communities, we can ask people what they feel. And here shared identity seems to be the necessary condition for community. Unlike the classic community contexts of prehistory, of Tönnies and Tocqueville, and of Middletown, shared identity in contemporary community can be bestowed on those who merely show up. No one can seriously presume to be able to assess someone else's sense of community identity. Contemporary communities are perhaps categorically less rigorous about boundary maintenance and member control than in the earlier paradigms. This may be why McMillan and Chavis's example of Puritan communities strikes a modern reader as perverted, not as revelatory of a design principle for community.

In contemporary terms, one might call Tönnies's notion of identity "embodied." Thus, he referred to bonds based on "the soil" where his successors have used more symbolic terminology such as sacred structure, emotional connection, and identification. This seems an important conceptual trajectory. For modern people, the soil itself is less important than the situated events and human interactions that transpire upon it. Identity, then, is constituted through the social/ symbolic interchange, through shared values and visions, through shared history and heritage, and the soil becomes essentially a vivid prop for this.

It is likely that this more symbolic conception of collective identity transforms the experience of community for contemporary people. If bonds are embodied, as for Tönnies, then they are universally, directly, and concretely experienced and enacted. The 50 members of a Paleolithic band and the 150 residents of a Neolithic village all knew one another immediately and intimatel and exercised their strong bonds daily. But such structures simply do not scale up. Contemporary people not only do not know all of their neighbors that well, they could not possibly know their neighbors that well. Even small towns are complex social systems that require several thousand residents to be sustainable. No one can exercise every potential dyadic connection. There just is not time enough in the day. Contemporary communities depend upon "systemic linkage" (Loomis 1960: 32); community ties are strengthened through the interactions of others with whom we share a community identity commitment. In other words, the strength of our communities is necessarily mediated by the successful interactions of people we may not even know. What we share with them is community identity.

Contemporary community bonds are also symbolically mediated in the sense that our community interactions characteristically entrain connotative significances beyond the literal interaction. Just as we experience ideals of love and other strong emotions through our instantiated relationships with actual people, we experience social ideals through our commitments to actual social entities. Thus, community interactions that are objectively somewhat mundane can mean much more to those who participate in them. Consider the example of exchanging small talk with a fellow resident at a community baseball game. Such an interaction hardly rises to the level of *Gemeinschaft*. It would never show up in Putnam's survey data, and might well be interpreted by Bellah as signifying an unmet longing for community. But it seems reasonable to conjecture that such interactions can also be concrete vehicles through which we experience the ideal of *Gemeinschaft*, albeit in a (merely) symbolic manner. It would be fair to say that this is not more than a shadow of what Tönnies described, but it may also be fair to say that this is an appropriate, and perhaps quite an effective, contemporary recontextualization of community. This point is potentially important since, if we are distracted by counting how many times the neighbors come to dinner or how many bowling leagues we belong to, we could easily underestimate the importance of a symbolically mediated community experience. This could be true for analysts as well as for community members.

The problematic of shared identity, as the touchstone facet of community, is that it asks for and evokes too little from members. This dilemma seems salient in the theorizing of McMillan and Chavis, leading to their focus on conformity and community sanctions. *Local participation* complements shared identity. It is the activity entailed by collective identity. Broad collective identity is necessary for community to exist at all, but it is not enough for a vital, creative, sustainable community. At least some of its members, some of the time, must also be prepared to enact the community's identity. Local participation addresses what Sarason thought of as the interdependence of giving and doing, and what McMillan and Chavis called integration and fulfillment of needs. It corresponds to what Lyon called interactions, and subsumes his subjective component of responsive government. It encompasses the many indicators of civic engagement analyzed by Putnam – being out in public, volunteering for community projects, socializing with neighbors, serving in nonprofit associations, and even bowling in leagues. It includes believing that one can and should have influence in the community, the flip side of McMillan and Chavis's influence.

Participation entails visibility, accountability, responsibility, and leadership: Active community members do not merely implement, they take initiative; they discuss and debate; they negotiate; they innovate. They expand the reach of the community with respect to self-determination and self-regulation, as in Warren's notion of horizontal integration. But they also expand the community into new realms of activity. Indeed, community informatics and community networking, the creation and management of Internet services for and often by community members – and a topic to which we will return in the balance of this book – has been an active arena for community learning and innovation during the past couple decades. Wenger, in his studies of communities of practice, argues that communities that do not innovate and learn eventually wither and die (Wenger 1998; Wenger, McDermott, and Snyder 2002).

Among other origins, perhaps, this idea of learning as an essential function for living entities comes from developmental theory (Vygotsky 1978). Learning in the developmental perspective is not merely aggregating bits of knowledge and skill, incrementally expanding a repertoire of concepts and capacities. In the interesting cases, learning means transformation, reorganization of what was previously regarded as known and well practiced. Significant learning is inherently disruptive; it drives the organism beyond the comfort zone of what can routinely be understood and accomplished into the so-called zone of proximal development, where outcomes are not certain, and where external help is typically required for progress. Community learning is an even more challenging prospect, since it involves a collection of differently skilled and motivated actors who may need also to learn to cooperate in new ways in order to achieve their new goals.

The importance of innovation and learning are modern developments. Traditional communities were comprehensive social entities that succeeded primarily by providing safety in numbers, maintaining critical mass to procreate and to develop and promulgate critical skills. They operated in a relatively static environment and evolved through the course of generations. Little of this traditional model maps very closely or usefully to contemporary society. Community development and innovation, learning and creativity, and intellectual and emotional vitality in communities have become more central and more critical to community sustainability. It seems increasingly common for engaged members to regard themselves as community designers, to see their role in the community as one of reshaping practices and steering trajectories, and not as merely honoring and re-enacting fixed ways of doing. This new attitude does not entail disrespect for folkways, traditions, and other totems; indeed, elderly members can be the most engaged designers, perhaps because they have attained a more expansive sense of the community through time and the confidence of being community fire keepers with respect to folkways, traditions, and so forth.

Because of vertical integration of many social and government services and societal functions in contemporary mass society, there just may be less to do for communities than there was during Paleolithic and Neolithic times. This is certainly not to say that people do all they could do in contemporary communities. Vertical integration and other forces, such as the generational and media effects analyzed by Putnam (2000), have surely undermined local participation. This in turn must eventually weaken community collective identity. Thus, identifying new community tasks is a critical challenge. These community tasks may themselves be quite symbolically oriented relative to traditional community-based social support. Potential examples are getting out the vote, deliberation of local issues, and addressing novel challenges for which there is no vertically integrated service delivery, challenges like developing new information technology infrastructures, including programs for community learning about how to use such infrastructures. Indeed, one might not bowl in a league or invite the neighbors over very often, but instead might write a community blog and use web-based collaboration to mentor middle-school science projects. There are new and emerging ways to participate in community (Resnick 2001).

Just as one cannot know everyone in the community, but can benefit with respect to constructing and maintaining community identity through the transitivity of systemic linkages, one cannot *do* everything in the community. Critical civic activity must occur, entailing the participation of some of the people some of the time. But much of the benefit from this activity flows through systemic linkages. Members need to feel that they can contribute to the community's effectiveness, that they have an impact on community decisions and initiatives; they need to feel community *self-efficacy*, in the sense of Bandura (1997). And, because members are visible, accountable, and responsible in a community, their fellow members know something about their contributions. But each member's contributions are limited; some may be completely invisible. Members need to believe that their community is sustainable and effective – that is, they need to feel *community collective efficacy* (Carroll, Rosson, and Zhou 2005). Influence, in the sense of McMillan and Chavis, becomes collectivized; members feel efficacious through seeing that the community can be effective.

*Diverse support* corresponds to what Lyon discussed as ties. Diverse support is an important facet of community, but it is a consequence of collective identity and local participation. As members participate within the community, they interact with one another in a multitude of ways. Two people are connected because both are parents or not parents, because they work at the same place or nearby one another, because they live on one side of the town center, or through many other potential types of social ties. These ties are continually facilitated and enhanced both by the construction and exercise of collective identity and by participation in community-centered activity. For example, the people one sits with at a local baseball game, if they are not already acquaintances, are nonetheless immediately acknowledged as neighbors, and thereby are more likely to be quickly integrated into one's social network. This point is in a sense the glass-half-full version of Putnam: Perhaps these neighbors will never be invited over for a dinner party, but in virtue of community collective identity, and whatever local community participation has managed to enhance it, one acknowledges these neighbors and interacts with them as fellow community members. This may be even less than a bowling league, but it is much more than *Gesellschaft*.

As Lyon emphasized, liberty and diversity are much more important to contemporary community than they most likely were or could have been in the prehistoric or medieval paradigms. In part this is because community is no longer a singular and comprehensive social paradigm, but is one relatively low-level rubric for social organization that is always embedded in mass society. Contemporary people may regard themselves as simultaneously members of several or even many communities. This repositioning of community in the overall organization of human social life reweights requirements for success and sustainability of communities. Those that do not foster and facilitate liberty and diversity cannot function effectively as components within mass society. They will tend to discourage innovation and change, and thus tend not to develop. They will drive members away, but not attract new members.

As Warren (1978) put it, contemporary communities are relatively dense clusters of social ties in a vast and sparse social network. These clusters are also quite diverse with respect to types of ties – for example, when contrasted to clusters corresponding to professional colleagues or even kin. Granovetter (1973) is often cited as emphasizing the importance of tie diversity, but he actually addressed only strength differences in dyadic ties, emphasizing the importance of weak ties – people we know, but with whom we do not have regular contact. Gans (1974a, 1974b) noted that, while weak ties are important, all ties are embedded in social contexts, and their meaning and significance in facilitating human activities derives from context. One needs to understand the history, practices, and attitudes of the community, and at least some of the key community actors, in order to make sense of patterns of ties.

Contemporary communities articulate social structure at many levels. A Paleolithic band community has relatively little internal substructure – parental dyads, groups that like to hunt together. There is not much utility in substructure for such a small community. However, the size and complexity of contemporary communities require vast amounts of substructure: municipal government, schools, hospitals, businesses, professional groups, sports clubs, associations, service groups, social organizations, Girl Scout troops, etc. These institutions are more than aggregations of current members; they are collective actors in their own right, and they define the persistent social structure of the community (Laumann, Galaskiewicz, and Marsden 1978; Porpora 1989). Community institutions articulate the range of the community's functions and interests, which both "institutionalizes" diversity and broadens the foundation for community cohesion from mere similarity to mutual interdependence within a framework of shared purposes and meanings (Durkheim [1893] 1947; Selznick 1996). Each of these clusters has numerous sorts of ties to other clusters. Thus, a community is a relatively dense cluster of social ties in a vast and sparse social network of persons, but also a relatively dense cluster of social ties among groups in a vast and sparse social network of groups. Both sorts of clustering are critical social resources for the members of the community.

To continue the earlier example, the tie of being parents of elementary-school children is different from the tie of being systems analysts or pharmacists, and those ties are different from the tie of living in the same subdivision or condominium. In community contexts, people regularly play a variety of defining roles, each entailing a variety of defining activities and ties. For example, the parent is a pharmacist, a condominium resident, a member of clubs and service groups, and so forth. Each of these roles entrains opportunities for community participation and interaction with other community members. In community contexts, these various arenas of activity and interaction often overlap. Thus, ties are rarely mere dyadic links; rather, they are rich in meaning and social affordances, they are multivalent and systemic. In Coleman's (1988) analysis, the *multiplexity* of social relationships in a modern community is critical to developing and facilitating flows of social capital.

This introductory discussion of community, and especially the three facets of the conceptual model that summarize and focus that discussion, help to frame questions we should pose about contemporary communities:

- How can communities appropriate new affordances of social life – for example those enabled by the Internet – for civic and social purposes?
- How can technologists and social scientists learn about and work with communities and their constituent groups to envision and create new possibilities for communities?
- What are the obstacles, challenges, early benefits, unintended consequences, and longer-term trajectories for such transformations of community with respect to collective identity, local participation, and diverse support networks?

In the balance of this book I report on a project investigating possibilities for community informatics and for American community. In the past 150 years, we have learned much about human community. We have learned that community is essential to human beings. And we have learned that community is contingent. It emerges from attitudes, beliefs, and actions of human beings. Many are concerned now that community is in crisis, at risk, deteriorating. But, as suggested above, community itself has changed, and no doubt is changing still. The crisis today is not any of the crises that have occasionally preoccupied social scientists during the past 150 years. And avoiding, resolving, or meliorating this crisis will certainly require and allow new insights and new approaches from this time. Our study involved observing, facilitating, implementing, and evaluating community innovations realized through information technology in an American community – Blacksburg, Virginia – in the context of a major community development project, the Blacksburg Electronic Village.

# 2    What are community networks?

*Community network* seems an intriguing oxymoron. Community networks are computer-based networks created by and for a local community. They support interaction among neighbors. They facilitate information dissemination, discussion, and joint activity pertaining to municipal government, public schools, civic groups, local events, community issues and concerns, commerce and economic development, and social services. But, given that we can directly interact with our neighbors – that is, interact with them face to face in the physical world – what would computer-mediated interactions buy us? Isn't physical proximity enough? Isn't it superior? We cannot shake hands or hug one another through the Internet, at least not very satisfactorily, and we surely cannot help one another clear rain gutters or shovel snow.

From the standpoint of networks, *community network* also seems inherently oxymoronic. The vision of the Internet, after all, is to bring people, services, and information from around the world into immediate conjunction through their desktops, laptops, and personal devices. One obvious meaning of the Internet is to question the modern conception of "mass society" as not inclusive enough unless it encompasses every human on Earth, or even reasonably near it. Given this vision of an all-encompassing mass society, why would anyone want to engage neighborhood people, services, and information through a computer? Approached from this direction, from the standpoint of the Internet, the notion of community network seems to impose quaint and obviated limitations on social possibilities afforded by new media.

This apparent contradiction is resolved by looking more carefully at what community networks are, why communities have created them, and their actual use. Community networks are created to facilitate the development and management of information and activity in a proximate community. The network and the community are coextensive. Members publish web pages for, send email to, and chat with essentially the same people they encounter as they shop, work, and move about in everyday activities. The motivations for and the consequences of participation in the network range from the purely pragmatic (finding current show times for movies, printing online pizza coupons) to the more communitarian (helping others learn about technology, organizing grassroots community action). In supporting these various interactions, the network becomes more than a medium. It becomes an institutional actor with relationships to other community institutions, as well as to individuals and their groups. The network is part of the persistent social structure of the community.

The puzzlement one occasionally still encounters about community networks derives from understanding both community and networks too exclusively and too simplistically. The Internet is not merely an *alternative* to face-to-face interaction, it also provides new ways to augment and enhance face-to-face interaction. For example, through the affordances of asynchronous interaction, such as email and discussion forums, people do not have to be available at a specific time and place in order to engage in a meaningful community interaction. Community members can expand their daily window of opportunity for interactions and collaborations with their fellow members by sending an email, editing a web page, or participating in a chat late at night or early in the morning. Community groups, like churches, service organizations, clubs, and associations, that comprise and contribute to the overall community can also benefit by creating special purpose communication channels and online workspaces to carry out their particular community activity.

This way of understanding community networks has a direct precedent in the history of the telephone (Fischer 1992). The telephone was originally regarded as a tool to enable voice communication over substantial distances, an improved telegraph. This was indeed an important role, but the telephone was also appropriated as a key tool for local communication – for example, coordinating activities among friends and immediate family that would be carried out face to face. Community networks can be regarded analogously as a global communication tool appropriated to facilitate and strengthen modern proximate community through affordances for asynchronous interactions, comprehensive information-sharing, public discussion and debate, special purpose interaction spaces for community organizations, and so forth. Of course, it is an empirical question whether community networks really do and have done this, or whether they merely have an unrealized potential to do it.

The simplest case of community is proximate, essentially face-to-face community. But, as described in chapter 1, direct face-to-face interaction for all member dyads is not possible in even a modestly sized modern community. Contemporary proximate communities depend on systemic links (Loomis 1960: 32) – that is, they already do and must transcend universal dyadic face-to-face interaction. And, in any case, proximate community lost its hegemony as a paradigm for community centuries ago through the emergence of various kinds of nonterritorial communities (Rubin 1969). As emphasized in chapter 1, community is a dynamic social arrangement that has evolved very rapidly in the last couple centuries. Perhaps *community network* would be oxymoronic for a Neolithic village of 150 people, all of whom know one another through many interdependencies, but this is not a typical demography for a contemporary community.

The simplest, most extreme case of networking is also a somewhat misleading stereotype. It is embodied in the apocryphal Peter Steiner cartoon published in the *New Yorker* on July 5, 1993, and captioned: "On the Internet nobody knows you're a dog." Of course it is true that the Internet is a playground for anonymous and irresponsible persons, and perhaps precocious dogs, carrying out pranks, including identity spoofing, and generally wreaking mayhem. But the more mundane and the more typical case is people honestly seeking information for everyday purposes, and interacting and collaborating with other people whom they know at least to some extent, and in many cases with people they know quite well.

There is no inherent conflict between community and computer networks. Rather, there are myriad possibilities for the interaction of the two, and perhaps even an urgency for communities to appropriate and better utilize the Internet. Community networks are a particular hybrid paradigm. They are virtual community infrastructures in which members can also regularly encounter and interact with other members face to face. And, at the same time, they are proximate communities in which Internet-mediated interaction and collaborative activity can augment and enhance what members do through traditional means.

This chapter briefly reviews the emergence and development of community networking during the past four decades, including the motivations, challenges, and key issues (see also Gurstein 2007). Like the Internet itself, community networks have evolved rapidly through this span of time, and very likely will continue to change. Because community networks are *designed*, their future is for people to consider and to create. The continuing challenge in community networking is to identify new ways of applying information technology to enrich and sustain community life. The chapter concludes with a design analysis, drawing on our conceptual model of community as embodied in recent, but now historical, community networks. This analysis is intended to help guide the future course of development for community networks.

## First-generation community networks

Community networking first emerged in the 1970s. The movement, if one can call it that, was not coordinated. Rather, the first community networks were purely local initiatives, part of a pervasive cultural Zeitgeist of discovery and exploration of new computer applications. Most of the early projects also had strong roots in community activism – jobs, housing, and veterans' issues in the Berkeley Community Memory (Colstad and Lipkin 1975; Farrington and Pine 1997; Rossman, 1975), community health in the Cleveland Free-Net (Beamish 1995), and problems of the homeless in the Santa Monica Public Electronic Network (Rogers, Collins-Jarvis, and Schmitz 1994). Public education, including informal education, has also been a major focus. Big Sky Telegraph supported teachers in rural Montana, linking one- and two-room schools with regional libraries, and providing computer support for the literary and artistic projects of Native Americans (Odasz 1993; Uncapher 1999). Social activism remains a strong theme in community computing (Schuler 1996).

Early community networks employed the technologies of their time. The Berkeley Community Memory, the first compelling example of community-oriented computer networking, was actually a mainframe service, implemented through a 110 baud link to teletype terminals. In the 1980s, implementations migrated to personal computers (PCs), at first connected only through daily bulletin board updates transmitted over telephone lines, and later through synchronous telephone modem connections. Today, community networks are accessed most typically through a variety of broadband network services, including telephone-based Digital Subscriber Line (DSL), cable Internet modem, fiber to the home, and various wireless infrastructures such as municipal wireless networks (Abdelaal and Ali 2009).

Innovation was a theme in community networking from the start. Indeed, the rationales attached to the Berkeley Community Memory in 1973 remarkably anticipate the World-Wide Web rhetoric that swept the world more than twenty years later:

> The system democratizes information, coming and going. Whatever one's power status in society – titan of industry, child of welfare recipient – one can put information into the system and take it out on an equal basis, provided its terminals are freely accessible and (relatively) free to use. It is a truly democratic and public utility, granting no one special privilege (provided its software can teach any user to operate it with sufficient skill for her needs). Put it another way: in this system no person or group can monopolize or otherwise control people's access to information. Information-power is fully decentralized. No editing, no censoring; no central authority to determine who shall know what in what way. Of course this means that no authority is responsible for providing "enough" information in the system; it must make do with whatever people choose to put in, on a democratic basis. Likewise this means that no authority is responsible for certifying, directly or implicitly, that any information is "right" or "accurate." Users of the system must take responsibility for their own judgments about its data, supported by whatever judgments other people offer to them through the system or outside it.
>
> (Rossman 1975: 7–8)

This short statement encompasses some of the key elements of community networking: On the one hand, an optimistic, techno-idealism that one can push information technology into public space with salutary consequences (equal control of and access to information) and, on the other hand, an aggressive commitment to participatory democracy and a somewhat fearless commitment to supporting democratic expression no matter what form it might take (no censorship, no central authority, total reliance on individual responsibility-taking).

The developers of the Berkeley Community Memory deliberately configured and presented the system to be as unstructured as possible so that its users could discover and invent its uses (Rossman 1975: 9). Thus, the first teletype terminal was placed under a bulletin board in a community record shop, and users started calling it an "electronic bulletin board," evoking a mental model for other users of what it was for and how to use it. People formed car pools, found chess partners, and reviewed local restaurants. Students used the system to find apartments, musicians used it to buy and sell instruments, and writers posted their poetry and essays. Community activists also appropriated the new medium – for example, posting the names of Alameda County's Vietnam War casualties in an online memorial.

A version of the Berkeley Community Memory system was subsequently implemented in Vancouver, British Columbia, and the core electronic bulletin board functionality had a huge impact on many subsequent designers. Bulletin board systems became widespread in the late 1970s and pervasive in the 1980s, as modems speeds improved to 1200 bit/seconds (Rafaeli 1984). Indeed, they continued to grow in popularity and user volume until the mid-1990s, when they were superseded by web forums. (See Farrington and Pine 1997 for additional discussion of the Berkeley Community Memory project.)

The Cleveland Free-Net developed from an online medical question/answer bulletin board initiated in 1984 at the Case Western Reserve University School of Medicine by Thomas M. Grundner and his colleagues, and called "St. Silicon's Hospital and Information Dispensary." This service, implemented on a single telephone line, was successful enough to attract attention and support from the university and from corporate sponsors. In 1986, the system was expanded to ten incoming telephone lines and renamed the Cleveland Free-Net. The scope of the bulletin board was expanded to include advice on law, education, arts, sciences, and government, as well as medicine and health. The Free-Net also provided discussion forums and free email accounts.

The popularity of the system grew more rapidly than expected, driving further development of the Free-Net infrastructure. In 1989, a scaled-up version of the system was released, capable of supporting as many as 360 simultaneous users. This version was also integrated with the campus network of Case Western – the first example of a community network spanning campus and town populations. That year the Cleveland Free-Net had 10,000 registered users. In 1995, it had more than 160,000 registered users and supported over 6 million user sessions. During the decade between the Berkeley Community Memory and the Cleveland Free-Net the telnet protocol was standardized (Abbate 1999). The Cleveland Free-Net was the first community network to offer free Interact access and was widely accessed through the Internet. The desirability of integration with the Internet was an issue debated in many early community networking projects, but the Cleveland model is the one that endured.

During the latter 1980s, Case Western was the center of the free-net movement. Starting in 1989, it distributed the software infrastructure for the Cleveland Free-Net, as FreePort, through the nonprofit National Public Telecomputing Network. This software greatly facilitated the development of several hundred free-nets during the 1990s, but increasingly it lagged user expectations about graphical user interface displays and functionality; FreePort supported only character-based user interfaces. As networked computing became less arcane, FreePort also had scaling and instability problems. As Schuler (1996: 483) put it in his overview of community networking, "There is fairly general agreement that this software – as it exists – is inadequate."

The Cleveland Free-Net project was taken very seriously by Case Western as a model. The university invested around half a million dollars in the project over more than ten years, but also investigated funding models for free-nets. A core principle was that access should be free, but any system has costs – hardware and software maintenance and replacement, administrative and user support staff, and so on. Case Western developed an operational model that included volunteers, resulting in an average per session cost to the university of less than 1 cent. An interesting implication of this financial analysis was that the cost of providing the free-net service was less than the cost of preparing and mailing invoices. Case Western received about $1000 per year in unsolicited donations and about $12,000 per year from licensing the FreePort software to other communities. This was by far the single most lucrative funding source for the Cleveland Free-Net, but it is tinged with an irony: Licensing infrastructure software to other free-net projects is surely a one-off funding paradigm. Not many free-nets could be funded this way! The Cleveland project explored the US public broadcast system "membership" model and the tax-based model that is used in many places to fund public libraries. However, neither of these models was actually ever implemented.

The Cleveland Free-Net provided a model for hundreds of other projects through its commitment to free access, through the FreePort software distribution, through its integration with the Internet, through its integration with the Case Western campus network, and through its exploration of funding mechanisms. Some of these positions became touchstones in the culture of community networking – for example, the principle of free access. Some became standard approaches – for example, most subsequent community networks have leveraged local colleges and universities, and almost all have been integrated with the Internet. Some of these themes remain open challenges – for example, the issue of sustainable funding models is a abiding issue for community networks (De Cindio and Ripamonti 2010; Siochrú and Girard 2005). (See Beamish 1995 for more detailed description and analysis of the Cleveland Free-Net.)

Big Sky Telegraph is an example of a very early rural community network. Big Sky was established in 1988 by Frank Odasz of Western Montana College (Odasz 1993). The network strongly and broadly emphasized educational opportunities. Its founding objective was to link Montana's 114 one-room schools together and to Western Montana College, though it eventually incorporated libraries, hospital, and other civic and service institutions in Montana. It directly leveraged the Internet. One of its signature initiatives was putting Montana students into direct contact with world-class centers of education and research. For example, a professor at MIT taught online high-school classes in chaos theory, leading to two Cody High School students enrolling at MIT. Another emphasis was helping teachers share lesson plans. By 1990, more than 600 lesson plans had been collected and indexed.

Big Sky also focused on vocational education programs. It worked with a network of Women's Centers in Montana to develop microcomputer training through the network. This was a highly innovative way to provide educational opportunities to people who were in many cases quite isolated, either literally homebound or just isolated in rural areas and without resources, including unskilled women divorced late in life, single mothers, and women dealing with domestic physical abuse. Beyond the direct benefits of vocational training, the women felt these opportunities enhanced their status in the community as well as their sense of themselves. Through the network, women from across western Montana could teach and support one other emotionally.

Another signature application of Big Sky Telegraph was its support for disseminating Native American artwork. Artists from the Assiniboine, Chippewa-Cree, Crow, Navajo, and Sioux nations created traditional artwork using the North American Presentation Level Protocol software (O'Brien and Bown 1983), enabling graphics encoding through ASCII. Eventually the artists created the online Native American Share-Art gallery, with the goal of making people outside the immediate geographic area more aware of tribal culture and to generate income for tribal artists. This project was an innovation in learning by teaching: The Native American artists used Big Sky and the Internet to make their work more available to the wider world, directly teaching that world about their culture and history. But, at the same time, this project was a vehicle for the artists themselves to use and develop English and computer skills in the context of indigenous expression. Moreover, the project provided a model for Native American children to learn more about, and perhaps to value more highly, their own heritage. (See Uncapher 1999 for additional discussion of Big Sky Telegraph.)

Santa Monica Public Electronic Network, known as Santa Monica PEN, was founded in 1989. It was the first municipal community network, directly administered by the Santa Monica city government. The initial vision for the PEN was chiefly access to public information such as bus schedules and events listings. It also provided a messaging system and forums, where residents could review and participate in city-sponsored discussions of local issues or initiate their own discussions. Access to public information proved to be the least used feature. Almost two-thirds of user activity took place in the discussion forums; most of other activity was email. Accessing public information comprised only about 10 percent of the user activity (Rogers, Collins-Jarvis, and Schmitz 1994).

The PEN was a closed network – that is, it was limited to Santa Monica. The original implementation was not integrated with the Internet, though eventually an Internet gateway was created. Nineteen public access terminals were established in libraries and other public space to make the system equally accessible to all citizens. And this seemed to work, as the user population was not skewed to younger, wealthier, and better-educated people as was and is often the case with new technology. Also interesting was that more than a third of the PEN users were female; this was at a time when female participation in online activities was often less than 10 percent (Rogers, Collins-Jarvis, and Schmitz 1994).

The fact that the PEN was a municipal system entailed interesting usage episodes (McKeown 1991). Perhaps the most famous incident in the project involved a community group concerned about the difficulties that homeless persons face in breaking out of the cycle of joblessness. The group, which included several homeless people, identified lack of access to morning showers, to clean clothing, and to safe storage space for personal belongings as key obstacles to homeless persons seeking employment. The group made a proposal to the Santa Monica City Council for public-access showers, washers, and lockers, and the council in fact appropriated funds to create such facilities. This is a wonderful vignette of how a community network helped segments of the population that might have otherwise remained disconnected and mutually invisible to interact and collaborate on a community proposal that enhanced life for everyone.

The PEN was also recruited for political campaigning and organizing. For example, in elections during 1990 statements from all 30 local candidates were posted on the network. One of the leading issues in that election year was a debate over proposed major hotel development that would have been located on the ocean side of the Pacific Coast Highway (it would have been the first such development). The proposal was extensively discussed in the PEN, and ultimately was defeated, despite being supported by powerful local interests.

Another anecdote, less positive, is the story of how a group of males, mostly adolescents, posted sexual scenarios on the network in which named local women were subjected to degrading acts. Because all contributors to the PEN were identified by their actual names, and because all lived within a couple miles of one another, no one had anticipated that such outrageous flaming behavior might occur, as it did and still does in anonymous network interactions (Hiltz and Turoff 1978). The city of Santa Monica felt cornered in that these citizens were, after all, exercising free speech. Interestingly, this incident was resolved at the member level, with no top-down administrative intervention. The women of the PEN used this misbehavior to strengthen their own organization (PENFEMME), expanding the range of female-oriented discussions and activities. Thus, even this case illustrates how the people of Santa Monica used the PEN creatively to address substantive matters. An engaging account of the early history of community networks can be found in Rheingold (2000).

## The Web and the second generation

First-generation community networks were uniquely inspiring grassroots technology initiatives (Agre and Schuler 1996; Anderson *et al.* 1995; Cisler 1995; Schuler 1996). But, like most applications of information technology, they were quickly overtaken by history. Several factors converged. In the early 1990s, the first-generation projects were succeeding. Networking was improving through the consolidation of the Internet, largely achieved by 1990, and through user-oriented tools such as the Internet Gopher (Anklesaria and McCahill 1993). Personal computers were becoming less expensive and easier to use. A greater variety of people were finding computing and the Internet to be approachable and community networking to be rewarding. This smooth growth curve was disrupted by the rapid ascendance of the World-Wide Web in 1993–4, triggered by the release and wide availability of the Mosaic browser (Vetter, Spell, and Ward 1994).

The first-generation community networks had emerged in an era of teletype terminals. Even as teletypes were replaced with cathode ray tube (CRT) displays, which seemed to be presenting full screens of information, many computer applications continued to use displays essentially as electronic teletype streams. PC software rapidly evolved in the early 1980s, implementing and widely disseminating graphical user interface techniques that had been leading-edge research just a few years before, and doing so on low-end hardware platforms – notably, the Apple Macintosh. Thus, by the early 1990s there was a gaping disconnect between user expectations about online interaction and information presentation, derived from experience with emerging PCs, and the teletype interactions available through Internet services. The PC application experience of the early 1990s was not much different from what it is today, whereas the experience of Internet services was not much different from what it had been at the start of the Berkley Community Memory. (See Kubicek and Wagner 2002 for a slightly different "generational" analysis of the emergence of community networks.)

The possibility of images, graphics, and fonts in web-based information accessible to all users brought these disparate user experiences into better alignment. Almost at a stroke, Internet services all had to be redesigned for the Web. This triggered explosive growth in Internet applications and technologies. For community networks it was a mixed blessing. These projects had evolved within the teletype paradigm with relatively little financial slack. They were in many cases viable as maintenance endeavors, but not staffed or resourced to undertake major redevelopment. It is often more cost effective to start again than to refit old technology into new technology paradigms. And, indeed, many of the first-generation community networks just disappeared, including all of the touchstone examples discussed above.

However, the excitement that the first-generation projects provoked lived after them and energized a second generation of web-based community networks. During the mid- to late 1990s many new community networks emerged, developed in the new web paradigm. The first of these second-generation projects was the Blacksburg Electronic Village, to which we will return in subsequent chapters. Perhaps because web-based systems were also more accessible for members of the press, these projects drew more attention to community networking than the first-generation projects ever had.

The web infrastructure entrained challenges of its own for community networking. Although web pages did a much better job with respect to presenting community information, including photographs and graphics, and eventually were far easier to create and maintain for amateur programmers, they were far poorer at supporting community interaction. First-generation community networks, from the Berkeley Community Memory onwards, had emphasized bulletin board discussions. Field studies like that of Rogers, Collins-Jarvis, and Schmitz (1994) showed that these tools were heavily used and effective in supporting community deliberation. But the early Web was all about static pages of information: The displays were far more attractive than teletype character streams, but there were no discussions. Web browser interaction, for the most part, was limited to following links.

This deficiency was identified almost immediately as a high priority area for further development of the World-Wide Web (Berwick *et al.* 1994). Early web-based discussion tools were indeed disseminated by the developers of the Web (Berners-Lee and Luotonen 1994), but they were not well supported. Nevertheless, by the mid-1990s web-based discussion forums were an active area of web development (e.g., Bentley *et al.* 1997; Rosson, Carroll, and Messner 1996; Suthers and Weiner 1995) and were incorporated into community networks (Carroll *et al.* 1995). As functionality for greater user interaction and dynamic display updating has been incorporated into the Web throughout the past two decades, web forums have become increasing popular throughout the world. There are now several hundred thousand web forums; in 2007, the top forum in Japan, 2-channel, received about 2.5 million posts per day (Katayama 2007).

One of the important vectors of development in the second generation of community networks was commercialization. As discussed earlier in connection with the Cleveland Free-Net, an abiding challenge for community networks has been the development of sustainable financial models. Beginning in the mid-1990s, the Web commercialized very rapidly; this period is sometimes called the dotcom boom. By integrating with the Web, second-generation community networks were integrated into this commercial frenzy in a variety of ways.

For example, since businesses were developing websites, the second-generation networks typically included links to local business sites. And, since many local businesses are franchises of large corporations, the local business links often pointed in fact to corporate sites. Moreover, users are invited to understand links in a web page as a sort of endorsement, or at least a recommendation; after all, the link was placed there deliberately so that visitors to the page could follow it. Thus, by trying faithfully to include local merchants within the community information space, second-generation community networks *ipso facto* put themselves in the position of recommending corporations! This is an interesting contemporary illustration of the tension between horizontal and vertical integration, as described by Warren (1978) long before the World-Wide Web. It also illustrates how quickly community networks moved down a slippery slope from their community activist role of the early 1980s to a hybrid role encompassing economic promotion in the later 1990s.

Indeed, the commercialization of the second-generation networks went much further than isolated links to businesses. America Online (AOL), the leading Internet service provider of the later 1990s, identified local entertainment information and local advertising as key growth opportunities (Bennahum 1996). AOL's Digital City service provided the first model for franchising community networks. Key to this service was a standard design template for listings of attractions, hotels, restaurants, amusement parks, day trips and itineraries, airport information, shopping, and so forth. Thus, each Digital City service reused essentially the same information design. AOL Digital Cities eventually built partnerships with more than 2000 other corporations.

The franchising model tends to stretch the notion of locality in order to maximally reuse information. For example, in 2002 the AOL service provided for Blacksburg, Virginia, was bundled into something called the Central Virginia community, a huge region to call a "community" (Carroll and Rosson 2003). Thus, the "local brew" discussion forum posting recommended a bar in Winston-Salem, North Carolina – more than two and half hours from Blacksburg. The franchising model tends to drive recognition and support for social interaction to relatively superficial and generic levels. Thus, the 2002 AOL service emphasized personal ads, email pen-pal listings, chat rooms, and dating services. Indeed, the 2002 "local brew" query returned much more information about meeting people in bars than about beer and ale. However, the people with whom one might meet and interact were distributed over a vast geographic area. The AOL service included no information on local community clubs, nonprofit/volunteer groups, church activities, or local politics.

The uniform web page designs employed for AOL Digital Cities conveyed lack of distinction, the sense that every place is just like every other place. This was also reinforced by the many generic AOL services that were promoted through Digital Cities, including AOL YellowPages, MapQuest, AOL Classifieds, and links to AOL corporate partners such as Match.com and Q Interactive (coolsavings.com). This uniformity made it easy to compare communities and to find information quickly when visiting a community. The AOL model was especially weak in ignoring the needs of community members, particularly in their roles as citizens and community leaders. Indeed, it directly undermined the possibility of community identity through its cookie cutter information model.

By 2010, the AOL service had evolved in several directions. It was much more complex. Through its citiesbest (citysbest.aol.com/) and cityguide (cityguide.aol. com/) portals, it emphasized the top 20 to 30 major American cities, though it described a wider range of communities in its when.com portal (www.when.com/). The current portals still emphasized local entertainment events and activities, including fairs and festivals, dance, concerts, movie listings, children's events, and so forth. However, the when.com portal also included nonprofit events – for example, a Humane Society bake sale, local Veterans Day speeches, church craft shows, and an Alzheimer's Association community meeting. The AOL portals continued to provide uniform web page/website design for all communities, and still stretched the notion of locality, though most events and activities listed in 2010 for Blacksburg were located less than an hour away. Curiously, the AOL site included no reference whatsoever to the Blacksburg Electronic Village, a well-known and well-established nonprofit community network.

In 2010, AOL was not the only commercial service provider addressing community information. There were other franchised services, essentially following the AOL model, but addressing more focused community information niches. As an example, consider the small university town of State College, Pennsylvania (where I resided at the time of this writing). Three tourism-oriented services provided State College information portals: WeGoPlaces.com, DiscoverOurTown.com, and Tripadvisor.com. Four other services, City-Data.com, RelocateAmerica.com, NeighborhoodLink.com, and AIMRelocation.com, provided relocation-oriented information portals on State College.

Indeed, State College in 2010 was served by *five* community-specific local information portals, all of them commercial in the sense that the majority of their content promotes businesses and business activites: Downtown State College (www.downtownstatecollege.com/), sponsored by the Downtown State College Improvement District, an association of town merchants; StateCollegeCentral (www.statecollegecentral.com/scc2/), maintained by a local web hosting and website design company; StateCollege.com, maintained by Lazerpro Digital Media Group, a local web hosting and website design company and Internet service provider; State College Online (www.state-college.com/), which listed two bulletin boards, neither of which had any discussion activity; and HappyValley.com, a local portal that emphasizes real estate information but which also points to most of the other local portals.

State College information sites also were maintained by its local newspaper (the *Centre Daily Times*; www.centredaily.com/), by its local municipal government (www.statecollegepa.us/), and by a regional nonprofit tourism entity (the Central Pennsylvania Convention & Visitors Bureau; www.centralpacvb.org/). A community-oriented calendar was maintained by the local public broadcasting service (www.wpsu.org/community), and a portal for local nonprofit services organizations is maintained by the local access community television service, C-NET (CentreConnect; www.centreconnect.org/). There were myriad other online local information sources – for example, the site of the local running club (the Nittany Valley Running Club; www.nvrun.com/). (NB: There were also many sites and services, not enumerated above, pertaining to and/or operated by the Pennsylvania State University, the main campus of which is located immediately adjacent to State College.)

One conclusion from this quick survey is that, at least for prosperous and active small communities like State College, the challenge of getting community information online is historical now. Community information in 2010 was pervasively and redundantly online and distributed through a hodge-podge of websites. Instead of a single community network trying to sustain critical mass, the touchstone challenge of the 1980s first-generation community networks, the circumstance of the later 2000s was a chaotic abundance of online information and a bewildering dilution of viewer attention. It is difficult to imagine that anyone in State College regularly used all of the sites enumerated above. Also, the chaotic abundance of online community information was redundant but selective: Information from or about local nonprofit groups and civic volunteer activities receded dramatically relative to community networks of the 1980s, when such information was at the core of community networking, and the 1990s, when it was considered an essential part of the community network.

This should not be surprising. The adoption of commercial models for community websites − both the local and franchise varieties − imposes a now pervasive advertising-based business model on web content: Churches, historical societies, food banks, and environment quality groups must "compete" directly for eye fixations and mouse clicks with movie listings, bar drinks specials, and shoe discounts. A predictable but unfortunate consequence of this is that civic and public information in community websites, and thereby our access to such information, has shrunk relative to consumer-oriented information. For example, in 2010 very little of the information on State College's five commercial websites was directed at nonprofit or community activity, even though State College has a large and varied collection of active nonprofit groups. Not one of the commercial websites pointed to CentreConnect (www.centreconnect.org/), the local portal for nonprofit organizations. This dramatic disconnect between civic/public life and information and consumer/commercial life and information is a disquieting characteristic of the second generation of community networks.

The very pervasiveness of web infrastructure ushered in a new challenge for second-generation community networks. In the decades before the Web, Internet access moved from being arcane to being elite. It grew steadily and rapidly, but the total number of users remained small with respect to the overall society. Conventional understanding of the early Internet was that it was populated by professionals and hobbyists. Most people ignored it. After the burst of acceptance and adoption in the early 1990s, the Internet was rapidly assimilated into broader conceptions of culture and infrastructure. Conventional understanding shifted to view access to web-based information as a socio-economic advantage (Denning and Kahn 2010). Indeed, this view was brutally validated by recognizing who was *not* participating avidly in the Web. Poorer people, the elderly, rural people, the less well educated, and members of ethnic minorities were excluded in far greater proportions.

The Pew Internet and American Life project (www.pewinternet.org) has surveyed these demographics repeatedly over the past couple decades, and it is remarkable how quickly some gaps have narrowed. However, clear disparities remain (the following data are from a Pew survey taken in May, 2008; see Fox and Vital 2008). Ninety percent of people aged 18 to 29 reported that they use the Internet compared with 35 percent of persons older than 65; other age groups were interpolated between these extremes. Ninety-one percent of college graduates reported using the Internet compared with 44 percent of people without a high-school degree; 63 percent of high-school graduates reported using the Internet. Ninety-five percent of people earning more than $75,000 use the Internet, compared with 53 percent of those earning less than $30,000. Seventy-five percent of whites and 80 percent of English-speaking Hispanics report using the Internet, compared with 59 percent of blacks and 32 percent of Spanish-dominant Hispanics. Seventy-seven percent of people who live in urban areas, and 77 percent who live in suburban areas, reported using the Internet, compared with 63 percent of people who live in rural areas. These patterns of differential access to Internet information and interactions are known as the *digital divide*.

There are actually several digital divides (another one is the worldwide disparity in access to information resources between people living in "advanced" countries and those living in "developing" countries). The domestic digital divide is specifically troubling with respect to community networks. Recall that early community networks promoted access and services for less fortunate community members: free medical advice in the Cleveland Free-Net, job training for battered women in Big Sky Telegraph, showers and lockers for homeless people in the Santa Monica PEN. As emphatically stated by Rossman in the 1975 quote reproduced above, a key goal of these projects was to pioneer new ways of enhancing equality. Thus, it is disturbingly ironic that second-generation community networks, succeeding in part through their adoption of the commercially based web paradigm, became part of the web establishment that implicitly, if inadvertently, excluded some groups. If the elderly, the poor, the less well educated, rural people, and ethnic groups participate less in the Internet at all, then they will *ipso facto* benefit less from and contribute less to community-oriented online information and services (De Cindio and Ripamonti 2010; Smith *et al.* 2009; Stephanidis 2009).

In the late 2000s, purely online communities, also known as virtual communities, became pervasive. Virtual communities originally emerged at about the same time as the Berkeley Community Memory project, in the form of the earliest Multi-User Domains (MUDs; Bartle 2003). In the 1980s, bulletin boards (based on the Community Memory model), newsgroups, Internet Relay Chat, and MOOs (Multi-user domain, Object-Oriented) were employed as communications infrastructures for virtual communities (Rheingold 2000; Smith and Kollock 1999). As in the case of community networks, the Web caused a massive reorganization of the landscape of virtual communities; many are now accessed through web browsers. Also as analogous to community networks, the Web rapidly and vastly increased the number and variety of virtual communities (for general discussion, see Kim 2000 and Preece 2000).

The distinction between virtual communities and community networks is far from a dichotomy. For example, Internet-based community networks attracted the participation of *former* residents, people who had moved away from the community, and therefore could participate in the community network only virtually (e.g., Carroll *et al.* 1999). They developed MOOs which modeled the actual geography of the community, but allowed users to engage in MOO-style virtual community activities such as building new objects and locations (Carroll *et al.* 2001; Kies *et al.* 1996). Conversely, early virtual communities sometimes directly leveraged members' knowledge of real places in MOOs (Bruckman and Resnick 1995), an approach that has guided contemporary large-scale virtual communities such as Second Life (Friedman, Steed, and Slater 2007; Wagner 2007). And studies of virtual communities often reported that members subsequently seek one another out in the real world (Preece 2000; Rheingold 2000).

In light of the discussion in chapter 1, it certainly is correct to see virtual communities as communities. Nevertheless, it is also useful to distinguish virtual communities from proximal communities. Communities that are purely or largely virtual are *socially bounded* in ways that are desirable, at least some of the time and with respect to certain goals, but that also limit how rewarding it can be to be members of these communities. Consider this in terms of the simple conceptual model of community sketched toward the end of chapter 1.

An essential property of community membership is the identity commitment of incorporating the community into one's construction of one's self. This is true for any community, but for virtual communities it seems inherently bounded: How committed could one be to images and messages in a browser window, especially when contrasted with the possible identity commitment one makes toward real people and physical interactions. Our correspondents on the Internet are under-identified. They tell us what they want us to know, and not more. The titillating cases of men posing as women online, or perhaps the reverse, are extreme cases. But, even in seemingly normal virtual community interactions, we do not know much about our correspondents. Extremely shallow self-disclosure is typical.

Indeed, members of virtual communities are always just one click away from never being seen or heard of again in their communities. Komito (1998) calls this pattern "social foraging." It is not just a possibility for or an affordance of virtual communities; it is an everyday event. Members abruptly disappear. Nothing remotely like this can happen in proximal community. The positive side of social foraging is that interaction and membership in virtual communities is unlikely ever to be coercive, as it can be in proximal communities. However, reciprocally, it is more difficult to develop broad and robust strong ties and to generate social capital with partners that can and do disappear any time the system updates.

Another essential property of community is member participation. In a sustainable and vital community, at least some members must enact the identity commitment, visibly and with impact. Their participation must be attributed – that is, other members need to know who is actively engaged and some of what they are up to. The inherent under-identification of our correspondents in virtual communities undermines the possible social consequence of their participation. Members do not really know who is doing what. But, even setting this issue aside, the activities in which members of virtual communities can possibly participate are rather limited – mostly, multiplayer games. Many of the most serious virtual community interactions involve only discussion (e.g., Preece 2000). Discussion is surely activity, and serious discussion often entails collaborative meaning-making and emotional connection. But, in virtual communities, discussion rarely has any collective action consequence beyond the discussion itself.

A third essential property of community membership is dense and diverse support networks. Virtual communities are bounded here by the fact that they generally focus on a fairly limited set of relationships and interactions. Even if these are quite intense (e.g., discussing one's cancer), they are still limited. They are not multiplexed, in Coleman's (1988) term; the person one knows intensely and poignantly as a fellow patient, one still most likely does not know as a voter, church member, parent, or Yankees fan.

I participated in a virtual community daily for six months. I helped others, and was helped. I had various social relationships with several dozen other members (albeit mediated by our made-up identities). I mastered various skills and I developed a reputation, which I defended. I joined a relatively integrated subgroup and contributed to the achievement of many of its collective objectives. Indeed, this group had unusually effective leaders relative to my real-world experience. But, one day, I decided to move on (and to write this book). I gave my account and resources to a fellow member. And I disappeared. As with the Lone Ranger, the most my virtual friends could say was "Who was that masked man?" They only knew me through what I said and what I did in the community. They did not know my age, my gender, my nationality, my politics, my profession, my hobbies, my family, etc. For a day or two after my disappearance, I was aware of a change in daily routine, and of course I knew what it was. But since I didn't logon, even that feeling remained rather muted.

Virtual community experiences afford identity commitments, participation, and support networks. They are authentic community experiences. They can be creative and rewarding both for the social forager and for the communities foraged. However, as my own experience illustrates, virtual communities are socially bounded, deliberately and specifically bounded. The balance of this book focuses on proximal communities and community experiences that are definitely imperfect, but that are not *socially bounded* in the sense I have described.

## Trajectories and rationales for community networks

In wrapping up this chapter, we should look toward the future. With even modest optimism, one should say that community networks, as we have known them, are just a beginning, that what we have seen to date in networking to support proximal human community are just the first few prototypes.

Moreover, it is important to pose the question as "Where shall we go from here?" rather than as "What might happen next?" Part of the excitement about community networking, both in the past and for the future, is that it has always been a *design domain* that has both allowed and required human initiative in order to move forward. People just like us invented community networks, and have continued to evolve them through the past four decades. The question now, given our social and technological tools, is where should we take community networking to enhance, or at least to preserve, characteristics we find indispensable, or at least desirable to community in our time? Most intriguingly, we should ask how community networks could strengthen communities in ways that were never before possible (Cooperrider and Avital 2004; Hollan and Stornetta 1992). And, conversely, what can we do to mitigate, or even remove, characteristics of community, or of existing technology to support community that we find intolerable or undesirable? For example, can we address undesired consequences of second-generation community networks with respect to the digital divide?

Designers need more than a highfaluting statement of intent to make substantive progress toward complex socio-technical goals like facilitating the creation of social capital in communities. In other work, I developed the proposal that designs can be viewed as embodying a nexus of specific hypotheses about people and their activities, that analysts can articulate these hypotheses in interpreting and assessing designs in use, and that indeed these hypotheses can be articulated within the design process *before anything is actually implemented* (Carroll 2000; Carroll and Rosson 1992; Rosson and Carroll 2002).

The proposal is often called *scenario-based design* because it involves analyzing designs as props for human activity scenarios (Carroll 1995, 2000). For example, a core design scenario for community networks would be the story of a citizen posting and/or accessing local information. Another would be the story of citizens discussing positions on a local community issue. A third would be a local nonprofit group carrying out its organizational activities such as managing volunteer staff hours at a food bank. And so on. Each of these scenarios could be detailed and specialized in a host of directions, but even at this coarse level of detailing they offer concrete contexts of community interaction through which to view the role that information technology plays and can play. An absolutely critical commitment of scenario-based design is to regard human activity as the ultimate object of design; thus, technology is manipulated and arranged, but only to transform and facilitate human activity in specific desired ways.

A scenario-based design analysis starts from core scenarios and tries to identify hypotheses about human activity that are implicit in the design. These hypotheses are often called *claims* because they are assertions about human activity that are implicit in the design (Carroll and Campbell 1989; Carroll and Kellogg 1989; Carroll, Kellogg, and Rosson 1991; Carroll and Rosson 1991). An example claim in the scenario of a citizen posting and/or accessing local community information is that interaction with such online information reminds all parties that the community is active and thriving – that is, community members are doing things that are being reported, they are planning things that are being announced, etc. This information also reminds everyone of community places where significant activity takes place; thus, people interacting with this information are reminded of those places, of the people in those places, and of other episodic details such as snow in the winter, lighting at night, and so forth.

Claims are empirical. They can be wrong. For example, if the community network presents only movie listings, bar drinks specials, and shoe discounts, it could not possibly convey to anyone that the community is active and thriving *as a community*. Could something like this actually happen? It is plain that it could happen, that it did happen, and that it continues to happen. Design is complex. People are amazing problem-solvers, but they can be overwhelmed by complexity. Even for relatively simple systems like community networks, designers can lose their way. Scenario-based design and claims analysis are lightweight tools for designers and analysts to plan and audit how people will experience systems.

The designer who may have set out to create a civic infrastructure, but nonetheless, through the exigencies and complexities of the design process, ended up with a commercial portal, may need to revisit and rebalance design goals. In this case, claims analysis of key interaction scenarios can provide specific guidance to recover or to strengthen specific aspects of the design. Or perhaps the commercial portal *is*, or became, the design goal. Obviously, not every web-based information system has civic objectives. Even in that case, it could *still* be useful to consider design consequences for the civic activity of people who might just be ordering shoes. The users are whole people, after all, and buying shoes is connected to other aspects of life.

Claims are also empirical in the more conventionalized sense that they are frequently corollary to, or perhaps deductions from, more general principles of descriptive science. Thus, the claim that posting and/or accessing local community information reminds members that their community is active and thriving derives from general principles of social self-perception and attribution theory. People are always observers of their own activity and reactions; they draw conclusions about themselves and the organizations of which they are part (Weiner 1992). This is a routine part of constructing and maintaining the self. Because claims are typically grounded in descriptive science, evaluating claims, by creating and evaluating designs, is a way of assessing and developing the descriptive science itself (Carroll 2000; Carroll and Rosson 1991, 1992; Carroll, Singley, and Rosson 1992).

Thus, scenario-based design and claims analysis is a program for integrating design analysis and action with standard hypothetico-deductive views of descriptive science. I have called this *design-based science* (Carroll 2000; Carroll, Kellogg, and Rosson 1991), by analogy with terms like *experimental science* or *ecological science*, because design work provides the empirical context for developing the science. Other investigators, especially in the learning sciences, have used the term *design-based research* as a somewhat less tendentious label for essentially the same thing (Barab and Squire 2004).

The claims in Box 2.1 describe possible consequences for the community and its members of posting and accessing community information online (an earlier version of this claims analysis appeared in Carroll and Rosson 2003). Claims enumerate the potential causal linkages between *design features*, in this case posting and accessing community information online, and *consequences* for people, such as reminding members that the community is active and thriving.

*Box 2.1*   Claims associated with the posting and accessing community information online scenario

---

Posting and accessing community information online

+ reminds members that the community is active and thriving (boosts collective efficacy) and that its activity is taking place in particular and significant places in the community (the town hall, the park, the community theater, the food bank, the high school, etc.)
+ illustrates how the community's core values, episodes, and traditions are embodied in its everyday activity; reminds people that this can happen, and should happen

*(Continued)*

*Box 2.1 (Continued)*

+ makes the community more visible; provides a shared information commons of experiences and reactions; celebrating, discussing, and developing shared values, episodes and traditions, mores, folkways, and experiences of community and world events
+ conveys to the community how some of its members and groups are enacting core values in community activities and provides social models how people can participate
+ projects the community's core values, episodes and traditions, mores, folkways, and experiences to the wider world
+ provides an additional channel or means (beyond face to face) for community members to participate in and become informed about community life
+ provides additional opportunities for members to learn about the community's social involutions, for example, to discover that a friend's sister also does legal defense work or that a local teacher is also a food bank volunteer and advocate, etc.

— But creating and using online information in itself is a relatively asocial activity and can promote a limited social relationship among community members.
— But managing online community information portals is a significant information design and maintenance responsibility, a technical challenge that entails financial costs.
— But the community's information is scattered across multiple websites, making it difficult to browse or to search for particular information, and diluting the critical mass of community activity reported in any one site, making it seem like less is happening.
— But commercial services providers and advertisers can influence or control what information is included and how accessible it is to users.
— But online information of local community service organizations and non-profits is sometimes left out of community network sites.
— But members posting their everyday information need to recognize and manually emphasize just how their posts exemplify the community's values, episodes, and traditions.
— But explicitly codifying core values to the community itself and to the wider world challenges community members, organizations, local government, etc., to live up to those values.
— But facilitating discussion of core values, episodes and traditions, mores, folkways, and experiences could make local conflicts more public and perhaps more polarizing.
— But authoring and using online information are not universal, literacy skills; some groups within the community may lack adequate online access (digital divide).
— But posting and accessing community information online could undermine established information forums such as local newspapers and other media.
— But it could entrain unintended, and perhaps destabilizing, changes in the social order (distribution of power, social networks, individual and institutional roles and relationships, etc.).

The conceptual model of community, presented at the end of chapter 1, was used to help identify these claims. The model does not cleanly decompose into independent clusters of claims because the facets of the model are mutually reinforcing in whole community behavior and experience. But we can still use the model to help structure discussion of the claims analysis. For example, some of the claims emphasize consequences for codifying community identity – what the community is in terms of people and places, what the community does, how it enacts values and traditions, how it evokes sharing, belonging, and emotional connection. Online community information describes how and where things are happening throughout the community, and how this activity promotes the core values and traditions of the community. It celebrates and develops the community's identity in everyday activity, and, because it does so in a global network, it presents the community to the wider world.

Some of the claims emphasize consequences for community participation – how individuals visibly experience community engagement, doing things and providing social models and leadership to others, and how members visibly have impact on the larger community through decisions and initiatives. Posting and accessing community information is an additional channel for community participation; people who might not be able to attend a public meeting on a weekend evening can post community information whenever they have spare time. The fact that the network makes this contribution public conveys to all that this is something anyone can do.

Some of the claims emphasize consequences for community support networks – how members use various social ties to provide, receive, and reciprocate support, how the involution of the roles members play crisscrosses the social landscape, how relatively deep social connections emerge. Posting and accessing community information creates an information commons in which information is exchanged, and which provides opportunities for people to encounter, and to be encountered by, their neighbors in a wide variety of community roles. For example, the post of a teacher who is also a food bank volunteer and advocate allows people who know her only in one of these roles to appreciate and come to know her in another role.

Claims analysis emphasizes inherent tradeoffs in design: A design is only a panacea when one has not thought enough about it. Features of designs – including software and hardware, use policies, social practices, and applications – entail design tradeoffs in the sense that a given feature always causes both desirable and undesirable consequences for members, groups of members, and other community institutions. For example, posting information so as to benefit from the many upsides listed in Box 2.1 depends on universal Internet literacy among community members, but we know that certain groups are still disadvantaged in various ways with respect to online information and services. The community benefit from the upsides also depends on the person doing the posting to manually emphasize the right community connections and themes. But this is a very significant demand, since the person might just be trying quickly to report a church outing, for example, and not have the time to reflect on the ways that such an activity exemplifies the values and traditions of the community. Also, living the enlightened life is often harder, at least some of the time; thus, conveying community values in posts, and enacting those values, could to some extent burden community members as they try to live up to the community values to which they are committed.

Another set of downsides has to do with infrastructure and system designs. For example, community information, especially the activity of local nonprofit groups, may have no distinct place in the community portal, or there may be many community portals, diluting the visibility and impact of any community information post. Even if there is an appropriate community network for posts, maintaining community networks has many costs in personnel and technology infrastructure. As emphasized since the Cleveland Free-Net, community networks are in need of viable business models. And if the community network thrives, this could undermine other currently viable community information forums, such as local newspapers.

Clearly, creating and using online community information could reduce time available to interact face to face in the community. Such time-budget reasoning has been seen as a critical downside to online community information (Neuman 1991; Kraut *et al.* 1998). Though its effect in those analyses was exaggerated (Kraut *et al.* 2002; Nie 2001), this is still a valid concern. Sharing perspectives is not always welcome by all; some legitimate and valuable community information can evoke controversy and conflict. In the longer term, this might not even be a bad thing, since it could lead to insight and learning throughout the community. But, in the short term, it could be unpleasant. More generally, there is a broad downside that innovative socio-technical transformations can be disruptive for the existing social order. Eventually, this can be a good thing for many in the community, but usually not in the immediate term, and never for established power bases in society.

The analysis in Box 2.1 may try the patience of some readers, but it is actually very abbreviated. Having worked through the claims analysis, many readers will have already generated a few additional significant potential consequences of posting and accessing community information online. It is indeed typical that claims analysis is open-ended, that it helps to raise new issues. The consequences for people and their activity, even limited to the posting and accessing community information scenario, go on and on. This open-endedness is not *caused by* scenario-based design or claims analysis; rather it is inherent to design problems. Thus, for example, Rittel and Webber (1973) argued that design problems address incomplete, contradictory, and changing objectives that are highly interdependent, and that design problems can be neither precisely formulated nor solved. Indeed Brooks (1975) argued that, because of this, designers must implement a design in order to adequately identify its goals. I have discussed the nature of design at length in Carroll (2000).

The "wickedness" of design, to use Rittel's term, is a serious disappointment for analytic approaches that presume closure and rely on strong forms of deduction. Indeed, it helps to motivate a conception of design as managing continually emerging consequences and relationships. In this view, a particular design is just a set of current moves in an ongoing dialectic between artifacts and the human activity they support and transform. For example, a community portal transforms posting and accessing community information. It may boost social capital and community engagement; it may energize citizens into establishing a strongly civic-oriented forum. But, in either case, the activity will be transformed and the changed activity will eventually provoke further designs. I have called this self-sustaining process the *task–artifact cycle* (Carroll 2000; Carroll and Campbell 1989; Carroll and Kellogg 1989; Carroll, Kellogg, and Rosson 1991; Carroll and Rosson 1991).

The implications of the task–artifact cycle are that designers should identify the most important causal relations in a current design proposal, as we have in Box 2.1, but be mindful that design arguments can only be codified at a point in time, and within a current socio-technical context of human needs, interests, expectations, and concerns relative to specific technology infrastructures, applications, services, and recognized short-term possibilities. If this seems uncomfortably vague, it is because it is. Nevertheless, this is how technology and activity have co-evolved throughout human history. What is substantively different in the modern era is that this co-evolution now occurs so rapidly and with such pervasive consequences.

A scenario-based design usually includes at least several key scenarios. Analogous to claims, there is no satisfying sense of scenario-closure. Even for systems of modest complexity, such as community networks, there are many creative and important things people might come up with to do, including quite a few that the designers most likely did not specifically anticipate. Moreover, as mentioned earlier, each scenario "type" has many, many variations. Box 2.2 presents claims for the story of citizens discussing positions on a local community issue. Deliberation among citizens is an important complement to becoming informed and sharing information, as in the posting and accessing community information online scenario of Box 2.1.

*Box 2.2*   Claims associated with the discussing positions on a local community issue scenario (claims carried over from Box 2.1 have been italicized)

---

Discussing online a local issue with a neighbor

+ creates a publicly viewable record of the discussion that can influence other neighbors (including local government) over a span of time
+ contributes to community decision-making by creating public content that others can react to and build upon in further discussions
+ reminds participants and viewers how community members have impact on community decisions (boosts self-efficacy and collective efficacy)
+ conveys to the community how some of its members and groups are enacting core values in community activities and provides social models for how people can participate

*(Continued)*

Box 2.2 (*Continued*)

+ *provides an additional channel or means (beyond face to face) for community members to participate in and become informed about community life*
+ provides a community activity through which members can meet others, and
   be exposed to the views of others, whom they might not otherwise encounter
   or become acquainted with
+ could trigger further follow-up interactions, including face-to-face meetings,
   and development of new relationships
+ *provides additional opportunities for members to learn about the community's social involutions, for example, to discover that a friend's sister also
   does legal defense work, or that a local teacher is also a food bank volunteer and advocate, etc.*
+ allows community members who might be busy with job, family, and other
   obligations to participate when they have free time.

− *But online community discussion forums are not always included or promoted in community network sites.*
− *But managing online community discussion forums is a significant design
   and maintenance responsibility, a technical challenge that entails financial
   costs.*
− But online discussions are susceptible to incivility (aka flaming).
− *But facilitating discussion of core values, episodes and traditions, mores,
   folkways, and experiences could make local conflicts more public and perhaps more polarizing.*
− *But discussing online a local issue with a neighbor could undermine established community discussion forums such as town council meetings, school
   board meetings, and other public face-to-face interactions.*
− *But the discussion could entrain unintended, and perhaps destabilizing,
   changes in the social order (distribution of power, social networks, individual and institutional roles and relationships, etc.).*

Quite a few of the claims in this analysis are literally or analogously carried over from the claims analysis in Box 2.1. Thus, the claim that the discussion forum provides an additional channel for community interaction is also part of the analysis of the posting and accessing community information online scenario. The claim that the discussion forum provides opportunities for neighbors to encounter one another in a wide variety of community roles, a claim about how the community network can facilitate and strengthen diverse support networks, is also part of both analyses.

Five of the downsides are also literally or analogously carried over from the claims analysis in Box 2.1: online community discussion forums are not always included or promoted in community portals; managing discussion forums involves significant skills and effort; the online discussion emphasize and intensify conflicts, including very fundamental conflicts about the community's identity; the online discussion could undermine established and currently effective community discussion forums; and the discussion could trigger unintended changes in the social order (for example, it might come to a momentous decision before the town council even has a chance to consider the issue).

These carry-over claims are relatively more general and therefore perhaps are more generally important with respect to consequences for the community, though we could assess that more confidently if we examined a dozen scenarios instead of just two. But their pervasiveness also creates visual noise in making sense of many claims; they make it more difficult to see what is distinctive about a given scenario. The carry-over claims were italicized here to distinguish them visually from claims more unique to the discussing positions on a local community issue scenario.

The conceptual model from chapter 1 was used to help generate these claims. Claims regarding community participation are especially important for this scenario, though some of these also flow from community identity. An asynchronous discussion carried out in a community network creates a public record of participation that can influence people through time, as they read it and think about it. The discussion evokes participation from others in that they can react to it and build upon it. All this serves to remind everyone in the community that members can have impact on community decisions through their participation. The discussion forum also supports participation by providing an additional communication channel for participation (a claim carried over from Box 2.1). And it specially facilitates the participation of people who are often busy during typical community times (weekday evenings), such as young parents or college students, by providing a channel for participating asynchronously.

Three other claims emphasize ways that the discussion activity can facilitate and strengthen diverse support networks. Thus, the discussion provides a new sort of community activity through which members can meet people and be exposed to views they might not otherwise have encountered. The online discussion could trigger face-to-face follow-up interactions and the development of new friendships. As mentioned above, the analysis also includes the carry-over claim that the discussion helps neighbors better appreciate the community's social involutions – that is, the variety of community roles through which any given person can be known.

This scenario of course also raises potential downsides. The five downsides carried over from Box 2.1 were mentioned above. One downside is more specific to this scenario: Online discussions are susceptible to incivility (flaming; Hiltz and Turoff 1978). People respond quickly; they get very delayed feedback from their interlocutors; they sometimes say things they would never say in a face-to-face encounter. However, such misbehavior would undermine both the particular discussion activity and relationships and reputations across the community.

These first two claims analyses – Boxes 2.1 and 2.2 – are a useful starting point for understanding the design space of community networks – that is to say, the core things people do with community networks, and some of the primary consequences of those interactions. It is just a starting point, though. For example, individual community constituencies such as churches, non-profit service groups, schools, and so forth have their own more specific scenarios for community networks. We will consider some of these later on.

The balance of this book is concerned with design research investigating new possibilities for community informatics and for American community. It uses the analysis of community, and the conceptual model of community, from chapter 1, and the analysis of community networks from this chapter, for example as summarized in Boxes 2.1 and 2.2, as a starting point for asking how community networks can be designed and developed to support local communities.

Community, as we saw in chapter 1, is an evolving and somewhat contested concept. This is not a deficiency in community or in social science; critical concepts are always contested and continually evolve. Community networks and the technologies on which they depend have evolved more rapidly yet, and will most likely continue to evolve rapidly. The introduction of web-based networking tools led to a reconstruction of what community networking was like, who used it, and even what it is was for. Such a context of socio-technical change suggests a research perspective that incorporates design and that poses proactive research questions.

Accordingly, we wanted to focus our investigation on design research questions such as the following: What are novel socio-technical features that could be incorporated into community networks and that might strengthen collective identity? What features might evoke or convey the values of a given community? What features might enhance feelings of belonging or emotional connection?

What is sustained participation in the context of community design, and what are its consequences for the participants? For example, does it enhance their sense of community, their belief that the community is competent and effective (community collective efficacy), and/or their individual beliefs that they can have an impact on the community (perceived self-efficacy)? What are new socio-technical approaches to engaging members in the continuing design of community networks and to sustaining community participation?

What are novel socio-technical features that could be incorporated into a community network to enhance social networks, cause them to become larger, denser, and/or more diverse? How can community networks provide new opportunities, more opportunities, and/or a greater range of opportunities for reciprocating support and developing a wide range of social ties? What are socio-technical features that entrain new social roles within communities and community networks that may appeal to a broader range of members?

Our study was long term and broad in scope. A team of faculty and dozens of students worked for a decade on projects in the context of the BEV, and our work has continued in State College, Pennsylvania, for what will soon be another decade. Yet we have not thoroughly investigated any of the questions above, and for some of them we have barely scratched the surface. We have made a start. We have learned some lessons. The technological and social possibilities for community networks have never been stronger or richer. The technology design pallet now includes better infrastructure for social interaction through so-called Web 2.0 services, as well as infrastructures for mobility and location-sensitive access to community network services. Better projects are more possible now than ever before. The goal of this book is to encourage and facilitate those projects.

# 3 Appropriating a community network

For many people, Robert Putnam's book *Bowling Alone* (2000) was the clarion of crisis for American community. Putnam assembled an awesome and alarming body of data indicating social and civic deterioration in American society. The book is largely the problem statement, the challenge, and the call to arms. While it does not presume to offer the solution, Putnam described a few hopeful signs in contemporary society. One of these was community networking. Putnam (2000: 411) was impressed with reports that community members used networks to strengthen their local face-to-face ties and increase their involvement in community activity. He specifically mentioned the Blacksburg Electronic Village (BEV) project (ibid.: 177): "Experience in Blacksburg suggests that ... social capital may turn out to be a *prerequisite for*, rather than a *consequence of*, effective computer-mediated communication."

The Blacksburg Electronic Village was the first example of a web-based community network. Only a few weeks after officially opening, the project achieved mass-media notoriety. Early high points were coverage of the project by the *New York Times* on January 16, 1994, and by NBC *Nightly News* on February 10, 1994. The storyline was that an idyllic but geographically isolated rural community was pioneering the electronic frontier of totally wired life. The incestuous nature of soft news, and the growing popular fascination with the Internet and the World-Wide Web during this period, led to a steady stream of derivative reports throughout the next two years.

Of course, the BEV did not pop out in January 1994, even if its myth did. It emerged from a tangle of visions about the future of telecommunications, curiously including the somewhat xenophobic fear of Japanese networking initiatives that pervaded the United States in the early 1990s. But the BEV was also about better computing services for students and faculty at Virginia Tech. It was about the town of Blacksburg making peace and moving forward in its relationship with its local telephone operating company. It was always concerned with providing innovative and high-quality services to the people of Blacksburg, and yet, because it was regarded as a critical infrastructure project, it was planned and implemented largely top-down, by institutional partners, and without broad community participation in its early stages. Nevertheless, the project succeeded ultimately in attaining widespread community participation, in demonstrating many new applications and concepts for online community information and activity, and in transforming daily life in Blacksburg.

The story of how the BEV developed, of what it became, and of how the community came to own it was the context for our design research in Blacksburg. But it is also an interesting story about participation in technology development, and specifically about participation in community networks. It is an important story for fully understanding the BEV and the second generation of community networks. And it offers lessons to emulate and to improve upon as community networking goes forward – for example, as it incorporates mobile/location-sensitive services and applications and so-called Web 2.0 social computing technologies.

Participation is absolutely essential to community, and to community networks. Participation is not simple, but simplistic views of it abound. There is a tendency to see it just as a matter of license or permission – that is, of powerful elites, somewhat reluctantly, allowing ordinary folk to have a say, and of the ordinary folk then happily playing more empowered roles. The assumption implicit in this is that people want to and can participate, if *only* the coercive power structures they live within would permit it. But this is far from true. Participation must be regarded as much more than merely an act of will or permission. It is a capacity, a skill, and an achievement. It requires understanding of the domain at issue – in our case, the expression of community activity through Internet technologies and applications. It also requires skills in effective collaboration, such as delegating, coordinating, and negotiating, among others. Not having basic domain knowledge and collaboration skills makes it impossible for stakeholders to recognize, articulate, or promote their own stakes, and thus impossible for them to participate meaningfully.

Even when participation is regarded as a complex and nuanced set of capacities and skills, it can be trivialized by being regarded too categorically. For example, there is a tendency to see it as *baptismal* – that is, to hold the view that, if key stakeholders (in this discussion, ordinary community members) are not involved, not empowered, not included from the very start and throughout the project, then participation has failed. It is definitely true that the most effective participation spans a project lifecycle, starting before goals are initially identified and ending when the use of the system has reached a long-term stability, or perhaps when the system reaches the end of its life and is decommissioned! Another trivialization is to see participation as *all or none* – that is, to distinguish between just two cases: (a) full participation, in which each stakeholder is fully involved in very facet of design, has just as much power as every other stakeholder, and energetically articulates that stakeholder perspective in planning and design discussions, and (b) any other participatory arrangement. In this view, any limits on the involvement and the power of any stakeholder group causes participation to fail, *tout court*. And, again, it is definitely true that full and equal participation of all stakeholder constituencies is the ideal case.

Categorical views of participation are ideologically elegant, but they are academic abstractions, paralytic in practice. They do a disservice to real stakeholders in real projects. They make meaningful participation *less* likely to occur. Thus, seeing participation as baptismal entails that, if some stakeholders are unprepared to participate meaningfully, there is no way forward for participation. It entails that, if full participation cannot be attained because some stakeholders choose to participate less than fully, there is no way forward for participation. In community networking, these are indeed the typical circumstances: Key stakeholders that must be engaged in the project are nevertheless initially unprepared to participate fully. Because of this, they may not appreciate the value of community technology to them or to their community. And when and if they do come to see the value of a joint endeavor, perhaps even to see their participation as a valid civic obligation, some may still never become as engaged in the community network as could ideally be the case.

Community-based participation must be cultivated in its context. Community members relate to the community and to the community network through their lives as a whole – raising their children, maintaining their homes, serving on school boards and in historical societies, and myriad other facets of real community life. From their perspectives, the community network, at best, is another worthwhile civic activity competing for a portion of their time and attention. Community members cannot be sent off to tutorials or to internships on participatory concepts and skills; they cannot be motivated to accept and engage the responsibilities of full participation in order to satisfy a definition. Community life is always already in progress, and any community initiative necessarily joins that ongoing context. Better participation can be evoked, facilitated, and supported. But this will always be a matter of working within a rich landscape of pre-existing circumstances.

In this chapter, we examine how the BEV emerged from a broad planning process, and how community participation emerged from and grew in the BEV project (Carroll 2005). More generally, we consider how capacities and motivations to participate develop in real community contexts, why people who can participate choose to do so, and why they don't, what facilitates mutual participatory relationships, what concepts and skills are most critical to successful participatory engagements, and in what ways participatory interactions facilitate productive outcomes.

## The field of dreams

The BEV project had its origins in a partnership among Virginia Tech (the primary research university in Virginia), Bell Atlantic (the regional telephone operating company), and the town of Blacksburg (Bowden and Wiencko 1993). A further key supporter for the project was US Congressman Rick Boucher of Virginia's 9th District. In two major press conferences, one in January 1992, announcing a feasibility study for the Blacksburg Electronic Village, and another in January 1993, announcing that initial deployment would occur in fall 1993, representatives of the three organizations plus Congressman Boucher were the four principal speakers. In fall of 1993, the BEV was operational, attracting about 1000 official community members during its first year. In July 1994, Reed Hunt, chairman of the US Federal Communications Commission (FCC) declared, "This private–public partnership sets an example for the rest of the nation" (Associated Press 1994).

A variety of issues motivated the various stakeholders to participate in the project. Congressman Boucher was motivated in part by concerns about US competitiveness in telecommunications. This was a high-profile national concern in the early 1990s, often articulated as a need to respond to well-publicized Japanese initiatives. In a 1992 interview, Congressman Boucher stated that part of the urgency to develop the BEV was to help the United States compete with Japanese networking initiatives (Smith 1992). In early 1993, as the BEV project was preparing to launch, the new Clinton administration announced its intention to promote a National Information Infrastructure (NII). At the January 1993 press conference, Boucher characterized the BEV as one model for the implementation of the NII.

In the mid-1980s Virginia Tech was rethinking its strategy for campus telecommunications. There was frustration in the university with what was perceived as out-of-date and expensive telecommunications services. At this time, ambitious plans for a national research network were being developed through the NSFNET initiative. The university wished to play a leading role in such national research and development initiatives, and obtained state support to install a campus telephone switch and to build a high-bandwidth telecommunications network.

The campus network initiative of the mid-1980s motivated the university's participation in the BEV project in two rather distinct ways. First, better campus computing created a demand for better home computing. As early as 1989 the concept of what was referred to as a "community networking service" was discussed at Virginia Tech, and a 1990 university-internal white paper discussed how campus-computing services could be extended to the community (Schorger 1997). Narrowly, the community networking service concept was that faculty and students should be able to obtain the same level of computing support at home as they had in their offices and laboratories on campus (Schorger 1995). More broadly, Virginia Tech saw the BEV project as an investigation of new ways of sharing knowledge. At the January 1993 deployment press conference, Virginia Tech President McComas envisioned networking as a means of bridging the gap between the university and the larger community, and of exploring new conceptions of literacy and citizenship.

The second way that the campus network development motivated the BEV project was that it provided an activity vehicle for restoring relationships with the other stakeholders. When Virginia Tech established its own telephone switch and campus network, Bell Atlantic lost the revenues associated with providing these services, and the town of Blacksburg lost the associated consumer utility taxes. The lost revenues were highly significant dimensions in the relationships among the three entities. For example, when my students interviewed Town Manager

Ron Secrist ten years after these events, he quite fluently cited the exact dollar amount of lost tax money (Park 1995). The BEV project presented an opportunity for the three stakeholders to cooperate in exploring the future of telecommunications, and thereby a means to transcend unpleasant aspects of their shared past. Candidly, though, this hinged on somewhat vague and optimistic expectations that the future would present new opportunities to all the partners.

Bell Atlantic (often acting through its subsidiary, Chesapeake and Pacific Telephone) was interested in the possibility that the BEV project could provide a model for future telecommunications services. Their vision was one of moving work, education, commerce, and leisure into the home. They saw their participation as investment in the development of future products and services. But they also regarded it as a risky investment that needed validation. They wanted to be the first of several corporate partners. Throughout the first two years of the project, 1992–4, Bell Atlantic waited eagerly to confirm their vision by seeing further corporate investors join. At the 1993 deployment press conference, they stated that further investments on their part would be made as new partners were identified. In 1995, it was discovered that Bell Atlantic had originally considered direct investments in the BEV project of as much as $5 million, but had decided to proceed more cautiously, in the end spending only about $700,000 (Schorger 1997).

Indeed, by 1995, Bell Atlantic was discouraged about the commercial possibilities of the BEV project, and was looking elsewhere for new technology initiatives. In a November 1995 interview, at a point when the company had largely withdrawn from the project, David Webster of Bell Atlantic characterized their motivation for participating as one of enhancing community and university relations (Park 1995). This was surely always a part of Bell Atlantic's motivation, but, based on statements made at the 1992 and 1993 press conferences, it was not originally their chief motivation, and was never the only one. In retrospect, it is clear that Bell Atlantic never got out of the BEV project what it wanted or expected. Unfortunately, and despite impressive and effusively positive national news coverage, no new partners joined.

The town of Blacksburg had two stated motivations (as summarized in a 1995 interview by Town Manager Ron Secrist; Park 1995). One was to provide new ways for citizens to access local government services and to participate in local government. The second was to create new possibilities for local economic development, and thereby also to improve and promote the town's image. It is worth emphasizing that these objectives are quite well articulated, particularly given early 1990s understandings of the Internet. One might have expected the town to be a relatively silent partner to technology heavyweights Virginia Tech and Bell Atlantic. However, from this early period the town stated specific objectives that indeed were achieved. A complementary observation, however, is that the town's objectives embodied a fairly narrow view of civic life as encompassing only participation in local government and economic activity.

The town was also the key partner with respect to the mythology of the BEV. The myth was not fundamentally about enhanced campus telecommunications or about new infrastructures and services from the telecommunications industry; it was about a new paradigm for community life. The early years of the BEV coincided with the run up to Blacksburg's bicentennial celebration in 1998. This bathed the community in romantic images of its frontier past. For example, the 1740s settlement was the site of the Draper's Meadow Massacre and kidnapping of Mary Draper Ingles. Her subsequent escape from the Shawnee and her 800-mile odyssey are known locally as the "long way home." In the 1990s, Blacksburg remained a beautiful, isolated place in the Appalachian Mountains. Combining this bucolic imagery with a plan to become a model community for the coming information society jolted Blacksburg into the national spotlight.

In two respects the town of Blacksburg was the most successful of the three partners. First, the town clearly achieved both of its original stated specific objectives, and in only a few years' time. It pioneered new ways of participating in and benefiting from local government, and it also created new possibilities for local economic development. Second, the town's role in the BEV partnership grew throughout the project, where the roles of the other two partners narrowed, as in the case of Virginia Tech, or declined, as in the case of Bell Atlantic. This makes it all the more interesting that at the outset of the project the town had the smallest and most narrow role.

The early years, 1992–4, were focused on infrastructure development, in several senses of infrastructure. The early BEV project was very focused on articulating the town–gown–industry partnership and a sustainable business model. Most concretely, it was focused on networking upgrades that would enable envisioned information services. Finally, and especially in 1994, the project focused on human infrastructure, actively and broadly engaging the population of Blacksburg in community learning and design to create the information and activity that would be the content of the BEV. This infrastructure development was not an organic, self-organizing process per se; rather, it was deliberately managed to respond to challenges and problems that had been identified in earlier community networking projects, that were devolved from recent history in Blacksburg, and that were anticipated based on rational analysis by the BEV planners.

The possibility of an effective town–gown–industry partnership was central to the identity of the early BEV. In part this was seen as a way to grow community networking beyond the first-generation models. First-generation projects had either a single institutional sponsor (the Cleveland Free-Net was sponsored by Case Western Reserve University and the PEN project was sponsored by the town of Santa Monica) or no institutional sponsors (as in the Berkeley Community Memory and the Big Sky Telegraph). Such management arrangements were efficient, but they ultimately limited access of the projects both to diverse stakeholder perspectives and to a broader range of stakeholder resources.

The BEV model was ambitious, but it was not easy to implement. Bell Atlantic was operating in an extremely competitive industry. It always regarded its participation in the project as investment in technology development and public relations, and it constantly evaluated its returns. Bell Atlantic was in no sense a local company. Its local stake in Blacksburg as the telephone operating company was quite narrow and generic. Thus, no matter how interesting the project outcomes – no matter how stimulating or impactful to Blacksburg residents, to local schools or Virginia Tech students, to local government and service organizations, etc. – they could only be rewarding to Bell Atlantic to the extent that they generated new businesses or truly glowing public relations. In retrospect, the triumvirate partnership model could only have been sustainable with a different business partner, one whose core businesses would have directly benefited from innovating and incubating commercial projects in a community network context (Carroll 2001).

Instead, and perhaps unfortunately, the BEV took its "national model" rhetoric literally and sought primarily large corporate partners, such as IBM. Reflecting on this in November 1995, Andrew Cohill, at that time BEV project director, suggested that the payoffs for corporate partners were not obvious enough to them. "Someone from IBM told us that nothing we're doing in Blacksburg has any relevance because we're not charging for the service" (Park 1995). Perhaps this should have been less surprising. In any case, a model for community networking that depends on gigantic corporate partners might be feasible for one or two touchstone projects, but could never be a general model for all community networks. There just are not enough Bell Atlantics and IBMs to go around.

The second institutional infrastructure focus was on a sustainable business model. As in the case of the town–gown–industry partnership, this was a deliberate response to the history of community networks. In 1990, inadequate institutional support and lack of sustainability planning were endemic challenges for community networks, and this is still the case. The BEV planners described two revenue-generating mechanisms to underwrite the costs of developing and maintaining the BEV. First, they proposed to franchise the model – that is, to provide consulting services and software packages to help other communities create electronic villages. This came to be known as "BEV in a box." This is essentially the same mechanism as the Cleveland Free-Net's distribution of its FreePort software through the National Public Telecomputing Network. As of 2010, this BEV service was still offered, though it is not clear that any significant revenue has ever been generated. The second revenue-generating mechanism in the business model was providing test-bed services to industry. Bell Atlantic was the prototype relationship for this mechanism. Indeed, this mechanism in the business model explains why the BEV planners focused on enlisting large corporate partners, such as Bell Atlantic and IBM. Large corporations regularly pursue projects of a size and complexity to need test beds and large-scale field trials. This also explains why the Bell Atlantic relationship remained important to the BEV project managers for several years after it was clearly shrinking and failing.

The BEV business model was also articulated on the cost control side. From the start, the project committed itself to building upon and integrating existing network technologies, as opposed to pursuing fundamental technological innovations in house. During the summer of 1992, a standard package of networking software, including ftp, gopher, a newsreader, and an email client, was developed and made freely available to Blacksburg residents. The goal was to enable easy distribution and installation from a floppy disk. Integration and accessibility of network client software was a challenging objective in 1992. Network access was by no means universal at the time; personal computers were not bundled with network client software as is now typical. In its context, this was an ambitious and farsighted plan. With respect to the business model, it was seen as seeding what would necessarily be a somewhat lengthy process of Internet adoption by the Blacksburg community. Over the next two years, the BEV software distribution was successively refined to improve both the tools and their ease of use. In early 1994, the BEV published its first web page, and in fall 1994 the World-Wide Web browser Mosaic was added to the BEV software package.

Of course, Virginia Tech faculty from various disciplines saw the BEV as a potential test bed for them to carry out research on novel networking tools and applications, as well as to study its personal, social, and institutional affordances and consequences. Through these initiatives the BEV wound up hosting innovative science and technology work that leveraged its infrastructure but which was formally outside the scope of the core project, and therefore which provided its own support. This was an efficient consequence of the business model and of the town–gown–industry partnership with respect to innovation.

The third infrastructure focus was networking. Bell Atlantic accelerated the installation schedule for a digital switch (Rosenberg 1992), laid 42 miles of fiber optic cable, and announced an Integrated Services Digital Network (ISDN) trial. There is some uncertainty about how direct the connection of some of this development was to the BEV project. For example, in 1992, Bell Atlantic stated that the switch upgrade had nothing to do with the BEV project, but in 1993 they stated that the upgrade was a key part of their contribution. The $6 million cost of the switch was frequently cited in 1993–4 to emphasize the magnitude of Bell Atlantic's contribution, but only the accelerated timing of the upgrade was affected by the BEV project. Over the summer of 1993, Bell Atlantic installed Ethernet service in four off-campus apartment complexes and a 10-megabit per second connection to the Virginia Tech campus.

In spring of 1994, Bell Atlantic agreed to provide four T-1 Ethernet network connections to the Montgomery County Public Schools, free for one year. This relatively modest donation had a large effect in helping to engage the school system more actively in the project, causing it to view the BEV and the Internet as educational resources "in hand" to be managed and deployed. Later in 1994, the Montgomery County school system created a new position of technology coordinator, and cooperated with Virginia Tech faculty on a successful proposal to the National Science Foundation for a $99,000 planning grant to develop concepts for a "virtual school." In spring 1995, the school system authorized $400,000 for school computing, and in fall of 1995 cooperated with Virginia Tech to win a $1.3 million award from the National Science Foundation to create a virtual school within the BEV infrastructure (discussed more fully in chapter 5).

The Bell Atlantic network connections also resolved lingering differences in visions for the BEV project. At the outset of the project, Herman Bartlett, superintendent of Montgomery County Public Schools, had argued that school-to-school interactive video would be a critical future technology. He initially resisted committing school resources to the BEV project and, more generally, to Internet-based technology. A liaison for the school system later commented:

> We didn't communicate, we ended up communicating a lot, but it was after everybody's sitting, thinking that everybody else is doing something without us [the schools] and that we were doing stuff without them – and we weren't. We weren't talking to each other, and finally we started talking to each other, but we had different agendas.
>
> (Schorger 1997: 47)

The donation of the four T-1 Internet connections mooted the discussion of whether to make use of the Internet.

Virginia Tech also initiated many hardware infrastructure improvements. In the summer of 1993, it established a high-speed modem pool for off-campus access. This was a relatively modest piece of infrastructure, whose primary initial users were largely Virginia Tech students and faculty. However, the modem pool was critical to enabling the BEV: Accounts were freely available to the entire Blacksburg community, creating universal community access to the Internet. Also in 1993, Virginia Tech began to install Ethernet in its on-campus student housing.

Starting in February 1992, the town of Blacksburg expanded the scope of its cable television committee, the Blacksburg Telecommunications Advisory Committee (BTAC), to encompass community network planning and management. The BTAC discussions, which after 1994 were posted in the BEV itself (Carroll *et al.* 1995; see chapter 6), provide an interesting vignette of community learning. The first discussions of 1992 focused on understanding what a community network might be, how the town could play a role in it, what role the BTAC should play, and of course what the town might be asked to do or to finance. At that time, the town had no Internet access and made very little use of information technology. However, by spring of 1992, the BTAC had already begun to define a leadership role, championing the installation of public access points for residents without home computers and supporting the BEV as a capital investment project for the town. Indeed, after 1992, BTAC meetings were concerned primarily with the BEV project. The town also coordinated the creation of BEV, Inc., a nonprofit corporation created to handle grants, and created a three-year technology plan; Blacksburg had never had such a plan before.

The fourth focus of infrastructure was community outreach and public education. At the inaugural 1992 press conference, Joe Wiencko, first director of the BEV project for Virginia Tech, said, "This is a project about people, not technology." Robert Heterick, vice president for information systems at Virginia Tech in 1992, had called the project a "field of dreams scenario," alluding to the 1989 hit movie that popularized the mysterious slogan "if you build it, he will come." The field of dreams statement conveys both the ultimate importance of local residents coming online and a confidence that, if the infrastructure were built, residents would come (Wiencko 1993). At the 1993 press conference, Dr. Erving Blythe, vice president for information systems at Virginia Tech in 1993, said, "in the end, the residents will define what the village is."

Clearly there is an irony here. The project was seen from the start as all about the people of Blacksburg, the ordinary folk, and indeed it did eventually end up that way. Yet, in 1992, almost no one in town knew anything about the project and, as the various facets of the BEV infrastructure were developed, the mystery just grew from the standpoint of ordinary folk. That said, however, it is also unclear that broader participation could have been truly meaningful in 1992. Blacksburg had never had a community network, and few ordinary citizens knew anything about the Internet at that time. Of course, the town of Blacksburg was the proxy for the population as a whole. But even the BTAC, the town's designated leaders in telecommunications, wrestled with the BEV concept for most of 1992 before firmly establishing the town's stake and leadership role in the project.

A conundrum of technology innovation is that the first applications are necessarily created in a vacuum of established practices: There can be no established "ways of doing" for infrastructures that heretofore did not exist. At the beginning of the BEV project, there were no online community services or activities. There was no community content to access. After the summer of 1993, the Virginia Tech modem pool enabled free Internet access, but few community members understood what this meant or how to use it. Indeed, the deployment of the web-based BEV so closely followed the deployment of the World-Wide Web infrastructure that it was even experienced as novel by Virginia Tech computer scientists and engineers. Only in November 1993 was basic community information on schedules and activities first placed on a gopher server. But, not surprisingly, no one had the job role of maintaining this information, and – foreshadowing the World-Wide Web – the information was not updated for more than a year.

Thinking counterfactually, it is interesting to imagine what the role of ordinary citizens might have been in the infrastructure planning stage of the BEV. The town of Blacksburg represented community interests in the original partnership model, and the BTAC faithfully reported on its own bimonthly discussions. But, in 1992, few people read these reports; BTAC reports became more accessible in 1994 when they were posted on the Web, but this begs the question! Thus, among ordinary residents the BEV remained exciting but mysterious during the early planning phase of 1992–3. Perhaps the planners could have shared more information with the larger community, but the planners themselves were uncertain. Indeed, the first specifications of hypertext markup language (HTML), the software technology that enabled the World-Wide Web, were being published as the BEV was being planned. No one in Blacksburg could have known how the project would be realized in any detail. The general lack of relevant knowledge throughout the non-Virginia Tech portion of the community, and the fact that the planners would have had to be very tentative in describing technological

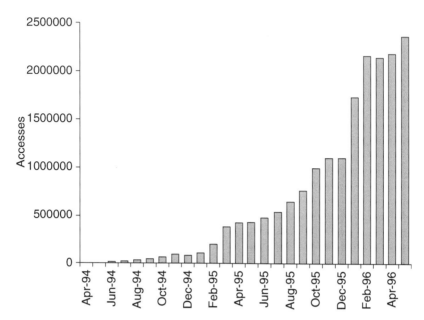

*Figure 3.1*    Accesses to BEV web pages over a 26-month period. The range is 2490
to 2,374,222 accesses per month. Monthly averages are 38,503 for 1994
(nine months); 597,625 for 1995 (twelve months); and 2,126,228 for 1996
(five months).

possibilities that were still emerging, would surely have led to relatively superficial and passive participation. It is arguable that at least part of the BEV project
infrastructure had to be implemented *before* meaningful participation could be
possible.

Perhaps because the local BEV mystery was so closely linked to the world-
wide mystery of new infrastructures for computing and telecommunications, the
community remained intrigued. From early 1994, the BEV developers began to
focus on community learning and engagement. Andrea Kavanaugh, director of
research for the BEV, said in an interview, "The community really has to take
charge if it wants to get a lot out of it" (Foster 1994). The adoption or diffusion
of the BEV in the Blacksburg community followed a characteristic exponential
pattern of growth (see Rogers 1983). Between spring of 1994 and spring of 1996,
accesses to BEV web pages grew by a factor of 1000. In April 1994, nearly 2500
BEV web pages were accessed – a modest number, but still reassuring that the
unprecedented commitment to a web framework could be acceptable to community members. In May 1996, there were nearly 2.4 million unique web page
accesses, as shown in Figure 3.1.

By the middle of 1994, after less than one year of operation, the BEV had
about 1000 community members and 40 businesses (Associated Press 1994).

The early adopters included many community leaders, and they brought great energy to the project of creating the BEV as information and communication activities as opposed to mere technology. These people really were pioneers – something easy to forget, as it has turned out that the rest of the world followed them during the ensuing five years. In 1994, home use of the Internet was almost non-existent. No one in Blacksburg was following a model; they were creating the model.

Infrastructure for community learning and engagement was provided by both the BEV project office in Virginia Tech and by the Blacksburg branch of the Montgomery–Floyd Regional Library. In January 1994, the library, with the support of a federal Library Services Construction Act grant, installed seven networked computers, allowing access to the BEV and to the Internet on a walk-in basis. An NBC *Nightly News* story in January 1994 featured images of people using the BEV in the library. Libraries in the United States are now typical sites for community computing, but this role had not been developed in 1993. Indeed, the installation of computers in the Blacksburg branch was achieved over the objections of two members of its board of supervisors. The library's central location in downtown Blacksburg probably contributed to its effectiveness in providing community learning. Over the first six months of 1994, the library trained about 500 community members through its short courses in networking, as well as providing *ad hoc* one-on-one support for user sessions. Between January 1994 and January 1996 the library public access terminals hosted over 75,000 user sessions (Carroll and Rosson 1996).

Box 3.1 summarizes design rationale for the scenario "learning about and using the BEV in the public library." Upsides are that using the BEV in a public space makes it easier to give and receive support from fellow community members, that this activity leverages the traditional information access role of the library in the community, that it promotes a new community role for the library of facilitating information exchange and informal learning among community members, and that it helps to make participation in such a community learning initiative more visible to other members of the community, perhaps inspiring their participation. The potential downsides of this type of BEV interaction is that one cannot save local work on a public access terminal, and there are a limited number of terminals available for use. Finally, it involves one actually going to the library.

*Box 3.1*   Claims associated with learning about and using the BEV in the public library

---

Learning about and using the BEV in the public library

+ enables getting support from fellow community members
+ leverages the traditional role of libraries in enhancing information access in communities

*(Continued)*

Box 3.1 (Continued)

+ promotes a new community role for libraries of facilitating information exchange and informal learning
+ makes participation in a community learning initiative more visible to the community.

− But it is difficult to save local work in public terminal sessions.
− But there are a limited number of public terminals.
− But to work at a public terminal one must physically go to the library.

The library initiative was very significant for the development of the BEV. The library was a purely community-based partner, entirely outside even the town government. Its hosting of the public access terminals showed how institutions beyond the original town–gown–industry partnership could appropriate key roles in moving the project outward and forward. In February 1994, the library began acting as a receiving station for BEV membership applications. In retrospect, the whole "membership" concept was slightly archaic from its inception. After all, why be a "member" of a free web service? The idea derived from the early concepts of the BEV as a panel of field testers for Bell Atlantic, and more broadly perhaps from a misjudgment about how open the Internet would become through the early 1990s. Nevertheless, BEV membership − circa 1994 − was symbolically meaningful in Blacksburg, and the fact that such a core function was partially delegated to and located in the library made the latter into a de facto core partner in the project. This was vivid to the entire community and opened the gates wide for other community groups and individuals to claim their roles in creating the BEV.

As mentioned earlier, the BEV project office in Virginia Tech had begun software distributions in the summer of 1992. All of these distributions were accompanied by instructional and documentation materials. In 1994, courses were started and individual user support to the community begun in order to help people make use of the BEV. Like the library courses and support, these were popular, though through much of this period the BEV project was located in a fairly distant corner of the Virginia Tech campus, basically accessible only by car. Later in 1994, the project provided a series of workshops for local businesses. These were also extremely popular, and generated a great deal of interested in the BEV and Internet in the local business community. Every workshop session offered in this period was run at capacity. In October 1994, the project office moved from its invisible-to-the-community campus location into space in the Virginia Museum of Natural History on Main Street, generating substantial walk-in traffic. It organized a BEV volunteer group that responded to approximately 44,000 help calls between October 1994 and January 1996 (Carroll and Rosson 1996). Andrew Cohill, the BEV project director in 1994, said that he had come to realize increasingly that building a community network was primarily a community learning project (personal communication, October 1994; see also De Cindio and Ripamonti 2010).

In the summer of 1995, the town of Blacksburg provided $15,000 for what was eventually 47 small grants, ranging from $90 to $390, to help local businesses establish or improve their World-Wide Web pages. Ken Anderson, a board member of BEV, Inc., the community nonprofit created to manage grants, explained that these were preferentially awarded to businesses that brought money into the town from outside, as opposed to businesses that "just circulate money inside the town" (Park 1995). However, the grants also required businesses to create their own web pages or to hire Blacksburg-based Internet Service Providers, and to agree to list their web pages in the Village Mall page in the BEV.

These infrastructure initiatives for community engagement and learning were very successful. During 1995, one-third of all businesses in Blacksburg had a listing in the BEV Village Mall web page, most of them including links to web pages maintained by individual businesses. By the end of 1995, fourteen Blacksburg companies provided web design, server space, and Internet consulting; twelve of those companies were founded during that year. No doubt the "field of dreams scenario" overstated things a bit; as far as anyone knows, Mary Draper Ingles never showed up to use a public terminal at the library. But the Blacksburg community beyond the anchor partnership of the town, the university, and the regional telephone operating company did come. Partly due to the BEV project's focus on human infrastructure, a wide variety of community members became informed and involved in local telecommunications discussions and initiatives.

## An experiment in culture, a culture of experiment

When the Electronic Village became vivid to the community at the beginning of 1994, it triggered a remarkable process of distributed community learning that continued for more than a decade, and eventually embedded the Internet into daily life as transparently as the telephone. One must concede that conditions in Blacksburg were quite favorable for this. The infrastructures were all developed – high-speed networking, Ethernet to the home, public access terminals and modem pool access, a well-educated population that by the end of 1994 was also quite sophisticated with respect to networking tools, and a strong town–gown partnership between Blacksburg and Virginia Tech, perhaps bolstered the more by Bell Atlantic starting to withdraw to pursue its commercial projects in interactive video.

The national publicity at the start of 1994, and the follow-ups that continued through the next two years, had large effects *inside* the community. This attention was an objective signal to Blacksburg residents that the BEV project was exciting and important to the outside world. It was a pervasive topic of conversation in the town, especially during 1994, and was a huge boost to community identity, but more specifically it fixed the BEV itself as a core element of that identity. Thus, remarkably, the BEV moved in just a few months' time from being a somewhat closed and mysterious planning and infrastructure project to being the most visible and most paradigmatic attribute of the community's self-perceived identity.

These changes in the community's self-perception were accompanied by dramatic changes in activity. A wide range of new community practices developed

*Figure 3.2*   BEV homepage in 1996.

in 1994. New social structures formed, such as the BEV-news listserv, a group that included technical support staff, early adopters, and new users with varying levels of computing experience and sophistication. During the first decade of the BEV, this was a very active group. Its email traffic and resulting archives became an important resource for community members, not only in their efforts to become more sophisticated users of the community network (the original intent of the listserv) but also as an additional channel for general social support and interaction (e.g., sharing successes or problems with community organizations). The listserv was a major feedback channel to the BEV project office.

By late 1995, a substantial proportion of the local community had access to the BEV and to the Internet. Based on town surveys, the BEV project office estimated that more than 45 percent of the population of Blacksburg, about 17,000 people, had access to the BEV at home or at work and used BEV information and services. This was far beyond the US national average at the time – less than 4 percent of the population (about 9.5 million Internet users, of whom 7.5 million reported using the World-Wide Web, out of a total population of 262 million; Interactive Services Association 1995). Users of the BEV were disproportionately affiliated with Virginia Tech: 85 percent of those with access to the BEV were Tech-affiliated (the town's population was 75 percent Tech-affiliated). There were approximately 4000 registered BEV members, 48 percent of whom were Tech-affiliated. Interestingly, 33 percent of BEV members were female, a relatively high proportion for Internet-based groups in the mid-1990s.

At this time, the BEV hosted fourteen community newsgroups on a variety of topics, four listservs, and its own chat room. Over 100 community groups and 200 local businesses maintained BEV sites. During 1995, accesses of BEV web pages grew ninefold; between April 1994 and May 1996, accesses to pages grew by a factor of 1000 (Carroll and Rosson 1996). As mentioned above, in 1995 all of Montgomery County middle and high schools (encompassing Blacksburg) had T-1 Internet connectivity. For reference, in 1995, 65 percent of US secondary schools had Internet access; the rate was less than 48 percent for rural and small-town schools (Cattagni and Farris 2001). The next year, all twenty schools in the Montgomery County school system – that is, including elementary schools – had T-1 Ethernet or Token Ring networking and had created some web content.

During 1995, the *Los Angeles Times* (Harrison 1995), the *Philadelphia Inquirer* (Farragher 1995), and the *Washington Post* (Chandrasekaran 1995) all ran feature articles on the BEV. The *Inquirer* referred to Blacksburg as "perhaps America's most wired municipality" (Farragher 1995: D1). This rhetoric was quickly assimilated into casual talk around town, and excitement fed excitement. Indeed, during 1995 the BEV project suffered some backlash from too much media exposure. For example, the Seattle Community Network, a more traditional first-generation community network launched by a group of computing industry professionals just after the BEV, limited its launch event to 100 persons specifically so that it would not appear BEV-like (Silver 2004)!

The rapid and broad engagement of the community was unlike anything seen before in community networking. The BEV became a clearinghouse for community groups of all sorts – local chapters of mainstream service organizations, such as Kiwanis, the League of Women Voters, the Lions, the Rotary, and the Humane Society, as well as organizations more unique to the Blacksburg community, such as Beans and Rice (a community development organization working with chronically under-served populations of Central Appalachia), the Blacksburg Seniors, the Citizens' Alliance for Sensible Gun Ownership and Legislation, Citizens Concerned about I-73, Friends of the Hand-in-Hand Park, the Montgomery County Christmas Store, and the New River Community Shelter. Local doctors posted health information. Local schools posted student projects. At this time, the BEV provided links to 60 local churches and many local arts organizations and clubs. Blacksburg is a cosmopolitan college town,

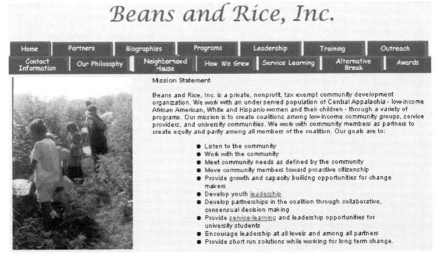

*Figure 3.3*   Homepage for Beans and Rice community group.

and can seem even more cosmopolitan given that it is surrounded by rural Appalachia, but the BEV made the diversity of the community more visible and accessible to every member. Three of the most active community group sites in the BEV in 1995 were those of the seniors, the Islamic Center, and the arts council (Carroll and Rosson 1996).

In 1995, the town of Blacksburg had developed an extensive website for municipal information, including digital maps and directions, dog licensing, parking, inspections and permits, road maintenance, parks and recreation, zoning and planning, and public transit schedules. The town provided some services directly online – for example, residents could request a vacation house check, participate in town and county surveys through a web form, or ask to have town announcements sent to them via email. The town also streamed video of council meetings over the Web, allowing residents who could not physically attend a meeting to see what was going on. Residents could send email to municipal officials and departments. For many other services, forms could be downloaded from the town's website.

In 1994, the World-Wide Web was strongly a publication medium. Its initial power was that it provided an easy user interface for the publication and reception of multimedia composite documents (basically, text plus images) – easier, that is, relative to the file transfer protocol (ftp). But, like most design innovations, the web paradigm was not merely an enhancement *tout court*: It facilitated publication-reception, but in doing this it de-emphasized and obscured tools for interactive discussion, such as email, listservs, newsgroups, Unix talk, and IRC chat. Moreover, publishing web pages requires one to have access to a server. Very few ordinary Blacksburg residents were in a position to run a web server in 1994. The BEV development group at Virginia Tech made server space available, but the university mandated that it exercise strict control over the contents of that web space. Thus, ironically, the "enhanced" infrastructure of the BEV, relative to first-generation community networks, biased participation in the community network to *publication over interaction* (recall the rationale for community network interactions in Boxes 2.1 and 2.2).

The BEV's commitment to be web-based also raised concerns that a web-based community network might become no more than an entry point to the World-Wide Web, to generic information and services having no connection to Blacksburg or southwestern Virginia. Beginning in 1993, Andrea Kavanaugh and various collaborators conducted a series of BEV surveys. During the first decade the surveys showed how local uses – participation in community listservs and accessing local web information – steadily *increased*. Indeed, the longer people used the Internet, the more likely they were to use it for local social-capital-building activities, more generally to feel identification with and attachment to the local community, and to be involved in community-based activity (Kavanaugh and Patterson 2001; Kavanaugh *et al.* 2003; Kavanaugh *et al.* 2005). The earliest surveys indicated more interest in local content and services than in global Internet content and services, though it is important to recall how undeveloped the World-Wide Web was in 1994, relative to entertainment, retailing, and other commercial services that are now sophisticated and inescapable.

Box 3.2 presents some of the design rationale for moving community network activities to the Web. This rationale builds on the claims analysis of Box 2.1, an analysis of interacting with community information independent-specific platforms. The web platform, relative to prior Internet tools typical of first-generation community networks, provides a better user experience through better fonts, graphics, and images. These richer information displays allow the community network to do a better job of codifying and promoting community identity through distinctive visual designs. Implementing on the web platform also integrates activities and resources with other web-based tools and information, and makes the community more visible both inside and beyond the community.

*Box 3.2*   Claims associated with accessing community information through the World-Wide Web (builds on Boxes 2.1 and 2.2)

---

Accessing community information through the World-Wide Web

+ creates a better user experience (relative to teletype interfaces of the first generation, including better-designed fonts and texts that incorporate graphics and images); this may motivate people to engage with the community network more

*(Continued)*

*Box 3.2   (Continued)*

+ promotes community identity by codifying in text and graphical displays the key structures and signature activities that comprise the community
+ increases the visibility of the community and the community network to the community itself, as well as to the broader society and the world beyond
+ enhances the visibility of local nonprofit groups, boosting community support, volunteering, and coordination among groups
+ integrates the network more seamlessly with a wide variety of Internet tools and resources, making the community network a richer media experience and suggesting technology learning possibilities to community members.

− But it requires greater technical expertise to implement and maintain sophisticated information and user interface designs (or entails contracting costs).
− But member-designed web pages and content may be visually inconsistent and otherwise uneven in quality.
− But accessing community information may tend to reduce the relative proportion of local information and communication in the community network.
− But this may draw the attention and activity of community members away from local content and toward more generic Internet content and activity.
− But it does not encourage or support discussion, deliberation, and debate among community members.
− But it may require or favor faster personal computer and high bandwidth network connections, thereby implicitly limiting participation of some community members.

There are also potential downsides of web-based implementations. The Web, especially in the mid-1990s, was a more complex software platform to manage, and non-experts frequently produced hideous designs that misused fonts and graphics. The Web required more computer power and network bandwidth, implicitly favoring community members with better computing resources, creating the possibility of a local digital divide. Finally, integration of the community network with the broader Web also increased the risk that community members would regard the network as just a launching point to worldwide information and resources and ignore the local content, though Kavanaugh's results suggested this downside was not a serious threat.

Through the next decade, the BEV contrived to develop. By 2001, 88 percent of Blacksburg residents and 79 percent of Montgomery County residents reported having personal Internet access at home or at work (Kavanaugh *et al.* 2003); of course, all residents could use the Internet through public access networked PCs in the library. According to the US Census Bureau's Current Population Survey (CPS) reports on computer and Internet use in the United States, slightly less than 55 percent of the US population had access to the Internet in September 2001. Indeed, even by early 2010, Internet access in the US was not yet 70 percent (US Census 2010). In 2001, more than 150 community groups and 550 local businesses in the greater Blacksburg community maintained websites. This represents more than 80 percent of all local organizations.

As the community appropriated the BEV, the community network evolved into a highly distributed confederation of community groups. These groups envisioned and implemented their own information systems and activities within the BEV umbrella, often inspiring other groups within the community, and broadening their own role within the larger community. Indeed, several groups that had played no role whatsoever in the early phase of planning and infrastructure development, such as the library and the Blacksburg Seniors, almost suddenly became community leaders through their own local innovations. This was quite striking to witness, both in how rapidly it occurred and in how thoroughly it changed the BEV from the inside out. The town and various entities within Virginia Tech became community participants in the overall activity of the BEV, but fewer and fewer were privileged participants or owners. The BEV project at Virginia Tech increasingly served a support function, not a central leadership role.

Blacksburg has a large, active, well-educated and well-organized population of elderly people. In recent decades, college towns have become popular retirement destinations. Blacksburg has a moderate mid-Atlantic climate. Its proximity to the New River and the Appalachian and Blue Ridge Mountains offers many outdoor activities; it is practically surrounded by the Appalachian Trail. Virginia Tech hosts many cultural activities, and the city of Roanoke, with a symphony orchestra, a zoo, professional sports teams and several theaters and museums, is less than an hour away. The Blacksburg community beyond Virginia Tech has community theater groups and several art galleries and historic sites. In 1993, as the BEV opened, the historic Lyric Theater was in the final phases of restoration as a community cultural center.

The Blacksburg Seniors, who quickly began calling themselves the BEV Seniors, were important early adopters of the BEV. Indeed, the BEV itself helped to solidify and energize a community of older adults who were beginning to associate through the town recreation programs. It allowed these older adults to interact with one another and with other community members more frequently and conveniently; they developed a rich set of online information and support services and became role models for other organizations in the BEV. The seniors saw the BEV as an important new source of information and activity. They also saw it as a self-educational project; they organized classes and support for fellow seniors. Eventually, they also saw the BEV as an opportunity for community service – for example, by providing tutoring – and an area in which the seniors could provide leadership to the larger community, by helping to design and explore new applications and services within the BEV. Since 1994, the seniors have maintained one of the core BEV pages, providing lists of local programs and national and worldwide resources for seniors, as well as links to the calendar of seniors' events provided by the local newspaper (e.g., walks, lunches, lectures). In the early years of the BEV, the seniors also managed a listserv discussion group of about 100 core members.

One early project initiated by the seniors' group involved their effort to gather and organize the recollections and artifacts of long-time residents. The Nostalgia Project began with discussions on the seniors' listserv, through the exchange of personal stories and reflections via email, and a series of organizational meetings. A form-based web application for collecting and annotating stories was announced in June 1996. Eventually, the Blacksburg Nostalgia system also supported sharing photographs. This project is discussed in chapter 6. Another project, CommunitySims, involved a reciprocal mentoring project in which pairs consisting of an elderly person and a middle-school student created and shared visual simulations depicting various community issues – for example, noisy fraternity parties or cars not coming to a complete stop at a particularly chaotic intersection. In these collaborations, the elderly person was the designated expert on community relations, while the middle-school kids were designated experts on visual programming. The intent of the project was to share skills and knowledge across generations. This project is also discussed more in chapter 6.

Another example involved a partnership among the town, the local high school, and the senior center. Blacksburg High School is located directly across the street from the town community center, which offers various after-school activities and which also houses the seniors' center. When the high school wanted to add Internet access to after-school activities, the town offered to provide computers and technology support funding to the seniors' center if the seniors would share the computer lab with the students and provide oversight for the after-school use of the lab. This made another half-dozen public access terminals available, for both old and young, in another public space. It also quickly provided a community learning experience for all the partners. Some of the high-school students wasted no time in misusing the computer lab to access adult materials and chat rooms. This alarmed the school, worried the town, and required the seniors to supervise the students more closely. The town also provided Internet-filtering software, which had the side effect of making network access more cumbersome. Some seniors felt that the deal they ended up with was less attractive than the one to which they had agreed, but it was clear that the role of the seniors in the Blacksburg community developed and expanded through this partnership.

Churches were another kind of community group that made innovative use of the BEV visible and inspiring to the larger community. More than 60 churches throughout Blacksburg developed homepages displaying a rich variety of information, church mission statements, schedules of events, monthly bulletins, email lists and directories, links to congregation community projects and to sister congregations, reports from missionaries, and translations of particular scriptural passages. At least one church made a weekly service available on the Internet for members who were traveling. In late 1995, one resident estimated that a majority percentage of his congregation's weekly communication was conducted by email; for example, the choir managed music selection, agreement on keys and chords, exchanging of lyrics, scheduling of practices, and so forth. He felt that these new channels increased communication among church members relative to how it had been before the BEV.

Church groups reported that their BEV information was often accessed by people moving to the Blacksburg area, or considering a move, and looking for a church. Some of the non-Christian denominations particularly emphasized the role of the BEV in enhancing "the diversity, richness, and quality of life in Blacksburg" by making their groups more visible to the larger community. This particular goal, of making one's group more visible to the larger community, was just pervasive in the BEV of the late 1990s: The mountain biking club used it specifically to broaden its membership beyond Virginia Tech students, a community theater group used it specifically to recruit from a wider community pool of potential actors and other participants, while the hunting club used it to recruit and to inform the broader community about training, safety, and services the club offered (Carroll and Rosson 1996).

The BEV-news listserv was a particularly interesting subcommunity in Blacksburg, in part because it was directly caused by the BEV. The original purpose of BEV-news was online community discussion of policies for the BEV. The project team members participated, sharing information with and fielding questions from about 350 community members (in 1996). The listserv was a vital forum for many policy discussions; for example, in early 1996 it was the primary forum for debates about how the BEV would be affected by a shift from Internet services provided mainly through the Virginia Tech modem pool to Internet services provided as well by commercial Internet Service Providers (this episode is discussed more fully later in this chapter). Thus, BEV-news was a critical for the community's appropriation of the BEV. It was a speaker's corner where interested community members could raise their questions and perspectives and stake their claim on the community network.

Over a twenty-month period during 1994–6, archived BEV-news contributions revealed a range of discussion topics far broader than BEV policy. Members raised and discussed help questions; they made announcements of current events and personal matters, such as a birth announcement; they discussed municipal issues, such as parking tickets and restaurant critiques; and they shared pointers to and discussions of Internet resources beyond the BEV. Overall, most of the contributions came from ordinary community residents; the input from the BEV project team was about 13 percent. Starting in 1995, the BEV-news group began organizing social gatherings, and thus became a community group in its own right – that is, not just a listserv discussion group.

Thirty-five percent of all BEV-news traffic pertained to help and education discussion, with less than 10 percent of this support coming from the BEV project team. In general, at this time, among all BEV subcommunities, self-help and education was a prominent activity. One of the main things people did in those early years was to learn about the BEV and the Internet, and to help their neighbors learn. And these mutual learning interactions evoked broader interaction and mutual cooperation throughout the community. This supports Cohill's conclusion that a community network is primarily a community learning project (personal communication, 1994).

Local economic development was a central theme in the BEV vision (Schorger 1995; Sears 1996). But business was slow to join. Some local merchants were concerned that their skills and resources were not sufficient to manage a serious presence. Some were concerned that shifting their customer interactions to the network would depersonalize and devalue the face-to-face interactions they had cultivated, were proud of, and enjoyed. And some worried that exposing information about their businesses to competitors and potential competitors could undermine their business in some way (Carroll and Rosson 1996). The BEV project's workshop series in late 1994 and the town's small grants program of 1995 were effective in helping to engage local business. By the end of 1995, over 200 local businesses (approximately one-quarter of all Blacksburg businesses) had some sort of presence in the BEV, in many cases a web page. Most viewed their participation both as supportive of the community initiative and as a means of advertising. Some mentioned "worldwide" exposure as a potential benefit. However, when pressed for specifics, no business we interviewed in this period could document concrete commercial advantages either locally or globally (ibid.).

Nonetheless, local businesses were quick to catch up and become a subcommunity of innovators. One example was a web form ordering service developed by the local grocery store, Wades. This allowed people to order various products online and have them delivered – for example, flowers or customizable "care packages" of food that parents could order for their Virginia Tech undergraduates. Variations on the idea soon appeared around town. A local travel agency began accepting itineraries and requests for accommodations, car rentals, etc., via web forms. At several restaurants, one could order ahead or reserve a table through the BEV. Of course, this kind of service later became fairly common, with web infrastructures make ordering products extremely easy and secure. But the idea was novel when Wades implemented it. In 1994, these services were available only in the little town of Blacksburg. It was impressive that even these commercial entrepreneurial activities manifested a strong community orientation. As one local garden store owner put it, their ambition was to be "the leading horticulture/plant info center in BEV." Interestingly, the goal is referenced to the community, and the community is referenced *as* the community network (Carroll and Rosson 1996). The design rationale for "moving local business information and services online" is summarized in Box 3.3.

*Box 3.3*  Claims associated with moving local business information and services online

Moving local business information and service online

+ contributes to the community's identity
+ provides local businesses a way of participating in the community's collective initiative
+ encourages innovative services not possible without the community network
+ potentially gives local businesses worldwide visibility.

*(Continued)*

Box 3.3   (*Continued*)

- But this could undermine face-to-face relationships between merchants and their clients and customers.
- But it could reveal too much about business practices to potential competitors.
- But it entails learning new skills, developing new resources, and incurring new costs.

Throughout the late 1990s, many group and individual initiatives regularly seasoned the BEV with innovation. A restaurant installed a networked PC at their bar. The owner said it would be "a useful and unique experiment" to facilitate informal peer learning through show-and-tell discussion. A local physician posted medical journal summaries to help neighbors better participate in doctor–patient interactions. The local Save Our Streams group helped to design geospatial software to annotate stream locations with water quality data gathered at those locations (Carroll and Rosson 1996; Carroll, Rosson, Isenhour, Ganoe *et al.* 2001; Schafer 2004). Community networks are always constructed by the community, in the sense that community members create the information in them. In the BEV, this was elaborated and applied to the level of services and applications: The Blacksburg community innovated a range of new community networking services and applications. And, quite typically, the overriding motivation was to stimulate and to enrich the participation of fellow community members.

Part of what was so exciting about the first decade of the BEV was surely a sense that one was living history. It seemed at the time, and events have proven, that the development of community web-based information, services, and activities was more than just a technology trial, a one-shot experiment. It seemed rather to be a point of inflection, the opening of a door to a paradigm for everyday life that was closely integrated with the Internet. No one could have known then that the model being developed and explored would become pervasive through the next two decades, but everyone seemed willing to work through investigation and help to create the model.

In 2010, the BEV was still operating, and was even more developed as a community portal for online information on local groups, businesses, and government. The central content of the homepage was a list of community events. In late March of 2010, it announced performances by a community theater company, a fundraising event by the Blacksburg Junior Women's Club to support local charities serving women and children, a cyber security competition by a Virginia Tech student club, an experiential art exposition to be held downtown, a free Internet program to help people make permanent healthier lifestyle changes developed by Virginia Tech psychologists, and a call for blood donors at the New River Valley Donor Center. At the end of the list, there was a link to a few other recent announcements: a link to a service to compare gas prices, a reminder that the Montgomery–Floyd Regional Library system offered free wireless

Internet connectivity (continuing to offer free wired terminal access), a note about the "computers for families" program that made refurbished PCs available to needy families, and a call for the Volunteer Emergency Families for Children program through which families provide short-term shelter and care to abused, neglected, runaway, and at-risk children.

A side bar on the right of the homepage presented a set of more persistent announcements. There was a call for BEV volunteers and a notice about COSMOS (Community Services Management System), an open source web-based system to manage client interactions and referrals for human service agencies developed by Virginia Tech, the Washington County (Virginia) Department of Social Services, and One Care, a regional nonprofit promoting health and human services for the people of southwest Virginia. There were two links (to the same page) warning people about spoofed emails and phishing scams, a set of quick links to BEV-news, newsgroups, etc., and two links to BEV research reports (alas, rather out of date).

At the top of the homepage, and repeated at the bottom, were sixteen primary content links, formatted at the top of the page into two ranks of eight buttons: E-Community, Visitors, Neighborhoods, Village Mall, Government, Youth, Services, Help/FAQ, Arts/Entertainment, Seniors, Calendar/News, Education, Organizations, Health, About, and Search. E-community, Services, Help/FAQ, About, and Search presented basic information about the BEV itself: BEV account maintenance functions (including registrations, email forwarding, password change, and access to a community directory), services provided by the BEV group (including websites, email accounts, mailing lists and online calendars for individuals and nonprofit organizations, pointers to help and training resources, classes, software, and the BEV FAQ), a repository of documents created by the BEV group through the years, and a search tool.

Visitors, Neighborhoods, Youth, Arts/Entertainment, Seniors, Calendar/News, and Health were fairly small and specific resources. The Visitors page had links to flying and driving directions, maps, lodging, dining, and parking information, and suggestions for things to do. Neighborhoods listed 25 Blacksburg neighborhoods, with links to four that maintained their own web pages. Youth was a single small page with graphics and a few links, some directed at children (Blacksburg Parks and Recreation, the regional youth symphony orchestra, the Virginia Youth Soccer Association, 4H, Boy Scouts and Girl Scouts) and a few directed at their parents (Virginia Tech Family and Work Life Resources, Blacksburg Daycare Centers). Arts/Entertainment pointed to the BEV events listings and to the Village Mall and community organization directory for lists covering arts, music, dance, etc.

As was always true of the BEV, most link paths from the homepage left the BEV web space after only one link. Seniors was an extreme case in that it was a top-level content link that *immediately* took the user out of the BEV. The page had a look and feel independent from the BEV pages, and did not even include navigational links to take the user back to the BEV site. It provided links to various community information sources, to online help and software downloads, to a seminar series for local seniors, and to websites and government information sites particularly relevant to seniors. The Calendar/News link displayed the second part of the events list that was on the BEV homepage, along with links to a calendar view of local events, a form for submitting events, and a list of local Blacksburg newsgroups, mailing lists, and listservs. The Education link displayed a small list of education-related resources, including SEEDS (Seek Education, Explore, Discover), a local educationally oriented nonprofit group, Virginia state agencies, the Kaplan test preparation company, two Blacksburg arts academies, several Virginia Tech programs, and the YMCA Open University. The Health page was a very extensive portal with hundreds of links to a wide variety of health resources. It was designed and maintained by the Edward Via College of Osteopathic Medicine, located in Blacksburg, as part of a public health project funded by the National Library of Medicine.

The Village Mall, Organizations, and Government links pointed to portals for local businesses, town/county government and political organizations, and non-profit groups, respectively. The Village Mall listed 728 businesses grouped into 116 categories, from accountants, adult living, advertising, animal care, and antiques to television service, transportation, travel, utilities, video production, and wedding services. The businesses ranged from the very small (Handyman Bob, John Tice Photography, Justin Scott Piano Lessons, Diane Green, CPA) to the anchor businesses of Blacksburg (Annie Kay's Whole Foods, Beamer's, Blacksburg Brewing, Boudreaux's Louisiana Kitchen, The Cellar, East Coasters, Eats, Heavener Hardware, Lyric Theatre, Macado's, Mish Mish, Moore's Body Shop, Sharkey's Grille, Vintage Cellar, Warm Hearth Village) to local franchises of national chains (Domino's, Holiday Inn, ING, Kinko's, Pizza Hut, US Postal Service).

The Organizations page listed 248 nonprofits grouped into fifteen categories (Arts, Civic, Clubs, Education, General, Health, Music, Political, Religion, Senior, Sports, Theater, Volunteer, Women, Youth). The organizations were also quite diverse, including local arts groups (Audubon Quartet, Master Chorale, Community Band, Community Strings, Cranwell International Center, Musica Viva, New River Valley Banjo, Fiddle, and Dance Club, Photography Club), sports groups (Saddle Club, Rugby Club, Blacksburg Striders, Mountain Bike Club, Special Olympics), service groups (Lions, Rotary), social action groups (Beans and Rice, a community learning and economic develop group focusing on chronic poverty in the Appalachians, Literacy Volunteers of the NRV, Montgomery County Christmas Store, Women's Resource Center), and support groups (Blacksburg Moms, Celiac Disease and Support Group, Survivors of Suicide). There were many churches in the list (Alleghany Baptist Church, Grace Covenant Presbyterian Church, Church of Christ, Mennonite Church, Seventh-Day Adventist) and a wide range of interest groups and clubs (Chess Club, Linus and Unix User Group, Master Gardener Association). Of course, quite a few of the organizations were local chapters of national groups (4H Montgomery County, Alcoholics Anonymous, Association for Women in Science–Virginia Tech, Boy Scout troops, Cub Scout packs, Habitat for Humanity, Humane

Society, La Leche League, League of Women Voters, Society for Creative Anachronism, YMCA and YMCA Thrift Shop).

The Government portal page had links to the towns of Blacksburg and Christiansburg and to Montgomery County, as well as to political groups and party sites. The town of Blacksburg has a very developed website including hundreds of pages. It encompasses not only the town government per se, but also public institutional services such as local hospitals and schools and various historical preservation sites and activities. Indeed, the town's information and services are so developed that in 2010 it offered a Citizens Institute, described as "a fun nine-week course," introducing the people and programs of the town.

There is really too much to inventory: public transit, town museum, community relations, engineering, financial services, housing and neighborhood services, human resources, parks and recreation, planning and building, police, volunteer fire department and rescue squad, public works, purchasing, technology, public access television, town attorney's office, town clerk, town manager. The Parks and Recreation topic (under "Living" on the town's homepage) describes the community center, including gyms, meeting rooms, a multipurpose room, and a game room, the aquatic center, the municipal golf course, and the municipal parks, picnic shelters, and softball fields. The community center pages describe facilities, including many photographs of locations, and ongoing and planned programs, and provide information on scheduling. The Refuse and Recycling topic itself consists of more than a dozen pages (Curbside Recycling Guidelines, Refuse and Recycling Schedule, Drop Off Recycling, Brush Collection, E-cycling Batteries and CFLs, Spring and Fall Cleanup, Leaf Collection and Giveaway, Household Hazardous Waste, Refuse and Recycling for Apartments and Townhouses, and a portal page of Recycling Resources with pointers to other sites, including Sustainable Blacksburg (a community nonprofit), Waste Management (a contractor), Virginia Tech Recycling, and the Virginia Department of Environmental Quality. Under many of the topics, the town provides a complete collection of its current master plan documents as pdf files.

Blacksburg has a well-developed geographical information system with a huge collection of local digital maps that can be downloaded, information on local water quality testing and a report that can be downloaded, information on water pressure and flows through fire hydrants, and information on land development and erosion and sediment control, including construction checklists, inspection protocols, and permits. It provides information on the management of storm water, including a description of the activities of the Storm Water Management Task Force – agendas, meeting minutes, committees, and a directory, and downloadable documents describing the town's storm water management ordinance, information on flood insurance, permits and information on floodplain development, and much more.

There are many interactive services in the town website. The 'I Want To …' system allows residents to request various services and get a rapid response from the town. Residents can pay for various services and obligations online: utilities, parking tickets, real estate taxes, vehicle license taxes, etc. The town has implemented a local emergency management system, Blacksburg Alert, that sends alerts via email, telephone, fax, and/or accessible teletypewriter to residents, covering emergency alerts, road closings, inclement weather announcements, refuse and recycling news, Blacksburg Transit notifications about bus arrival times, and general town news. Users can request alerts from any or all of these categories.

As the second decade of the BEV is coming to an end it is interesting that, while the frenzy of innovation and boasts of being the "most connected" town are now gone, the community is still benefiting from that distant field of dreams. It has assimilated the Internet to carry out community functions and remains a leading example of community networking in the United States, though, instead of breaking ground five to seven years ahead of other communities, its distinctiveness now resides more in how long and how pervasively the people of Blacksburg have been living the routine life of a web-based community network. In March 2010, I noticed an evolution in rhetoric: The BEV – once the newest and most advanced – now refers to itself as "one of the nation's oldest community e-networks."

## Participation requires appropriation

The BEV project occurred at a specific time and place. We should and must try to learn from singular case studies, but we must also recognize that many external factors, either historical and one-of-kind or idiosyncratic, were significant in this case. For example, the World-Wide Web, HTML and other basic web tools emerged just as the BEV was being launched. This was critical infrastructure to the BEV, and directly facilitated the active appropriation of the network by the community. Indeed, being the first web-based community network was key to the BEV's initial identity. However, the role of the Web was historical and singular. No similar project undertaken in the future could expect the same boost. Similarly, there was a context of government policies and initiatives, such as the US federal emphasis on the Internet and applications of networking during the Clinton administration, and the dramatic cuts to state university budgets in Virginia during the administration of George Allen. The federal policies facilitated the BEV project by evoking much more attention than would have occurred in other circumstances, and by opening up federal funding opportunities that underwrote the BEV initiatives. The severe Virginia state policies caused the BEV to focus intently and steadily on developing a standalone business model. These forces were both historical and idiosyncratic. Such factors make it unwise merely to push the BEV template onto other projects in other contexts.

From the start, the field of dreams scenario sounded just a bit romantic, perhaps even an excuse for not involving the full community in the early planning for the project (Carroll and Rosson 1996). However, as things turned out, engaging the whole community only after the initial planning and infrastructure development worked impressively. During 1994–6 the BEV unleashed one of the largest and most diverse participatory design projects ever. In 1994, the cables and modems – and more importantly, perhaps, the software and instructional support – were in place to allow community members not only to imagine what a community network might be or mean, but actively to discover and define the network and to find their own meanings in it. As we have seen in this chapter, the appropriation of the BEV by the Blacksburg community was not merely an act of receiving permission or an invitation; it was not circumscribed in a meeting, or a series of workshops. Rather, it was the result of a relatively long-term mutual commitment on the part of all the stakeholders – the BEV project, community members, and local institutions. It was critically enabled and facilitated by the infrastructure: One cannot appropriate unless one can meaningfully engage.

The appropriation of the network by the community made the BEV part of the identity of the Blacksburg community. This was achieved through many relatively modest appropriations, such as the BTAC identifying how the town could contribute to the project or local merchants reconciling their concerns that email might erode face-to-face relationships. Each of these separate episodes was itself a small crisis, a local resolution, a modest insight, a development in how one or several community members understood the network, and in how they would use the network going forward. But the effect of these modest appropriations over a few years was transformational. The community's sense of its own identity was altered, as in the Blacksburg Seniors becoming the BEV Seniors. People's expectations about possible roles they could play in the project and their actual engagement and participation changed dramatically, as in the massive community learning project and the diverse innovations across various community groups through and beyond the latter 1990s.

The design rationale for the "posting and accessing community information online" scenario in Box 2.1 included the upside claims that such activities could provide a shared commons of experiences and reactions, could illustrate the role of core values, episodes, and traditions in community activity, and could remind the community that it was active and thriving. These developmental trajectories were quite evident in the narrative of emerging practices in the BEV, which eventually became a multi-authored working representation and public inscription of the community's identity. This achievement entrained further challenges, accommodations, and development. For example, various education, training and other technical support programs were initiated to allow more of the community to participate more fully. And the new tasks of managing online information for local businesses and community groups caused new roles to emerge and a new sort of expertise network in the community.

These appropriations and the development of participation they enabled were rapid but also broad and profound; they took place over years. One of the most dramatic episodes of community learning through a crisis that triggered insight and growth occurred in March 1996. The BEV was well underway, when suddenly, it seemed, Virginia Tech announced that it would cease providing free Internet services to non-university BEV subscribers as of July 1. This course of evolution had indeed been designed into the original BEV plan, but the timing was partly political: The state government of Virginia had been cutting university budgets for several years, and Virginia Tech felt it could not afford the appearance of squandering state resources. Along with the new policy on Internet services, the university significantly reduced its funding for the BEV project, and most of the staff were made part-time. Ironically, the decision was enabled by the economic development successes of the BEV: Local businesses were emerging in the Internet services area. These companies were eager to become Internet Service Providers for Blacksburg residents, organizations, and businesses. Indeed, Bell Atlantic began offering ISDN services in August of 1996. The university wanted to support such private initiatives, and definitely not to compete or to be seen to be competing with them. (This episode foreshadows the private–public tensions over municipal *wireless* networking infrastructure that were to occur a decade later; Dao 2005.)

From an objective standpoint, the decision to transition non-university members to commercial Internet Service Providers was perfectly sound. The Internet services area was becoming a business in 1996, and Virginia Tech was a public-sector institution. Legally, it is a state agency in Virginia. However, the immediate meaning of the decision to the Blacksburg community was that Virginia Tech seemed to be pushing them out of what had been a collective town–gown partnership. Moreover, the community was not involved in making the decision, which was merely announced to them. Perhaps this reminded some residents that the whole project had to a significant degree been sprung on the community in the first place. Misperception and mistrust were inevitable. There were outcries that non-university residents had been "kicked off" the BEV. The issue persisted for months, and the discontent in the community was intense (Sears 1996). Some residents complained that Virginia Tech had tricked the community into embracing the BEV. The project that President McComas had envisioned as creating a new model for campus–community cooperation had accidentally triggered a classic town/gown schism.

In the end, the decision was implemented in a curious way. The BEV itself was made more independent of Virginia Tech – for example, it ran on dedicated BEV servers, not general Virginia Tech servers, thus blunting the potential complaint that state resources were being mismanaged to support a Blacksburg community project. BEV policies were changed to distinguish more sharply between commercial accounts – local business – and personal or community nonprofit accounts. The BEV continued to offer fairly inexpensive accounts and other services to individual residents and to nonprofit organizations, but business users were indeed forced to rely on commercial Internet Service Providers. The crisis reorganized the BEV, refactoring roles throughout the community. For example, the BEV Seniors took on the new role of investigating and posting advice on local ISP options. The role of the BEV group in Virginia Tech was narrowed somewhat to accommodate its reduced funding and staffing, and it now focused on maintenance of the core web pages and commercialization of the BEV model for other communities. Interestingly, in March 2010, the BEV was announcing that it planned to withdraw from offering personal web page accounts. It no longer accepts new requests and urges existing account holders to move their web content to commercial web page service providers.

In activity theory and in other developmental theories, it is argued that any significant growth in humans and groups is triggered by crisis (Piaget and Inhelder 1969; Vygotsky 1978). The many instances of appropriation by individuals and groups throughout the community illustrated how small crises in adopting new patterns of activity lead to insight and learning. The "kicked off the BEV" episode is of course the signature example of this. The "field of dreams scenario" only created the possibility for the BEV as envisioned. The community had to appropriate the BEV, to create it through resolving inevitable crises that arise whenever assumptions about social practices and the social order are fundamentally challenged. Invitations to participate, however sincere, and however accompanied by guidance and support, do not categorically change underlying ownership and responsibility relations. By 1996, the community had certainly accepted the invitation. It had populated the content and innovated some of the core activities of the community network. Through this the community increasingly was coming to own the BEV, and after the "kicked off the BEV" crisis there was no question that the community owned it. From that point forward, Virginia Tech was just a community group.

Box 3.4 summarizes the design rationale for the "kicked off the BEV" scenario. The upsides for this scenario are that dissociating the community network from a particular community institution such as Virginia Tech encourages community members to see the network as community owned and independent of the university. Community members can be more engaged by and take more responsibility for their own community network, as opposed to a university project in which they participate. For example, the seniors helped fellow community members find Internet Service Providers. The downsides include feeling that one has been "kicked off the BEV," that one has lost support and services that one had and relied on before, and the technical challenges of taking more responsibility for managing the network. Finally, the shift to personal Internet Service Providers differentially affected Virginia Tech employees and other residents, creating the potential for a community digital divide. (See Hampton 2003 for discussion of an analogous episode of crisis in a community network triggering development.)

*Box 3.4*  Claims associated with the "kicked off the BEV" scenario

Shifting from a Virginia Tech BEV account to a personal Internet Service Provider (dissociating the community network from a particular configuration of anchor community institutions)

> + encourages community members to see the network itself as an independent civic institution

*(Continued)*

Box 3.4   (*Continued*)

  + allows more direct citizen engagement and ownership of the community network
  + is eased by support from community groups, such as the seniors' posting of information on ISP accounts.

  − But it feels as if one has been kicked off the BEV.
  − But it removes the comprehensive infrastructure support derived from institutions such as local universities, municipal government, and business groups.
  − But the community may experience difficulties in assuming the responsibility for managing such an information and communication infrastructure.
  − But it selectively disadvantages some community members (e.g., those not employed by Virginia Tech), creating a local digital divide.

The design rationale for the "discussing online a local issue with a neighbor" scenario in Box 2.2 included two downsides – namely, that such discussions can make conflicts more public and perhaps more polarizing, and that they can entrain destabilizing changes in the social order. And, indeed, the BEV itself facilitated such online discussions of the "kicked off the BEV" episode and of many more routine crises in community practices. In doing so, however, it also directly helped to engage more people more rapidly and more thoroughly in the debate, to codify issues and positions more clearly and more publicly, and to remind the community that, ultimately, it was responsible for and capable of moving forward. These are some of the upside claims for "discussing online a local issue with a neighbor." The successful confrontation and management of community crises can be a key resource for community sustainability and development. And that is just what happened.

The BEV was a large-scale and long-term participatory design research project. It raises fundamental questions about the nature of effective participation in design. In the BEV project, effective participation was crucially enabled by infrastructure that was developed in advance and without direct user involvement. Community members were presented with a set of technological possibilities that intrigued them and that helped them learn about networks and network services. Through this motivation and learning, they were able to manipulate and appropriate the core BEV capabilities. This, in turn, allowed them to participate actively in the BEV as content developers and as developers of new applications and services, eventually coming to own the BEV, in the sense of managing most of its content, services, and applications. Notably, the BEV development process took years and involved complex relationships and negotiations among stakeholders – for example, ranging from mutual support to unilateral withdrawal of support.

These are not typical parameters for participatory design interactions. Participatory design always directly involves future users with designers/developers and accords autonomy and power to the users. Any serious implementation of participatory design produces disruptive outcomes and transformative learning. Generally, this is accomplished through participation in design meetings and workshops (Muller, Haslwanter, and Dayton 1997). Such engagements are relatively focused and brief, and do not culminate in the users becoming systems administrators. They may therefore require less appropriation on the part of the users than we observed in the BEV case, and which we have argued was critical to that case. The design of the BEV ultimately transcended the typical and limiting a priori scoping of roles in participatory design. On the other hand, the BEV project required five to ten years to reach fruition. Longer-term participatory design engagements might indeed be a distinct category of participatory design (Carroll *et al.* 2000).

# 4 Community consequences of a network

Chapter 3 described why and how the BEV project was launched, how the Blacksburg community appropriated the network, and how the BEV developed through nearly two decades. Various stakeholders raised a wide variety of motivations and rationales for the BEV at different points in time. Many expectations were articulated as to what people would do with a community network and the kinds of attitudes and interactions it would facilitate. Such statements serve many purposes in the development of socio-technical systems like the BEV. They energize stakeholders to get involved, to make commitments, and to carry through on commitments. They reassure stakeholders that highly desirable consequences, or at least not undesirable consequences, are being pursued and can be achieved. They attract attention and support from potential allies. And they help everyone involved make more sense of the project.

Motivations and rationales are the front end of consequences. Some of what is intended is achieved, but intending is not the same as achieving. It is important in any design project to try to clarify what the outcomes actually were, and to compare those outcomes to motivations and rationales. However, for complex and ubiquitous systems like community networks, this is difficult. As discussed in chapter 2, rationales for community networks encompass myriad claims about consequences for interactions and experiences throughout the community, many of which are highly nuanced and ultimately quite subjective. Moreover, because community networks are embedded in social life, they cannot be evaluated using the strongest empirical methods – namely, controlled experiments. There is no community network without community contexts.

Second-generation community networks, such as the BEV, are also inherently distributed Internet systems with vague boundaries, increasing their complexity. They consist of a relatively small core website with hundreds of links out to community resources, created and maintained by a wide variety of members. These community members are designers, but they are not following a single design. Nevertheless, the resources they create, and the ways that these resources are appropriated and integrated in use throughout the community, are fundamental to what the community network is – namely, a bricolage of separate efforts. It may be possible to have consensus as to where the network starts – for the BEV, www.bev.net – but it is vague at best to say where it ends. This open-endedness is also inherent to what community networks are. Evaluating a community network is necessarily evaluating an open system.

Thus, investigating the consequences of a community network entails evaluating an embedded infrastructure, not separable from the community itself. It is evaluating a bricolage of personal and collective innovation and appropriation, so loosely integrated that it may appear integral to no one. It is essentially investigation of the whole community with special attention to how people think about, talk about, engage with, and even avoid the Internet, and with what consequences. There was not and cannot be a doppelganger of Blacksburg, identical but for the BEV infrastructure. Thus evaluating infrastructures and other complex socio-technical designs must rely on detailed descriptive analysis and sense-making to link possible causes and effects through systematic analysis, such as scenario-based design rationale techniques. The story of the BEV in chapter 3, the anecdotes and vignettes of life in the BEV community, is such a descriptive evaluation, grounded in direct participant observation.

The economics of community networks is a further practical obstacle to definitively evaluating outcomes. Community network projects have always been pursued with extremely limited funding. In the case of the BEV, despite careful planning and public relations, the project never attracted large-scale commercial interest, never developed significant revenue sources, and, indeed, was eventually separated organizationally from the original partner institutions. No surprise then that community network projects have tended to focus the limited resources they can marshal to developing and maintaining services and to providing training and other user support, and have typically paid much less attention to evaluating outcomes. Where there has been evaluation research it has tended to focus on population demographics, case study anecdotes, and opportunistic satisfaction surveys and interviews, often conducted by the project designers or managers (Carroll and Rosson 2001).

In this context, the BEV project is a relatively strong example of sustained evaluation efforts. From 1993, there was a director of research in the BEV project team (Andrea Kavanaugh) carrying out and publishing regular community surveys (e.g., Kavanaugh and Patterson 2001). From 1994, a group of Virginia Tech faculty – the BEV Research Advisory Group – was formally charged with instigating and coordinating BEV research in the university. Through the years, dozens of papers and several books appeared, evaluating the BEV project from various standpoints (e.g., Carroll 2005; Carroll and Rosson 1996; Cohill and Kavanaugh 2000).

In 2001–3, my colleagues and I were able to carry out a study of the BEV community. For community networking, this was a relatively large-scale and complex empirical study. Though, of course, we barely scratched the surface. The study design sought to respect the embedded, open-ended, and participatory nature of the BEV by engaging community members through a variety of methods, minimally disturbing emerging practices, habits, and patterns of life. This evaluation study complements the narrative overview in chapter 3, highlighting lower level details of how the BEV was used by the community and how the latter was affected by these interactions. It provides context for the more specific design research projects discussed in subsequent chapters.

## The EPIC study: Experiences, people, the Internet, and community

In 2001, the US National Science Foundation provided support for a broad evaluation study of the BEV, focusing on household use and impacts of the BEV and the Internet for the population of Blacksburg and Montgomery County. We recruited participants as household units, not as individuals. The study involved multiple methods and gathered multiple types of data. It included *a two-wave survey*, with the second survey administration approximately twelve months after the first, *a logging study*, in which we directly monitored household email and web activity, and *an interview study*, in which we carried out a series of four household interviews throughout a twelve-month period. At the end of the project, an online discussion was created to share and discuss the results within the BEV community. The various components of this research design are summarized in a timeline in Figure 4.1.

Our research design incorporated a random sample of 100 households. We stratified the sample by *residence* (residing within the town of Blacksburg or elsewhere in Montgomery County), *technology* (access to the Internet from home only, from work only, from home and work, or no access), and *education level* of head of household (elementary school, high school, one to three years of college, more than four years of college), representing each category in proportion to the actual population of Montgomery County, as described by US Census data and other demographic studies of the local area (see Carroll and Reese 2003).

We used random sampling to avoid self-selection or "opportunity-based" recruiting practices, which can lead to systematic biases in the data, such as the over-representation of more educated persons. We started with a sample of 1250 Montgomery county residential addresses generated randomly by zip code, using telephone directory records, post office records, and Department of Motor Vehicle data. We removed 380 invalid addresses and recruited households into

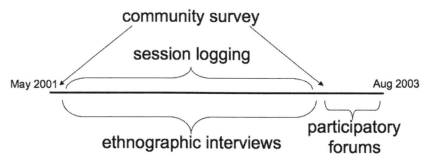

*Figure 4.1*  Overall research design of the EPIC study.

our study from the remaining 870, using a ten-item survey that allowed us to classify households with respect to the three stratification variables – residence, technology, and educational level. This produced a pool of 188 respondent households (22 percent response rate), from which we constructed the 100-household sample.

From this overall sample, we created subsamples for the logging and interview studies. Using the three stratification criteria, we constructed a subsample of twenty households to participate in an interview study (Dunlap *et al.* 2003). Only 75 households in the overall survey sample were qualified for the home logging study: Ten of the households in our sample were deliberately selected to represent the 10 percent of the local population without Internet access, and fifteen were selected to represent households with Internet access only at work or at school. In 32 other cases, we were unable to gather logging data. In twenty cases this was because the household's Internet Service Provider (AOL) employed a proprietary Internet protocol. In four cases, the household had a complex Internet access configuration that we decided not to tamper with. And in eight cases households elected not to be logged for personal reasons. Thus, 43 households participated in the logging study (see Carroll, Snook, and Isenhour 2009 for additional methodological details).

Participating households were enrolled in the study through a face-to-face visit to their homes. We made every effort to ensure that all members of the household were present for this meeting. The goals and procedures of the study were explained, and questions and concerns were answered. The survey portion of the study was distributed to participants, and, if it was convenient, the participants completed the survey at that time. Otherwise, we went over the survey with members of the household and left a mail-return envelope with them. As part of this initial meeting, we installed the software to log Internet use. This included setting proxies in the household browser and email clients if this was technically feasible. If the household had been selected for interviewing, we carried out the initial interview.

We followed a similar home visit procedure to administer the second-wave survey, at which time we removed logging software. Arranging and carrying out the enrollment procedure was quite time-consuming. We enrolled households during the period August, 2001, through February, 2002, and decommissioned them during the period August, 2002, through February, 2003, on a rolling basis. For households selected for interviewing there were two additional home visits scheduled between the enrolling and wrap-up visits. The final activity in our study was a participatory evaluation forum. We summarized some of our initial results and posted them on a web forum, inviting members of the participant households to comment (anonymously). Subsequently, we opened up this forum to the larger Blacksburg/Montgomery County community.

Our sample differed from random samples of Americans in specific ways, presumably reflecting differences between Blacksburg and the larger US population. Our sample of Internet users was somewhat older, more affluent, better educated, and involved more females than males. In 2001, 18 percent of US

Internet users reported incomes of $50,000 to $75,000; in our sample, 31 percent reported incomes in this range. Nationally, 71 percent of Internet users reported some college, college degree, or graduate degree; in our sample, this was 88 percent. While, in 2001, 18 percent of US Internet users were 54 to 64 years old and 29 percent were aged 17 to 29, 27 percent of our Internet user participants were between 54 and 64, and only 17 percent were between 17 and 29. There were 10 percent more women among our Internet user participants than men; in the overall population, Internet use was fairly even with respect to gender at that time (Kavanaugh *et al.* 2005).

## Logging home use of the BEV

The objective of our logging study was to broadly and quantitatively characterize activities of the BEV community at a fairly mature point in its development. In the period 2001 to 2003, the BEV had been operational for nearly a decade. We wanted to characterize BEV interactions in the context of other logging studies at that time, and we specifically wanted to assess whether the Internet was being used for local purposes.

We logged participants' email and web activity using proxy software (the specific configurations we used are described in Carroll, Snook, and Isenhour 2009). The use of proxies allowed us to monitor activity without requiring the participants to change their Internet Service Provider (ISP) or to use a different email reader or web browser. Our non-invasive approach also meant that we could only monitor behavior to the extent it was articulated. For example, most of our participants had *household* Internet accounts – that is, one Internet account used by all members of the household. Thus, we were unable to differentiate activity of individual household members.

The 43 households that we logged, during a full year of interaction for each household, produced 1.7 million URL requests (NB large multimedia files were not logged due to performance issues). There was substantial redundancy in people's accesses of Internet sites. A total of 369,047 *unique* URLs were accessed, meaning 78 percent of http requests were for URLs already accessed by one or more participants, including being accessed by the same participant more than once. There was an average of 745 accesses of 165 unique URLs per household per week throughout the study period. There was also considerable clustering among the unique URLs accessed by our participants with respect to Internet hosts (for example, http://www.vt.edu/academics/ and http://www.vt.edu/admissions/ are unique URLs, but share a common host: www.vt.edu). A total of 27,314 unique Internet host names (for example, www.vt.edu and www.webmail.vt.edu are unique hosts) were accessed. Finally, a total of 19,390 unique domains were accessed (for example, vt.edu is an Internet domain that includes both of the unique hosts www.vt.edu and www.webmail.vt.edu).

Even in 2001–3, the Internet was vast. At the level of Internet hosts, most traffic was not in common across different households – that is, different households

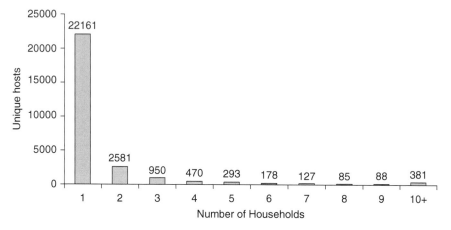

*Figure 4.2*   Household access to unique Internet hosts.

*Table 4.1* URL substrings used to identify local traffic

| Zip codes | Municipalities | Idioms/domains |
|---|---|---|
| 24060, 24061, 24062, 24063, 24073, 24068, 24087, 24111, 24138, 24149, 24162, 24091 | Blacksburg, Christiansburg, Floyd, McCoy, Montgomery, Riner, Roanoke, Shawsville | montva, newriver, Hokie, Beamer, BEV, bburg, nrv, mcps, swva, mfrl, techfcu, thelyric |

accessed different hosts. More than 80 percent (22,161) of the roughly 27,000 unique hosts were accessed by only a single household (i.e., one household, one or more times; Figure 4.2).

We were particularly interested in local Internet traffic. The BEV can be thought of as a neighborhood of URLs, listservs, email addresses, and so forth. However, this neighborhood is difficult to define in terms of network topology; not all "local" sites are on local servers. For example, we found that movie show times for one local theater were served by a machine in California. Similarly, people in Blacksburg could order a pizza for delivery from the local Papa John's franchise, but to do this they accessed Papa John's national website. Conversely, not all content on local servers is actually local. For example, much of the content served from machines at Virginia Tech would be general science and engineering material with no significant connection to Blacksburg or Montgomery County.

We developed a method to estimate logged activity pertaining to the region within a one-hour travel radius of Blacksburg by searching URLs for distinct substrings: zip codes, municipality names, and local idioms and domains, as listed in Table 4.1.

Several iterations of the keyword list were required to maximize the number of local sites identified while minimizing misses and false alarms. Several keywords originally included, such as "Pilot" (a local city name), were eliminated because they occur so much more frequently as general terms. Other keywords, such as "BEV," proved useful and were retained even though they produced some false alarms (bevnet.com was a beverage industry site).

We classified 79,816 URL requests, to 545 distinct hosts, nearly 5 percent of our log data, as local. To put this in perspective, at the time of our study, the Internet consisted of more than 147 million distinct hosts (Internet Systems Consortium 2009). Thus, requests to local hosts were approximately 10,000 times more likely than chance in our data (i.e., the 545 local hosts comprised less than .0004 percent of the Internet as a whole). Six local sites were among the 100 most frequently accessed in our data. Five of these were Virginia Tech websites (for university webmail, homepage, libraries, file storage, and learning resources) and the sixth was client.msn.com, which provided local multimedia content associated with customized my.msn.com homepages, maintained by nine households in our sample.

We divided local traffic into university traffic (pertaining to the three universities and colleges within our target radius: Virginia Tech, Radford University, and New River Valley Community College) and non-university traffic (civic organizations, local information). University traffic was the preponderant category, comprising 62,732 URL accesses – about 3.7 percent of the total, and 82 percent of local accesses. Non-university traffic comprised about 1 percent of total traffic logged; some of the most frequent hosts in this category were the city of Roanoke, a regional ISP cooperative, a local credit union, the Montgomery County school system, the Montgomery–Floyd Regional Library, the town of Blacksburg, and the BEV.

A special focus for our analysis of local traffic was use of the core BEV pages. Logged traffic on the BEV totalled 649 accesses across the participant pool, with just over half of the households (23) accessing it at some point during the study. On a per household basis, this is comparable to access rates for other major sites logged in our study, such as Amazon (29 distinct households) and Virginia Tech (30 distinct households). The households that accessed the BEV did so about every other week during the study (28 accesses per household).

Table 4.2 presents a breakdown of BEV activity by host. Most accesses request the BEV homepage, which is updated fairly frequently and provides headlines and pointers to community information (outside the bev.net domain). The balance of accesses was divided between community and civic pages. Community traffic included directory listings to local products and services (www.bev.net/mall), local job openings, and personal homepages (www.bev.net/ecommunity). Civic traffic included directories of homepages for organizations such as churches, the Humane Society, and a fencing club. The Arts directory of local performances, art shows, and other events was accessed less frequently. The Calendar, which lists events such as local road races, book signings, festivals, and classes, as well as art shows and performance events, was accessed even less, though by more households.

*Table 4.2* Accesses of BEV hosts

| BEV host | Accesses | Distinct households |
|---|---|---|
| www.bev.net | 338 | 22 |
| community.bev.net | 97 | 11 |
| civic.bev.net | 88 | 9 |
| www.civic.bev.net | 59 | 3 |
| arts.bev.net | 33 | 3 |
| calendar.bev.net | 22 | 7 |
| www.bburg.bev.net | 2 | 2 |

Our logging data quantified the growing importance of commercial websites at this time; three-quarters of all URLs accessed in our study were in the .com domain. Search engines (Lycos, Yahoo, Google, Infoseek, Altavisita, Excite, AlltheWeb, AskJeeves) were a very important category of commercial site, accounting for 4 percent of all accesses.

Pushed commercial advertising – that is, http requests not manually generated and resulting in pop-up displays – was another important category of commercial website. We created a URL substring analysis to identify pushed advertising, consisting of "ad." and "ads." with manually added specific URLs (e.g., advertising.com, atwola.com), and identified 461,488 accesses – more than a quarter (27.7 percent) of all Internet activity we logged. Pushed advertising sites comprised 28 of the 100 top sites accessed in our study. Among the 72 sites in the top 100 that were *not* pushed advertising sites, 60 were .com sites.

Another important category in our analysis of web activity was email service from browsers. We identified webmail traffic through a keyword search on the term "mail," which returned 102,402 accesses. All 43 households logged some amount of webmail traffic. Household levels varied from over 29,000 hits to just two. With every message, reply, and forward counting as a hit, the average household logged just under 2,400 webmail hits. Not surprisingly, hotmail.com, msn.com, and yahoo.com were among the top five webmail hosts used by our participants. However, Virginia Tech and the Montgomery County School system were also in the top five. While all 43 households logged at least some webmail traffic, only half (21) logged POP3/SMTP mail activity. There was no relationship between email and webmail traffic volume.

Our logging study is most directly comparable to the HomeNet study (Kraut *et al.* 1996). The HomeNet study examined the Internet behavior of 48 families during their first year online, using equipment purchased and managed for them by the researchers. It employed several methods of data collection, including questionnaires, analysis of archives (newsgroup messages and help requests), interviews, and data logs of web traffic. Each participant was assigned an individual account, allowing the team to articulate individual usage for every member of every household, a total of 157 individuals.

HomeNet participants accessed 9,912 unique Internet hosts, or about .2 percent of the Internet at the time; 55 percent of these were accessed only once,

while fewer than 2 percent were accessed by more than 20 percent of the participants. Internet portal and search sites such as Lycos and Yahoo were the most
frequently accessed hosts, making up half of the top ten websites with the
most distinct users. The HomeNet participants were selected for having *not*
established home use of the Internet prior to that study, and were provided with
equipment and support. This might have inflated rates of home Internet use, as
relatively more of the use observed might have been novice exploration.

However, the HomeNet access patterns are fairly consistent with the distribu-
tions we found. Our participants accessed about six times as many unique
Internet hosts per capita as did the HomeNet participants, but because the
Internet had grown so much the 27,314 unique Internet hosts they accessed com-
prised .02 percent of the Internet at the time, or one-tenth the proportion of the
HomeNet panel (Internet Systems Consortium 2009).

By articulating individual family member usage, the HomeNet project was
able to show that children were disproportionate users. The median teenage boy
accumulated over 320 hours on the Net during the first 55 weeks of the trial,
compared with less than 32 hours for the median adult male. Teens made use of
the Internet for communication using various MUDS and chats. Anecdotally, it
was reported that HomeNet participants accessed local content, such as movie
times, bus schedules, local sports scores, local community group information,
and local school information. But this was not quantified.

## Community survey

The EPIC community survey was a 27-page paper form, generally administered
in a face-to-face meeting of household members with researchers. It took about
50 minutes to complete. A shortened survey was created for household members
aged ten through sixteen years, but the discussion below focuses only on responses
of 157 adult household members. The survey drew upon a variety of validated and
reliable items from earlier survey studies, and was developed and refined by iterat-
ing through multiple cycles of group review and pilot testing.

Most directly the survey built upon Kavanaugh's series of BEV survey studies
and incorporated report measures for community-oriented activities, such as the
names of civic organizations to which respondents belonged, as well as the extent
of their involvement with these groups, including whether they attended meetings, contributed money to the organizations, and/or had held leadership offices.
We classified community groups as one of four types: civic/political, religious/
charitable/support, educational/professional, or social/recreational (Edwards and
Booth 1973; Kasarda and Janowitz 1974; Putnam 2000). The survey extended
Kavanaugh's prior report measures by asking participants to describe methods of
communication used among members of each group, including computer-mediated
methods (email, newsgroup).

The survey also incorporated a set of community involvement items adapted
from Rothenbuhler (1991) and Shepherd and Rothenbuhler (2001), asking how

frequently people keep up with local news, get together with others who know what is going on in the community, have ideas for change in the community, and work to cause change.

We used factor analysis to group survey items and construct reliable composite variables (indicated by Cronbach alpha greater than .7). This discussion focuses on four composite variables for community membership and participation – informedness, activism, associations, and belonging. Table 4.3 enumerates the items comprising each of these variables, along with the Cronbach alphas for each variable obtained in each of the two waves of data collection for the survey study. (Note tha,t in the second wave, the obtained alpha for associations was less than .7; for the other cases – see also Table 4.5 below – obtained alphas were roughly the same in both waves of the study, and met our criterion of .7).

These constructs were developed *before* the conceptual model presented in chapter 1, analyzing identity commitment, participation, and diverse support networks as the three critical elements of community. Thus, the EPIC study is not a direct assessment of that conceptual model. The model was based on a critical reading of decades of research literature and analysis of the phenomenon of community. The EPIC constructs derive from statistical analysis of data pertaining to survey items adapted from recent studies of community.

Nevertheless, it is interesting to consider how the four constructs of Belonging, Informedness, Activism, and Association correspond to the three constructs of the conceptual model. The Belonging construct can be mapped to community identification (feeling part of the community, spending time in the community, belonging

*Table 4.3* Community membership and participation constructs

| | |
|---|---|
| Informedness; alpha = .7; .7 | Know what is going on in community |
| | Keep up with news in community |
| | Know what is going on outside local community |
| Activism; alpha = .9; .9 | How active and involved in local community |
| | Work to bring about change in local community |
| | A lot of time working with others to solve local community problems |
| | Get together with people who know what is going on in local community |
| | Have ideas for improving things in local community |
| | Frequently participate in community activities |
| Associations; alpha = .7; .5 | Belong to many organizations |
| | Number of group memberships |
| Belonging; alpha = .7; .7 | Spend a lot of time helping friends and neighbors |
| | Belong to friend group that takes part in common activities |
| | Spend a lot of time with friends |
| | Spend a lot of time alone (reversed) |
| | Don't really belong in my local community (reversed) |
| | Feel part of the community |

to a friend group in the community); the Informedness construct can be mapped to relatively passive community participation (being aware of what is going on, both in the community and in the large societal context in which the community is embedded); the Activism construct can be mapped to relatively more active community participation (having ideas to improve things, solving problems and working to bring about change); and the Associations construct can be mapped to diverse community support networks (belonging to many community organizations). We will return to this correspondence below.

Our survey pioneered a new report measure, a subscale of seventeen community collective efficacy items, listed in Table 4.4. Community collective efficacy (CCE), based on Bandura's (1997) construct of collective efficacy, measures the beliefs people hold that the groups to which they belong can achieve specific outcomes. Constructing such a scale involves making an analysis of the key *capacities* of a kind of group, and then asking people to judge the extent to which their group has these capacities. For a neighborhood community, one such capacity might be establishing and maintaining high-quality public education. In the United States, this is a local community responsibility. Members of a community with high collective efficacy should believe that their communities can achieve this specific outcome.

During the first two years of the EPIC project, we revised and refined the CCE scale. The items in Table 4.4 present seventeen core community capacities, each of which is presented with a relevant obstacle, intended to help evoke a more vivid context for the respondent and thereby a more considered and valid judgment. For example, one capacity is preserving parklands, which is generally desirable, but the wording of the item highlights the potential for conflict with population pressures: Land preserved for parks cannot also be developed for housing. The seventeen-item scale obtained an overall Cronbach alpha of .9 (in the second survey wave), indicating that the set of items reflect and measure a coherent underlying construct.

We used factor analysis to identify four first-order factors in the scale, as indicated in Table 4.4. Each of these factors had a Cronbach alpha of .7 or more. We interpreted the first factor as "managing conflicts and dilemmas," especially with respect to shared access and resources. The second factor was identified as "sustainable development," in the sense of balancing goals and policies with respect to growth and environment. The third factor was called "consensus and united action" – ways of cooperating, working together, agreeing, and constructively handling mistakes and disappointments. The fourth factor was identified as "autonomy in social services" and pertains to the community's ability to care for vulnerable populations with limited support from higher levels of government. (For additional details, see Carroll and Reese 2003; Carroll, Rosson, and Zhou 2005).

In other domains it has been found that beliefs of group members about collective efficacy predict their actual performance as a group (Bandura 1997). Part of this is no doubt because highly specific judgments about collective capabilities, as in Table 4.4, can be more grounded and therefore more valid, versus

*Table 4.4* Community collective efficacy (CCE) scale items

| | |
|---|---|
| Managing conflicts and dilemmas; alpha = .8 | Our community can enact fair laws, despite conflicts in the larger society. |
| | I am confident that our community can create adequate resources to develop new jobs despite changes in the economy. |
| | Our community can present itself in ways that increase tourism while maintaining its unique character. |
| | Despite occasional problems with the economy, we can assist economically disadvantaged members of our community. |
| | We can resolve crises in the community without any negative aftereffects. |
| | I am convinced that we can improve the quality of life in the community, even when resources are limited or become scarce. |
| Sustainable development; alpha = .7 | We can greatly improve the roads in Blacksburg and Montgomery County, even when there is strong opposition from adjacent counties and states. |
| | Despite a growing population, our community can preserve parklands in Blacksburg and Montgomery County. |
| | We can ensure that the air and water in our community remain clean despite commercial development. |
| Consensus and united action; alpha = .8 | Our community can cooperate in the face of difficulties to improve the quality of community facilities. |
| | Despite work and family obligations, we can commit ourselves to common community goals. |
| | As a community, we can handle mistakes and setbacks without getting discouraged. |
| | I am confident that we can be united in the community vision we present to outsiders. |
| | The people of our community can continue to work together, even when it requires a great deal of effort. |
| Social services; alpha = .8 | Our community can greatly improve the quality of education in Montgomery County without help from the Commonwealth of Virginia. |
| | Our community can improve quality and access to services for people with disabilities without help from federal government. |
| | Our community can greatly improve services for senior citizens in Blacksburg and Montgomery County without help from the Commonwealth of Virginia. |

asking for an aggregate judgment of whether one's community is strong or weak. Bandura (1997) argued further that specific beliefs about capabilities guide the self-regulation of agency, and thereby help determine learning and performance outcomes. In this view, high efficacy for a domain *causes* people to set more challenging goals, to work harder on more difficult aspects of tasks, to master new competencies, and to achieve more.

Along with the foregoing measures of community membership and participation, the survey included a range of report measures of Internet experience and daily use, changes in interests and activities since getting onto the Internet, and activities that directly involved the Internet. The overall Internet experience construct combined self-rated experience with computers and the Internet with a person's estimated average hours of Internet use per day (Cronbach alpha = .8 in both survey waves).

The survey's self-perception items on changes since getting onto the Internet, originally developed by Pitkow and Kehoe (1996), were adapted by Kavanaugh in earlier BEV studies. Participants were asked whether, since beginning to use the Internet, they were:

- more, less, or equally involved in the local community and beyond the local community;
- more, less, or equally involved with local issues and with national issues;
- more, less, or equally connected to local people and to people not in the local community;
- more, less, or equally connected with a diversity of people in the local community and beyond the local community;
- more likely, less likely, or equally likely to attend community meetings and events.

These items formed a coherent construct that we called Involvement Since Getting Online, with a Cronbach alpha of .8 in the first survey wave and .9 in the second survey wave.

The survey adapted the Internet behavior and attitude scales developed for the HomeNet survey instrument (Kraut *et al.* 1996). Participants were asked to summarize their BEV-oriented activities – for example, newsgroups in which they participate, web pages they have designed, how often they access the BEV from public access sites (such as the public library), from work, or from home, and how their community-oriented activities are influenced by use of the BEV. Non-users of the community network were included, and were asked to describe their knowledge of the BEV and its services, why they are not currently using the BEV (e.g., lack of access, lack of interest, specific concerns about network applications), and to imagine how use of the BEV might impact their community-oriented activities.

There were other items in the EPIC survey to characterize type and frequency of online activity for the respondent during the preceding six months, on a frequency scale that ranged from "almost never" to "several times per day," for politics (emailing officials, discussing issues), recreation (watching videos, playing games, posting art work), health (getting information, giving or receiving personal health support), work/school (carrying out tasks, learning new skills), commerce (banking, investments, purchases), civic and social use (see Table 4.5), and general online activity (searching, browsing, downloading). Indeed, all of these items are intercorrelated and form a single composite variable with a Cronbach alpha of .8, suggesting that people use the Internet for a wide range of

*Table 4.5* Use of the Internet constructs

| | |
|---|---|
| Civic use; alpha = .8; .8 | Getting the news |
| | Looking for information on national or global events |
| | Answering questions or providing information |
| | Posting factual information |
| | Looking for information about local events/activities |
| | Accessing a community website |
| | Expressing ideas or opinions |
| | Participating in a local interest group online |
| Social use; alpha = .8; .8 | Communicating with coworkers about non-work issues |
| | Communicating with family in the local area |
| | Communicating with friends in the local area |
| | Communicating with friends not in the local area |
| | Communicating with family not in the local area |
| | Meeting new people |

purposes, and that using it for any purpose suggests one might also use it for other purposes. None of this is surprising, and results and discussion further articulating some of these purposes for using the Internet can be found in Kavanaugh *et al.* (2005) and Kavanugh *et al.* (2007).

The discussion below focuses on two specific composite variables describing use of the Internet: *civic* use and *social* use. Table 4.5 enumerates the items comprising each of these variables, along with the Cronbach alphas for each variable obtained in each of the two waves of data collection for the survey study.

The survey also incorporated several standard psychological scales to characterize participants with respect to perceived social support and introversion/extroversion (Bendig 1962; Cohen *et al.* 1984; Kanner *et al.* 1981). These scales have been used in many survey studies. Here social support and extroversion obtained Cronbach alphas of .8 and .9, respectively, indicating that both scales reflect and measure a coherent underlying construct. Finally, the survey captured basic demographics for participants such as years of education, gender, and age.

The survey study produced a large number of results. Further analyses of the EPIC survey data, and further details on the analyses described here, can be found in Carroll and Reese (2003), Carroll, Rosson, Kavanaugh *et al.* (2006), Carroll, Rosson, and Zhou (2005), Kavanaugh, Carroll, Rosson, Reese and Zin (2005), Kavanaugh, Carroll, Rosson, Zin and Reese (2005), Kavanaugh *et al.* (2003), and Kavanaugh *et al.* (2007).

The EPIC study started when the BEV was already well established in the Blacksburg community. However, we found evidence of continuing community development with respect to use of the Internet and involvement with community groups. People in the EPIC sample belonged to an average of 2.4 community groups – slightly above the US national average of two (Edwards and Booth 1973; Perkins, Brown, and Taylor 1996). We found that, between the first and second survey wave, community members who participated in at least one community group significantly increased their reported use of network communication tools, including email, email lists, newsgroups, chat rooms, and web-based discussions. Indeed, this pattern was true for all four types of community group (civic/political, religious/charitable/support, educational/professional, and social/recreational), though it was statistically borderline for social/recreational groups ($p = .05$; see Kavanaugh *et al.* 2007, for details).

We also found that, between the first and second survey wave, community members who participated in at least one community group significantly increased their reported level of involvement in their group or groups. Level of involvement in this analysis was based on a four-point coding scale, in descending order, from (1) a group leader, (2) attended meetings, (3) contributed money, (4) a group member. This pattern of increasing level of involvement was numerically true for all four types of group examined separately, though it was statistically significant only for religious/charitable/support and social/recreational groups. (For more details, see Kavanaugh *et al.* 2007.) These data, of course, do not tell us that people became more involved in community groups *because* they made greater use of Internet communication tools, or that they made greater use of the Internet *because* they had become more actively involved, just that the two trends co-occurred in the context of the BEV.

Converging evidence was obtained from other parts of the survey data focused on understanding what sorts of community beliefs and activities could predict the composite variable of Involvement Since Getting Online. We carried out a series of multiple regression analyses on data from the first survey wave, identifying sets of variables that together explained significant proportions of the variance in Involvement Since Getting Online. We built path models, first regressing variables that are obviously exogenous (in our case, years of education, extroversion, and age) on mediating variables (such as Informedness, Activism, Civic Use of the Internet, Social Use of the Internet and CCE), and subsequently regressing mediators on one another and on the outcome variable Involvement Since Getting Online. Of course, only significant regressions were included.

We developed two different path models. One model, the Civic Effects Model, showed that Activism and Civic Use of the Internet jointly predict 38 percent of the variance in Involvement Since Getting Online (Kavanaugh, Carroll, Rosson, Reese and Zin 2005). The other model, the Social Participation Model, showed that Activism and Social Use of the Internet jointly predicted 29 percent of the variance in Involvement Since Getting Online (Kavanaugh, Carroll, Rosson, Zin and Reese 2005). Based on this exploratory model-building, we ran a confirmatory analysis, using the data from the second survey wave. In that analysis, the Civic Effects Model showed that Activism and Civic Use of the Internet jointly predicted 20 percent of the variance in Involvement Since Getting Online. In the confirmatory analysis, the Social Participation Model showed that Activism and Social Use of the Internet jointly predicted 42 percent of the variance in Involvement Since Getting Online.

These analyses showed that Activism is a very important predictor of increased community involvement after getting online. Specifically, people already interested and actively engaged in community life, and who already use the Internet for civic or social purposes (Table 4.5), report becoming even more involved after beginning to use the Internet.

We decided to turn the analysis around, focusing on the four community membership and participation constructs of Belonging, Activism, Informedness, and Associations (Table 4.3). We are interested in what activities and person characteristics enhance the utilization of the Internet for community-oriented purposes, but we are also interested in how activities and characteristics enhance community itself, and the community's sense of community.

## Modeling the community's sense of community

We constructed a set of path models using the four community membership and participation constructs as outcome variables. As in the other models, we began with clearly exogenous variables – years of education, extroversion, and age. We regressed these on CCE and Internet Experience, which we regarded as relatively persistent personal characteristics. Then we regressed the exogenous variables, together with CCE, and Internet Experience on Social and Civic Use of the Internet as mediating variables. Finally, we regressed the entire ensemble of variables on the four community membership and participation outcome variables. We repeated this procedure for the second-wave survey data to obtain four additional models. One complication in this analysis was that we continued to refine the collective efficacy scale between the two waves of data collection and used the refined scale in the analysis of the second-wave data. The four path models for the second-wave survey data are displayed in Figure 4.3 (all results

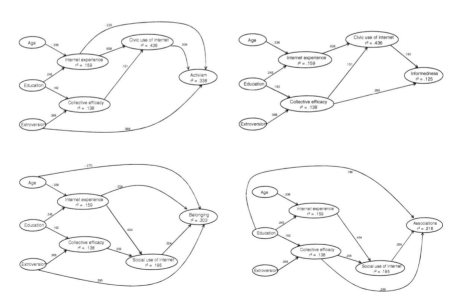

*Figure 4.3*   Path models for Activism, Informedness, Belonging, and Associations.

and relationships are statistically significant; see Carroll, Rosson, and Zhou 2005 for details; see Carroll, Rosson, Kavanaugh *et al.* 2006 for the path models for the first survey wave data).

These models describe a number of general demographic and psycho-social relationships. For example, younger and more educated persons tend to have more Internet experience. Better-educated and more extroverted persons tend to have stronger community collective efficacy beliefs. People with more Internet experience and stronger beliefs about community collective efficacy tend to make more social use and more civic use of the Internet. These patterns are similar to those we saw in the path models from the first survey wave data, with three exceptions: In that analysis, we did not find significant paths linking education to CCE or linking CCE to social and civic use of the Internet (recall that, in the second-wave analysis, we used a refined CCE scale).

Of more interest are the relations between Internet use and the community membership and participation constructs. The upper left panel of Figure 4.3 shows that people who are extroverted and people who make greater civic use of the Internet tend to be more activist – that is, to participate more actively in the community. When the mediating effect of civic use of the Internet is removed, Internet experience by itself is a *negative* predictor of Activism. Thus, civic use of the Internet is associated with greater community activism, but Internet use by itself – that is, for purposes including non-civic activities – is associated with *lower* community activism. We found this same pattern in the first survey wave analysis.

The path model for Informedness in the upper right panel of Figure 4.3 also shows an enabling relationship with civic use of the Internet. In this case, there is no negative relationship with Internet experience. Also, instead of the direct relationship with extroversion, the relationship of extroversion is mediated by CCE, which has a direct facilitative effect on Informedness. This is interesting with respect to the conceptual model: Earlier, we suggested that Activism could be associated with active participation and Informedness with passive participation. The path models emphasize how the former is directly related to an action orientation toward community life – namely, extroversion – where the latter is directly related to having strong beliefs about the community's capabilities – namely, community collective efficacy (CCE) – and related to extroversion only through CCE.

The lower left panel of Figure 4.3 shows that people who are extroverted and people who make greater social use of the Internet tend to feel greater belonging, and perhaps identify more with the community. Rather analogous to the path model for Activism, when the mediating effect of social use of the Internet is removed, Internet experience by itself is a *negative* predictor for Belonging. Thus, social use of the Internet is associated with greater community identification (Belonging), but Internet use by itself – that is, for purposes including non-social activities – is associated with lower community identification. A curious feature of this model is a *negative* path from age to Belonging, suggesting that younger community members report more belonging than do older members. In the analysis of the first-wave data (Carroll, Rosson, Kavanaugh *et al.* 2006) we found no such direct relationship between age and Belonging. We did find the analogous facilitative effect of social use of the Internet on Belonging, but we did not find a significant negative (or positive) path from Internet experience to Belonging.

Finally, the lower right panel of Figure 4.3 shows the path model for Associations from the second-wave data analysis. Here we found a facilitative path relation from social use of the Internet, analogous to that in the path model for Belonging and consistent with data presented earlier: People who make greater use of the Internet for social purposes tend also to participate in a greater number of community groups. We also found a significant path from CCE to Associations, analogous to that in the Informedness model, and quite consistent with Bandura's (1997) conception of efficacy as a mechanism for self-regulation: People who have stronger beliefs about the capabilities of their community tend to participate in more community organizations. We also found a direct path from education to Associations, suggesting that community members who have more education participate in a greater number of community groups. In the analysis of the first-wave data for Associations (Carroll, Rosson, Kavanaugh *et al.* 2006) we found no direct relationship between education and Associations. However, we did find a direct negative path from Internet experience to Associations, which we interpreted analogously with the Activism and Belonging models discussed above.

To summarize, the exploratory models of the first-wave survey data (Carroll, Rosson, Kavanaugh *et al.* 2006) are largely confirmed by the models of the second-wave data (Figure 4.3). Civic use of the Internet is a predictor of greater Activism and Informedness; social use of the Internet is a predictor of greater Belonging and Associations. An interpretation of this, based on the conceptual model of chapter 1, is that participation, identification, and social support networks all can be facilitated through Internet interactions, but not necessarily through the same types of interactions. Participation (Activism and Informedness) is related to using the Internet for information-seeking and discussion, where community identification and diverse sources of social support (Belonging and Associations) are related to using the Internet for social communications.

Community collective efficacy (CCE) had a facilitative relationship, mediated by social or civic use of the Internet, with all four of the membership and participation constructs, and, in the case of Informedness and Associations, a direct relationship as well. Extroversion also had a facilitative relationship with all four constructs, in this case mediated by CCE, and a direct relationship with Activism and Belonging. A possible interpretation based on the conceptual model is that less active participation (Informedness) and maintenance of social networks (Associations) rely more directly on having beliefs about community capacities, but that relatively active participation (Activism) and community identification (Belonging) rely more directly on taking initiative.

In order further to explore and validate interpretations for the community membership and participation path models, and specifically to articulate the role of the community collective efficacy construct in these path models, we constructed another set of four path models using the first-order factors of community collective efficacy – managing conflicts and dilemmas, sustainable development, consensus and unified action, and autonomy in social services (Table 4.4) – instead of the overall construct. These models are displayed in Figure 4.4.

These four new path models are analogous to those in Figure 4.3, with similar path coefficients and explanatory power internally validating the analysis. The four factors definitely do articulate the role of CCE. For example, the fourth factor, autonomy in social services, plays *no role* in any of the models. Notably the items that comprise this factor all pertain to the community's relationship with external governmental entities. Such relationships do seem appropriate as part of a CCE construct, but perhaps this type of relationship is not primarily important in shaping community-internal relationships of identity, participation, and support in the sense of Belonging, Activism, Informedness, and Associations.

Comparing across the four models in Figure 4.4, several general patterns emerge. Managing conflicts and dilemmas (factor 1) and sustainable development (factor 2) both play a role in the Activism model. Sustainable development has the same paths as the aggregate factor CCE did in Figure 4.3: Strong beliefs that the community can effectively manage growth and development has an enabling relationship with participation, mediated through civic use of the Internet. The direct path from managing conflicts and dilemmas to Activism is new in this model and articulates a new role for CCE: A strong belief that the

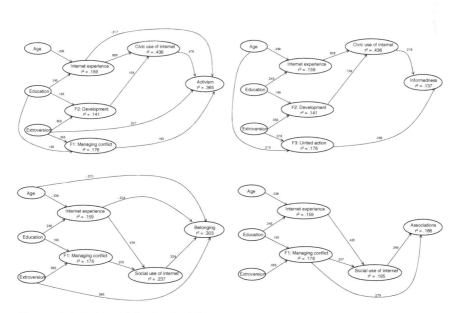

*Figure 4.4* Path models for Activism, Informedness, Belonging, and Associations, illustrating the involvement of three first-order factors of CCE.

community can manage conflicts and dilemmas is directly related to active participation. This pattern supports the interpretation that active participation depends directly on community capacities for problem-solving, planning, and negotiating, and that civic use of the Internet depends more specifically on directing such collective capacities toward sustainable development debates.

In the Informedness model, sustainable development and consensus and united action each assume one of the two outbound paths that the aggregate CCE factor had in Figure 4.3. The role of sustainable development in the Informedness model is just the same as it is in the Activism model, suggesting a common foundation of active and passive participation – namely, that a strong belief in the community's capacity to effectively manage growth and development has a direct enabling relationship with civic use of the Internet. The direct path from consensus and united action to Informedness suggests that strong beliefs about community solidarity, cooperation, and constructive handling of mistakes and disappointments are positively related to staying informed. This second path is an interesting contrast to that of the Activism model: In the latter, participation is correlated with actions such as achieving goals, settling conflicts, and managing resources, whereas, in the Informedness model, participation is correlated with values such as cooperation, perseverance, and solidarity.

In the path models for Belonging and Associations, the single first-order factor of managing conflicts and dilemmas has all the same inbound and outbound paths as the aggregate CCE factor had in Figure 4.3. It is interesting that, for both of these constructs, the relevant first-order factor is the one that emphasizes community capacities for problem-solving, initiative-taking, and active engagement, and not, for example, consensus and united action, emphasizing cooperation, working together, agreement, and constructive handling of mistakes and disappointment. This suggests that the beliefs about community capacities that are most instrumental to a sense of belonging or identification, and to building and sustaining social networks through community groups, are beliefs about facing and making tough decisions, achieving goals, settling conflicts, and managing resources.

## Critical people

We included the interview component in the EPIC study to provide richer, qualitative glimpses into how family and community life were affected by the Internet and the BEV and, conversely, how the BEV was affected by family and community life. These are necessarily anecdotal and, indeed, based on a relatively small subsample of twenty households. Each household was interviewed four times over the course of the study. In most cases, two researchers conducted the semi-structured interviews in the homes of the participants. Each interview was recorded with a digital audio recorder and transcribed. Interviews lasted from about 45 minutes to several hours and covered a variety of topics relating to participants' interactions with the Internet and their involvement in community organizations and local activities.

The first interview concentrated on basic information about the household, their professional work, daily life, leisure activities, and feelings about the local area and community. The second and third interviews focused on their local community contacts, community involvement, and the use of the Internet in facilitating those community activities and ties. The final interview investigated the role of the Internet in the home, exploring household rules and habits relating to computers, family concerns about the Internet, and typical routines and behaviors involving their use of the Internet (Carroll, Rosson, Kavanaugh *et al.* 2006; Dunlap *et al.* 2003).

Information from the interviews was intended to support two general goals. First, rich descriptions of participants' attitudes and behaviors involving the Internet helped to confirm, elaborate, explain, and augment survey findings. Second, ongoing dialog with participants provided opportunities to discover patterns and relationships that were not anticipated when developing the surveys.

The interviews provided an opportunity for participants to describe their own attitudes and understandings of the Internet in their own words. In-depth interviews were opportunities for researchers to document the discourse, language, and understandings of participants. The purpose was to describe the Internet as participants made sense of it in their lives. The stories and experiences that they conveyed reflected the meanings that they used to understand, engage, and explain the Internet and community. The language they employed helped researchers make better sense of answers and patterns in the surveys. Participants expressed personal feelings about how email, Internet chat, and the Web had changed and functioned in their work, hobbies, friendships, and local government. The interviews helped researchers describe the participants even when their answers did not seem reasonable or internally consistent.

Flanagan (1954) famously described the "critical incident" method for gathering vivid retrospective episodes of human performance. In our study we were focused not so much on episodes as on aggregate life patterns of our participants. We thought of them as critical people, vividly animated through their own reports and reflections on daily life.

In one of the interview households, we found an interesting generational contrast that resonated with our models for Activism and Belonging. This was a relatively large household of five adults, including two teenagers, who made heavy and varied use of their home computer. There was a particularly striking contrast between the father and one of the daughters: a younger extrovert versus an older introvert. From his survey responses, the father represents an introvert with low activism, low community belonging, and few associations, who is moderately well informed. According to his wife, "he uses [the Internet] a lot at work, a lot of communication with [business relations] and stuff like that." At home, he tended relax with computer games, some Internet-based, and also to use the Internet to access music sharing (Napster) and history websites.

The daughter, in contrast, was an extrovert with high activism, high belonging, many associations, and low informedness. She played soccer, softball, and basketball; she swam and juggled, and was member of science fiction, adventure, and sign language clubs, as well as Girl Scouts and the Baptist Church. She was a leader in four of these community groups. The daughter was very oriented to Internet-based communication. Her local community social circle was greater than 100. She emailed and chatted with a large group of friends, among them many people from her from sports teams, clubs, and church. From her point of view, her father was a less-than-adequate Internet user: "He's not into the Internet. ... He knows nothing about the Internet. ... At work, all he does is email. [At home,] he usually just uses the computer to play games."

A special circumstance in this case was that the daughter had a slight hearing disability, which made text-based interaction especially effective for her: "[The Internet] is better for me because I can't communicate very well on the phone with certain people. It is so much better when I get on the computer with them 'cause I understand them so much better." In this respect, the daughter is also a vivid example of how the BEV infrastructure enhanced opportunities for community participation for specific categories of people who might have been relatively more excluded without these interaction options.

Another household we interviewed illustrated how the Internet can be used to withdraw from the social world, perhaps to recharge. The household consisted of a married couple, both of whom were mid-career social service professionals who worked very long hours and with people throughout the day in their jobs. Thus, the husband described a typical twelve-hour workday that he enjoyed despite feeling exhaustion when he arrived home. After a long day of social interaction, his typical routine was to wind down with the Internet: "I don't want to go to the mall to see people."

Use of the Internet was central and significant in this couple's home life. The home was well equipped, with high-speed cable access and multiple desktop and laptop computers. The couple explained that, since adopting the Internet, they visited the library and local stores less, instead searching for information and shopping online. They enjoyed using the Internet to stay current with the news and latest technology. They shared the Internet-based activity of keeping up with news from the husband's former hometown. However, neither of them used the Internet for social purposes: "We use the Internet for information and not as a communication tool." They specifically did not use the Internet for activism or politics: "We shy away from those kinds of issues."

This couple is an example of work life merging with home life: The husband had his laptop on most of the time, and used the machine for both work and personal purposes, interleaving the two. The laptop contained critical software he had developed to manage some of his administrative work tasks. With respect to the community membership and participation models, this couple illustrates how high Internet experience that is *not* directed at civic purposes or social purposes can entail lower Activism and Belonging.

In some cases, interviews revealed underlying contradictions and limitations in the survey study. One participant seemed a paragon case of the Belonging model; he was well-educated sales manager who had been an early adopter of the Internet, online for several years, and had made extensive use of the Internet for social purposes. His survey responses were high for extroversion and CCE and indicated strong feelings of community belonging and identification. His home was well equipped. One computer in the house was designated for work purposes, while the other was a personal machine for everyone, including his wife and daughter. He made widespread use of the Internet for his work. His company used the Intranet extensively and has installed an extra phone line for a dial-up Internet connection for the business. He and a friend had organized a local youth sports event via the Internet. He communicated with his friends and most of the people involved in the event by sending email messages and attachments. This allowed them to coordinate the event with a minimal number of physical meetings. He acknowledged the utility of the Internet for streamlining both his work and community activity.

However, in interview discussions, this individual bemoaned the erosion of face-to-face communication, which he blamed on email: "My biggest complaint is what the computer has done with social interactions … in my regard more business related. Where I used to do a lot of face-to-face, you know, interpersonal, now it's a lot of emails and phone calls, and I hate emails." He believed that online interactions were being used inappropriately: "We're sending and communicating stuff that we should not be communicating by email." Indeed, he described how he often took day trips to visit customers within a couple-hour radius. This concern illustrates the claims enumerated in Table 3.3.

Some interviews reminded us that survey items are not always responded to as intended. For example, one working mother's survey responses classified her as middle-high for Activism, Associations, Informedness, and Belonging, and low for Internet Experience. During the interview she announced, "I don't think I'm in any clubs." However, in the course of the discussion it emerged that she was a member of the Middle School Parent–Teacher Association, the High School Parent–Teacher Association, Habitat for Humanity, Boy Scouts, the Methodist Church and its Sunday School, and several university club committees. She was a project manager for Habitat for Humanity, and was responsible for planning and coordinating Sunday school lessons and after-church coffee. Relative to our sample, this is an extremely high level of associations.

This woman also considerably underestimated her Internet experience. She was part of our logging study, and it turned out that she was one of the heaviest users of the Internet for community purposes in our sample: She was the top-ranked user of email, which she employed to coordinate meetings of her groups, and she had the fifth-most community website accesses.

Another participant, a 76-year-old widow, also rated herself as rather average for activism and use of the Internet for civic purposes. However, in the interviews we discovered that she was a member of eight community groups, and the leader of two, and that she was heavily involved in driving around senior citizens who were unable to get around on their own. She was also in the logging study, and we found that she was the top-ranked user in accesses to community web pages and that overall her household web use, which was just her, was in the top third of our sample.

The interviews helped us understand how life changes were reflected in people's use of information technology. In one young family, the wife had recently taken leave of absence from her job to care for her new baby. She discovered that this gave her time to expand the range of her use of the Internet. She was already relatively high for community activism, belonging and informedness, and had many community associations. But during the period of leave her use of local websites increased, both in frequency and range. She began sharing photos with friends and started an online Bible-study project with her mother and sister. She also began to explore shopping online.

Our stratification procedure deliberately involved ten households in which no member used the Internet at home or at work in order to represent the part of the Blacksburg community that did not participate directly in the BEV. This group proved to be interesting in the interviews. We initially included two of these households in the interview study subsample, but later added others. We discovered that most of the households we classified as non-users were actively wrestling with the question of what computer equipment to buy, and therefore were actually on a trajectory to obtaining Internet access or were already accessing Internet services through other people. Thus, most of our non-users really were "marginal" users (Dunlap *et al.* 2003).

An example of the first kind was a young couple, well-educated professionals, who had decided not to have Internet access specifically *because* they had young children: "With the kids being small, I didn't want them locked into video games. I grew up playing outside and I built this house here so the kids would have a nice place to play and encourage them to go outside and play outside and play games. Do creative art things or pretend stuff." At the same time, these parents worried that their children needed Internet access: "The kids desperately need it for school."

The parents were both knowledgeable about Internet tools, but were clearly struggling, seeing home computing as a sort of Pandora's box: "Email is convenient to use, but I like talking to people because you can tell keywords and voice inflection and so on. I guess that's maybe why, I don't want to say I rebel against it, but I'm not a strong proponent of it at this point in time." During the study, this family did in fact purchase a home computer, though at the final interview they still had not unpacked it.

An example of the second type of marginal use was a young single man who made regular but vicarious use of a variety of Internet services: He downloaded lyrics and lead sheets; he sent and received emails, including attachments; he tracked local and regional sports in which he was a participant. However, he did not carry out these tasks directly: "Instead of me doing it, I just ask, 'can you get it online'?" His brother sent and received emails for him, forwarding them to a coworker who printed them. A friend who works in the same building regularly printed out web information for him: "I get copies from people. I don't actually go get it myself. They always pull it up and check it. I get the hard copy." This person had developed a fairly elaborate support network to maintain a proxy Internet connection.

Another example of second-hand use of the Internet was a middle-aged woman who got access to the Internet through her sister. The relationship started when the sister and a brother living in California started emailing. The sister then passed on information about their brother: "Most of the time it isn't worth passing on, but that is how I learn things." Subsequently, she asked her sister to look up an increasing variety of web-based information – "pages and pages" – on the breed of her dog, her favorite NASCAR driver, possible vacation destinations, and so on: "My sister looks up anything we want to know." Through the course of our study, this participant admitted that she had considered getting a home Internet connection, but at the end of the study she was not seriously moving toward that: "I could do stuff for myself instead of getting somebody else to do it for me. I might go on to the dirty websites and nobody would know but me."

Many of these second-hand use relationships occurred *within* household units. For example, we interviewed a wife who managed her husband's email: "He has a couple of friends he likes to email, but he doesn't do it. He tells me, and I type it out." We also encountered several examples of people who depended on other people for particular aspects of their Internet access. Thus, one young man engaged in some direct use of the Internet but delegated more complex interactions to his girlfriend. For example, he found items on eBay that he wanted, but then asked his girlfriend to carry out the bidding process.

## Bridges

As our data analysis progressed, we identified a category of critical people that we called *bridges*: people who participate in more than one community group. This concept is related to our construct of Associations, but it is a binary distinction instead of a scaled variable. Intriguingly, we found that the 75 bridges in our sample were significantly higher than the 83 non-bridges on *all* of our critical personal characteristics and constructs: Bridges were better educated; they were higher on Informedness, Activism, and Belonging (by definition, of course, they are also higher for Associations); and they have higher CCE. We looked, further, into the distinction between the 23 leader bridges in our sample – persons who are *leaders* in two or more community groups – and the 52 member bridges. Leader bridges were numerically higher than member bridges for all of our measures, but, probably because the number of participants left in the analysis was small, only a couple measures were statistically significant (for further details and results, see Kavanaugh *et al.* 2003).

We also found evidence that using the Internet affects bridges and non-bridges differently, and that bridges make distinctive use of the Internet. Overall, bridges were higher for Involvement Since Getting Online than non-bridges, and leader bridges were higher than member bridges. More intensive use of the Internet was associated with different activity for bridges and non-bridges. We found that bridges and non-bridges who were light users of the Internet were not statistically different with respect to Social Use of the Internet and Involvement

Since Getting Online; however, bridges who were heavy users of the Internet, relative to our sample, made greater Social Use of the Internet and reported attending more local meetings and events since going online compared with the non-bridges who were heavy users.

Finally, we found evidence that bridges developed differently than non-bridges during the EPIC study. Earlier in this chapter we described the result that members of community groups increased their use of Internet collaboration tools during the study period – that is, between the first and second survey waves – and that they also reported increased levels of involvement in their community groups. When we looked separately at bridge and non-bridge community members, we found that this effect is largely due to the bridges (in this analysis, a member was considered a bridge only if he or she was a bridge – a member of two or more groups – for *both* survey waves). Between the two survey waves, both bridge and non-bridge members increased their use of Internet collaboration tools and reported increased levels of involvement in their groups. However, only for bridges were these differences statistically significant.

In summary, we came to see bridges, and especially leader bridges, as key community members, integrating the community by integrating community groups.

The term *bridge* was originally introduced by Harary, Norman, and Cartwright (1965: 198). However, they defined it more severely than we did, as a person providing the *only* connecting path between two groups in a social network. Our study did not comprehensively map the social network of Blacksburg, but it is doubtful that many or perhaps any of our bridges were bridges in this severe sense. Indeed, it seems there usually are redundant linkages among people and groups throughout a community (see also Granovetter 1973).

Bridges in our sense are related to several concepts discussed in chapter 1. Thus, Simmel (1972) had argued that ties among groups in society (*Gesellschaft*) provide critical integration and balance the potential for social isolation that might follow from ties strictly within groups. And Loomis (1960) introduced the concept of *systemic linkages* to refer to arrangements in which ties between community members whom one does not even know can still be beneficial. Community groups could be said to have a systemic tie if they share a bridging member and most strongly if they share a leader bridge.

In more recent literature, Putnam (2000) distinguished between bonding and bridging social capital. The former is the more obvious: Strong bonds among friends or within a group are important for generating and circulating social capital. But Putnam pointed out that bonding social capital is also self-limiting. It cannot integrate the community because, by its definition, it operates within self-selected coteries and not across social boundaries. This details the earlier concepts with respect to how patterns of linking can allow social capital to flow throughout a community. Granovetter's (1973) contrast between strong and weak ties is driving at a similar idea: In his view, a set of strong ties is always a closed subgraph in a social network. Weak ties are important because they span these strong clusters. Granovetter's study showed that, when people need to access a social network broadly, to find a job, weak ties can be more important to success-ful outcomes. (See Williams 2005 for a meta-analysis questioning Granovetter's "strength of weak ties" claim.)

Community bridges are scientifically interesting because they seem to con-ceptually differentiate Putnam's notion of bridging social capital from Granovetter's notion of weak ties: Bridges integrate the community through bridging social capital (Putnam), but they do this through *strong ties*, not weak ties (Granovetter). Indeed, Granovetter famously argued that, if A is strongly tied to B and also strongly tied to C, it is "most *unlikely*" that B and C will not share a strong tie (Granovetter 1973: 1363). This is an interesting conjecture about friendship networks, which is what Granovetter appears to be thinking about, and perhaps other kinds of networks. But it is not true of community groups.

Consider a hypothetical case in which a person is a leader bridge – that is, a leader in two small community groups. It is difficult not to imagine that this would entail that this person has strong ties to every, or very nearly every, mem-ber of both groups, using Granovetter's own operational definition of strong tie, which is social contact more than once per week. However, it is most *unlikely* that every dyad spanning both groups shares a strong tie. No community could be that well integrated. It is indeed very likely that some of these dyads have no strong tie at all, precisely the network arrangement Granovetter ruled out.

One of the distinctions Granovetter himself proposed between strong and weak ties is that removing a single strong tie leaves a network pretty much intact, because of triangles of redundant connections like A–B–C above. However, removing a weak tie can change the network dramatically with respect to which nodes are reachable from which other nodes, and in how many jumps. Granovetter's tie removal test further demonstrates that bridges integrate com-munities through strong ties: Removing any single tie from a set of ties that integrate two community groups through a bridging member really does not change anything. The bridging member still integrates the community by inte-grating the same set of community groups, just one tie less densely.

There is a weak tie story here, however. Our hypothetical leader bridge inte-grates community groups through the strong ties that he or she has with members of the groups. But this arrangement of social ties creates the possibility for *weak* ties between dyads that span the two groups. Indeed, this is a variation of Granovetter's triangle: The bridge A has strong ties to B in one group and to C in another group. This provides insufficient foundation for a strong tie between B and C, but it is a paradigm case for a weak tie: B might know only that there exists a C in A's other group, and C might know only that there exists an analo-gous B. Thus, in addition to integrating the community by directly spanning community groups with strong ties, bridges mediate weak ties across group boundaries for all other members.

In recent decades, Burt (1992) has extensively investigated bridging in the context of networks of business professionals. In his work, a tie is a "frequent and substantial business" interaction (Burt 2002), a significant tie that he argues is a strong tie relationship, though it seems a weaker tie than simultaneous membership/leadership of two distinct groups, as in our study. Burt finds that bridging ties among organizational peers are important. For example, managers with bridging ties are disproportionately the source of recognized good ideas in their organization. Yet these bridging ties are also rare, comprising less than 5 percent of ties among managers in different business units (Burt 2004). This is interesting, since the proportion of bridges in our study was 47 percent; again, though, in our case the people themselves were bridges, as opposed to merely having a bridging tie.

Bridging ties, as described in the preceding paragraph, decay rapidly; Burt (2002) found that nine out of ten bridge relationships disappeared within a year. His interpretation is that new bridging ties are often allowed to decline after they have served some initial purpose; by definition, they cannot be supported by a network of supporting ties. Babchuk and Booth (1973) reported that bridging individuals are more likely than other members to change group affiliations over time. In this case, the mechanism may be that membership in two or more groups weakens one's sense of group boundaries, perhaps creating broader awareness of what other groups exist and about opportunities for defection or additional memberships. Indeed, this flux could be an additional, longitudinal mechanism through which bridges integrate the community by integrating groups. Nevertheless, in our second survey wave, 59 of our 75 first-wave bridges were still bridges, a decline of 21 percent. This is a more modest decline than we would have expected based on prior literature. It may be, for example, that many of our bridges were already well established as such, and thereby less susceptible to the processes described by Burt and by Babchuk and Booth. We have to leave these questions for further research.

## Conclusions

The work described in this chapter does not settle questions about the potential consequences of community networks for community, or conversely. It helps to supplement the narrative of chapters 2 and 3, and it raises a range of questions for future investigations of community networks. We found evidence that the BEV had indeed transformed community life and created new possibilities for strengthening community. The people of Blacksburg, during 2001–3, accessed local Internet content, and specifically BEV content, disproportionately. To this extent, Internet access in Blacksburg was indeed used for community networking. Consistent with this, we found that participation in community groups was correlated with increased use of online collaboration tools and with greater involvement in the community through the course of the study.

The Social Participation and Civic Effects path models showed that active community participation, along with social or civic use of the Internet, predicted involvement in the community since getting online. This further suggests that a community network can be a catalyst for community participation.

In a series of path models analyzing the four keys constructs of Belonging, Informedness, Activism and Associations, we found that civic use of the Internet entails greater community participation, and that social use of the Internet entails greater community identification and diverse social support. However, mere use of Internet did not strengthen these key community feelings, beliefs, dispositions, and experiences. For community identity and active participation, it was a direct negative factor.

Our construct of community collective efficacy (CCE) was an important factor in the path models for all four community membership and participation constructs, and a direct predictor of diverse support networks (associations) and passive aspects of community participation (informedness). Strong beliefs that the community can manage conflicts and dilemmas are a key aspect of community collective efficacy for sense of belonging, active community participation, and diverse support networks. In contrast, beliefs that the community can reach consensus in action facilitates the relatively more passive participation of being informed.

Our consideration of case studies and types of people highlighted several key patterns: We described the conservatism of self-reports, which can rather dramatically underestimate a respondent's community activity and technology. We described several patterns of marginal use in which participants who self-classified as non-users actually were making regular use of the Internet through the help of friends and family members. Finally, we discussed the bridging pattern. Bridges, and especially leader bridges, are key community members, integrating the community through their roles in multiple community groups. The many tie relationships in which bridges participate, and that they systemically mediate for others, strengthen the community as a diverse support network.

# 5 Learning in a networked community

The BEV became a far-flung participatory design project, energizing pockets of innovation throughout the community, transforming the community's sense of its own identity, and catalyzing community learning about information technology. This provided an incredibly conducive context for smaller-scale, more focused community design research initiatives. In the decade from the mid-1990s through the mid-2000s, our research group worked with various community groups and institutions on a series of community networking systems and applications.

We approached these projects as participatory design research: We wanted to learn about effective processes and technological tools through creating software with real people in and for real-world situations. We saw these projects as community-oriented service learning and research, since our goal was to better integrate the learning and research activities of ourselves and our students with civic engagement, with meaningful contributions to the everyday concerns of our neighbors. The BEV itself was a large and complex participatory design research project, involving many key actors. Knowledge can emerge from historical analysis of such projects, as argued in chapter 3 with respect to the relationship between appropriation and participation in a "field of dreams" scenario. But smaller-scale and more focused projects afford more articulated analysis of processes and tools – and thereby the possibility of more articulated design knowledge. This is what we wanted to achieve in our projects carried out within the BEV context.

With respect to design processes, we wanted to explore participatory design techniques in community contexts. Prior to our work, most participatory design work had focused on relatively brief and structured exercises directed at understanding the role of information technology in commercial workplaces, and most had concentrated on mediated participation – workshop exercises often involving labor union officials representing workers and their concerns (e.g., Bødker et al. 1987). As participatory design techniques were adapted in North America, they were even further simplified, eventually becoming very brief, one-shot brainstorms between designers and users (Muller 1992). We were impressed with the results of early participatory design studies, as well as with the theoretical and moral rationale for participatory design, but we were deeply skeptical that designers and users could meaningfully engage, share their practices, and work collaboratively through only brief and mediated or relatively superficial encounters.

The overarching context of the BEV project made it possible for us to pursue a very different approach to participatory design. The BEV had already made the important point that pre-existing, appropriable socio-technical infrastructure is a prerequisite for meaningful participation. We wanted to explore this further with respect to more specific designs and design techniques. We wanted to explore ways of working directly with community members, and we found that our community partners expected this level of engagement. We wanted to collaborate over greater spans of time and with respect to a wider range of design issues, and we found that our community partners in Blacksburg were eager for this also. Indeed, we came to understand that the keenest concern of community partners in university–community collaborations is that the university researchers will suddenly appear, seemingly out of nowhere, and talk about broad visions with scholarly empathy, but actually carry out fairly focused projects within a semester or a year and then vanish. In this regard, the BEV was very useful to both sides of town–gown engagement: It helped our community partners to see themselves as innovators, not merely as props or supporters of someone else's innovation, and it constantly reminded us that our projects were part of a bigger and more significant movement in the community.

With respect to technological tools, we wanted to elaborate the second-generation paradigm for community networks in the direction of supporting interaction. The World-Wide Web made networking services more usable; second-generation community networks leveraged this to make local information more accessible. Indeed, the BEV is the original demonstration that providing basic tools, notably training and other technical support, can evoke a broad-based exchange of online community information in a web-based community network. However, an irony of second-generation community networks is that they traded accessibility for interaction. In making it easier both to publish static content as web pages and more pleasant to browse and read the text and graphics in web pages, second-generation community networks implicitly emphasize this more passive kind of community activity. But what about other touchstone scenarios for community networks? What about discussion, debate, and deliberation? What about reacting to and developing a neighbor's ideas (Box 2.2)?

Support for interaction within the Web paradigm emerged rapidly in the mid-1990s, especially support for asynchronous discussion forums (Berwick *et al.* 1994). And a wide variety of new interactive technologies and tools for web-based information systems have continued to emerge. These technologies made the Web paradigm even more attractive to users, but at a cost in complexity relative to static HTML pages. We wanted to explore how community members could appropriate these new technologies and deploy them in interactive BEV services and applications. We wanted to elaborate the second-generation paradigm by helping to make the BEV a collaborative medium for community members, and not merely a collective repository for community information.

Our first and, it turned out, our longest-lived collaborative design research project was a partnership with a group of middle- and high-school science teachers in the Montgomery County school system, a project we called "Learning in a

Networked Community," or LiNC. We initiated a participatory design collaboration that was both more deliberate and more focused than that of the overall BEV project, as well as more directly guided by prior research on participatory design. Our goal was to investigate participatory design as a methodological framework for community networking, as a way of working across boundaries in a community. We wanted to further articulate participatory design processes in a case where those processes were not mediated or abridged, as in the earlier work, but where those processes involved substantial and continuing commitment from actual practitioners.

One of the most important arguments for participatory design is the possibility of mutual learning: When participants seriously engage, share their understandings, and jointly create outcomes, they are transformed with respect to understanding one another, but also with respect to their own practices. Unfortunately, in most reports of participatory design, the nature of this learning – what is learned, how the learning is organized, and the transformative nature of the learning – is not made explicit. We wanted to explore what it would take and what it would be like for participants in a design collaboration – including ourselves – to experience transformative learning.

We did not find any of this to be simple or quick. But we found it to be possible. We achieved a participatory process that continued to evolve and develop through a decade of collaborative endeavor and that was quite effective in producing innovative school technologies. This chapter focuses on the development of that participatory process and the design prototypes this process produced. We employed this participatory process in a series of other design research projects that are described in subsequent chapters.

## Engaging a practice

In 1993 the US National Science Foundation (NSF) announced a Networking Infrastructure for Education program, which supported research initiatives exploring how networked computing could enhance science and mathematics education. A large interdisciplinary group of Virginia Tech faculty began meeting in the winter and spring of 1993–4, sometimes with teachers and administrators from the county public school system, to discuss project concepts that could leverage the BEV infrastructure in addressing nationally articulated challenges for public schools, such as supporting collaborative, project-based learning in classrooms, increasing community involvement with schools, improving access of rural schools to educational opportunities, enhancing gender equity in science and mathematics education, and controlling material costs in science education (American Association for the Advancement of Science 1991, 1993; National Science Teachers Association 1992; US Department of Education 1994). In the first round of awards under the Networking Infrastructure for Education program, our group obtained a planning grant, which allowed us to provide several teachers with networked classroom computers and to continue and expand our discussion and planning process.

Just setting up those first few computers in classrooms advanced our collaboration with local teachers tremendously. Stuart Laughton, a Virginia Tech PhD student I was advising at the time, began working with two of the teachers to explore how ethnographic interviews could work as a technique for understanding teachers' concerns and requirements, and how interaction scenarios could work as a tool for exchanging and developing visions of how networks and software could impact teaching and learning interactions (Fetterman 1989). Laughton worked with two teachers from the Montgomery County school division, one a middle-school physical science teacher, the other a high-school physics teacher. His work involved tight cycles of interviews and discussion, development of interaction scenarios embodying solution approaches, and implementation and evaluation of interactive software prototypes. Laughton continued and studied this iterative process of direct teacher participation in the development of classroom software for the next year. Eventually, it became one of the field studies reported in his PhD dissertation (Laughton 1996).

Laughton's study was limited but produced intriguing results. First, it showed clearly *how* teachers could be direct and effective partners in the design and development of new technological approaches. The single prior study of participatory design with teachers, by M. G. Williams (1994), had focused just on customization of off-the-shelf software in which teachers interacted only indirectly with engineers through a "translator." Thus, the participation was mediated, and the space of design possibilities was quite limited. Laughton's study showed that more ambitious design collaboration could be achieved, and that the participants themselves could cope with "translation." Indeed, his study suggested that the interpersonal work required to bridge the communication gap between public school educators and software engineers was beneficial in the longer term. It helped to develop trust and mutual understanding, which in turn afforded more revealing exchanges. Second, it was interesting to us that *all* of the projects designed with the teachers involved support for interaction versus mere posting and sharing of content. The teachers were interested in support for online discussion, online submission and management of homeworks, and so forth. In 1994, web-based interaction was a relatively advanced functionality. As software design, it was beyond customization of off-the-shelf software. Based on Laughton's study, we were encouraged that participatory design of new networking infrastructures and applications for collaborative education was desirable and feasible.

Public schools are ideal in many ways as partners for participatory design research on community technology. Every American community has a school system, and for every community the school system is a key community institution. To a great extent, the importance of schools follows from their primary role, to educate and enculturate the next generation of citizens. However, it also derives from the American model of public finance and local control: Communities largely finance their own local schools. Indeed, for many communities, funding for public schools is the largest single category for local public spending. The budget for the Montgomery Country school system, for which

Blacksburg is the major population center, is roughly double the entire town budget, covering all local functions other than education. Schools also frequently serve as public spaces. They are used as election polling places and for large public meetings. Important school events are often open to the community, such as basketball games and science fairs. These factors place the public schools at the center of American community identity.

Traditionally, individual teachers have considerable professional discretion about pedagogy and classroom management. The work of teaching is, after all, carried out in individual classrooms, largely in isolation from peers and from school administrators. Yet teaching is inherently social. It is fundamentally about stimulating, shaping, and helping to develop young people. In the culture of teaching, experienced teachers mentor younger faculty members. Experienced teachers have well-established personal practices and philosophies of education. This mentoring can be highly intellectual and inherently reflective. Of course, not every teacher is actively concerned with innovation or with sharing practices and resources among peers, but many are. The public school workplace provides some mechanisms for teacher professional development, such as free periods and periodic professional development workshops. But many teachers feel that these mechanisms are insufficient and that innovative practices are not adequately encouraged, acknowledged, valued, or disseminated. It is not surprising that relatively large and well-established public institutions, such as school systems, would tend to be somewhat inertial; rather, it is impressive that a substantial proportion of teachers nonetheless remain committed to and immersed in educational innovation.

Teachers are also traditionally regarded as pillars of the local community. Those we worked with in Blacksburg all seemed to be bridges, in the sense explained in chapter 4. As relatively well-educated members of the community, teachers were traditionally seen as an intellectual resource to the community. Typical community-based associations, such as the School Board and the Parent–Teacher Association, engage parents in planning and implementing educational programs and reciprocally engage teachers in the concerns and activities of the broader community. Many standard learning activities, particularly in elementary education, involve community engagement – for example, supporting local charities or social service agencies, or inviting various community members to visit the school and explain to the students the roles they play.

Nevertheless, there are unique and formidable challenges for participatory design in public schools. Technology in general has been chronically problematic in the culture of schools. Throughout the past century, teachers have been repeatedly challenged by government and by society to make better use of technology, to teach technology, to teach effectively with technology. Yet, from the teacher's standpoint, classroom technology itself is often more the problem than the solution. The history of classroom technology is largely a history of singularly ineffective technologies pushed into the classroom context: Film and radio in the 1920s, television in the 1950s, computer-assisted instruction in the 1980s, among others, have been notable failures (Cuban 1986; Hodas 1993; Tyack and

Cuban 1995). Based on history, teachers in the early 1990s could have been skeptical that the Internet would be anything more than the next distracting and ineffective technology panacea.

In finer analysis, the problematic recent history of classroom technology can be seen as deriving from a profound *lack* of teacher participation. Thus, it is remarkable that, among the many failed classroom technology innovations, none supported collaborative learning pedagogies, and most implicitly limit the teacher's role with respect to pedagogical interactions. Indeed, most previous technology innovations were merely broadcast media for one-size-fits-all static content and, to that extent, can be seen as pedagogically regressive, even if technologically innovative. Moreover, in all these earlier cases, the technological innovations were delivered to and imposed upon teachers. The role of the teacher was one of being trained, and then performing, as an operator; the technologies and the content and activity they supported were already defined. In other words, these technologies were designed to be difficult or impossible to appropriate. Such a strategy not only fails to leverage the pedagogical expertise of teachers, it specifically undermines that expertise. Given this, it is predictable that, inside the "black boxes" of classrooms, these technologies were often just not used, and eventually they went away (Tyack and Cuban 1995).

In recent decades, the professional discretion – and isolation – of teachers in classroom practices has become an issue. The black box of classroom practice makes outstanding and derelict performance equally opaque. Many "school reform" initiatives in effect are attempts to open up the "black box" of individual teacher practices (Cuban 1993; Davies 1991; Dunlap, Neale, and Carroll 2000; Mitchell 1997; National Research Council 1996; Rosenholtz 1989; Shields 1994). School reform is a very complex topic. It ranges from bureaucratic regimes of teacher performance assessment (see immediately below) to encouragement for innovative practices, among them the strengthening of teacher professional cultures within schools and greater engagement with the community in which a school is embedded. This latter current in school reform has helped to raise awareness of and interest in teacher collaboration and broader community engagement. It directly facilitated a receptive attitude in the Montgomery County schools to our proposal for a long-term participatory design research project investigating how the schools could better leverage the BEV infrastructure.

However, the complementary thrust of school reform toward teacher accountability and objective performance assessment has had exactly the opposite effect. At a high level of analysis, such as the view of state overseers, schools and school systems are also "black boxes." And, again, the basic concern is not misplaced; it is reasonable to ensure that all children have comparable educational opportunities. A common approach to this uncertainty has been to create bureaucracies of standardized testing. In the mid-1990s, public schools in Virginia were being introduced to state-mandated standards of learning, enforced by high-stakes tests: Poor performance of a class or a school would be taken as evidence that its teacher or teachers were not performing well, while poor performance for a school would lead to loss of accreditation. The Virginia standards were bundled with class plans and other materials, suggesting pretty transparently that the safest course for teachers might be to follow the standard curriculum. This is an unfortunate downside of standardization – namely, deskilling professional work and undermining innovation. Indeed, statewide results for the standard testing rose so dramatically in Virginia that it is difficult to see it as anything other than teaching to the test: In 1998, only 2 percent of Virginia schools met the standard for full accreditation; however, in 2005, 92 percent of the schools met the standard (Virginia Department of Education 2005).

The real world is a messy place for socio-technical research, but there is no alternative. School reform initiatives that emphasize the need for teachers to engage and reflect are highly compatible with participatory design. Indeed, it could be argued that they uniquely require participatory design. But high-stakes standard tests are an obstacle to participatory design or any other mechanism for identifying and supporting innovative practices, for trying anything new and therefore risky, because they place a high penalty on failure at any point but reward plodding approaches that produce mediocre outcomes. The Virginia standards of learning were a looming threat and a constant challenge for our participatory design collaboration.

In the fall of 1994, as part of our continuing planning process and to help focus the development of a research proposal, we created what we called the Marissa scenario, named for my then six-year-old daughter, a narrative vision sketching how a networking infrastructure could transform the learning experiences of children (Box 5.1). The scenario was written to convey our starting vision of what computer-based collaborative learning could be like from the perspective of the students who would experience it. The learning activity in the scenario is student-driven, collaborative, and project-based; the students construct and analyze a series of simulation experiments, learning self-initiative and socially constructive approaches by engaging in them. In our proposal, we suggested that community members – parents, for example – could also visit this virtual school, and thus more easily become involved with school activities. We thought of this as an ongoing "science fair" accessible via the BEV, and in that way opening up the schools to broader community visibility and participation.

*Box 5.1*   An envisionment of learning in a networked community: The Marissa scenario

- Marissa, a tenth-grade physics student, is studying gravity and its role in planetary motion. She goes to the virtual science lab and navigates to the gravity room.
- In the gravity room she discovers two other students, Randy and David, already working with the Alternate Reality Kit (Smith 1987), which allows students to alter various physical parameters (such as the universal gravitational constant) and then observe effects in a graphical simulation world.

*(Continued)*

Box 5.1    (*Continued*)

- The three students, each of whom is from a different school in the county, discuss possible experiments by typing messages from their respective personal computers. Together they build and analyze several solar systems, eventually focusing on the question of how comets can disrupt otherwise stable systems.
- They capture data from their experiments and display it with several visualization tools, then write a brief report of their experiments, sending it for comments to Don, another student in Marissa's class, and Ms. Gould, Randy's physics teacher.

The Marissa scenario was probably a bit *too* visionary, or at least too radical, and it was perhaps also a bit naive. It clearly puts students at the center of their own learning – surely a good thing. Indeed, the teacher enters into the learning only in a minor supporting role at the end, to review and comment on the student-initiated work. One could reasonably question whether the Marissa scenario presents a comprehensive paradigm for education – that is, whether student inquiry *alone* can drive the whole process. But this would miss the point of the scenario as an envisionment. The most important role of such a scenario is to get design work started and focused (Carroll 2000; Rosson and Carroll 2002). The Marissa scenario did this quite well; it energized our entire team and shaped our NSF proposal. Later, it provided a concrete starting point for developing and implementing more comprehensive design proposals. In our case, a critical role of the envisionment scenario was to inspire NSF reviewers to the extent that they might award us a major research grant to investigate collaborative learning mediated by a community network. And it did that too.

Indeed, the scenario proved to be remarkably inspiring. A couple years after our successful NSF proposal, Virginia Tech created the image in Figure 5.1, highlighting the bucolic landscapes of Montgomery County, and suggesting that collaborative learning over networks could bring science concepts and experiments to the student even if she was sitting in a cow pasture. This image was used in university promotional materials for a new advanced technology center, and in the late 1990s it became iconic for human–computer interaction and learning technologies research at Virginia Tech.

Interestingly, later in the project, one of the teachers revealed to me that the Marissa scenario shocked her at the time. She saw this entirely student-driven learning episode as farfetched. Of course, one has to acknowledge that the scenario is rather iconoclastic with respect to the teacher-centered nature of schools. Any teacher looking at this as a vision for the future of education would have to wonder, "Where is the teacher?" In the Marissa scenario, the students drive all the learning and engage with the teacher only after the important intellectual work is finished. In creating the scenario, I was indeed deliberately trying to be provocative, perhaps even farfetched, because that is how one identifies and develops new ideas. And, in my experience, provocative visions evoke more energy and better ideas from one's colleagues. But I was not trying to shock or

*Figure 5.1*   Visualization of the Marissa scenario.

upset anyone. I was not even challenging teacher-centered conceptions of school. In our proposal, the Marissa scenario is framed as something the children do after school; they are using the community network to collaborate when otherwise it would have been impossible to do so.

When I learned of my colleague's initial reaction to the scenario, I was struck that at the time she had said nothing remotely like this. Even though she had been a member of the university/school system planning group longer than I had, and, more importantly, even though she had vastly more experience in designing and implementing learning activities for children than I had, she had not questioned my idea at the time, not even a tiny bit. To me this is a striking vignette of how participatory design can silently fail. We never know what our partners do not tell us. I would never have learned of her reaction if I had not continued to work with her for several more years after the envisionment scenario, eventually reaching a point of mutual trust where she could reveal her original skepticism to me. By then of course, it was a humorously ironic footnote on the years we had spent working together. Recalling this episode always reminds me that participatory design can be a fool's paradise: Everyone on a diverse design team can seem so empowered, just so long as you complete the collaboration before they tell you the truth!

## Sharing a vision

In late 1995, the US National Science Foundation (NSF) made a major award to Virginia Tech and the public schools of Montgomery County to develop and investigate a high-quality communications infrastructure to support collaborative science learning. The large interdisciplinary planning group was suddenly a much smaller group of the people committed to carry out the work we had proposed. I was the principal investigator for the NSF grant and the leader for the LiNC project (Learning in a Networked Community). I took Laughton's work as the process starting point for our project. I wanted us to pursue a participatory design approach, but more deeply and completely than Laughton had been able to do in one year or than was typically ever undertaken in participatory design projects. My intention was to start from the Marissa envisionment, to challenge, to change, and to deconstruct it, and ideally to develop technological innovations both more appropriate to real contexts of teaching and learning in public schools and more radical than the original envisionment. This was a lot to aim for, but we had more than a million dollars. In 1995, that was a lot of money.

Our project work started with an extended ethnographic investigation of teaching and learning practices in the classrooms of the four LiNC teachers. Beginning in the 1995–6 school year, university faculty and students became regular visitors to the schools. In the spring of 1996, with an influx of graduate-student research assistants funded by the NSF grant, we spent many hours observing and videotaping classroom activity, interviewing teachers and students in the classrooms, and gathering a variety of educational artifacts such as lesson plans and science journals. We used ethnographic methods, classifying and analyzing these materials with the teachers (Button and Sharrock 2009; Clifford 1986; Fetterman 1989). More details can be found in Carroll *et al.* (1998); the definitive report on the early phases of this work is George Chin's Virginia Tech dissertation (Chin 2004).

We learned a lot about schools and about teachers in that first year. The classroom scenario in Box 5.2 is drawn from the science learning activities we observed in the middle schools. It summarizes a lesson on waves given by one of the LiNC middle-school teacher participants, incorporating a set of learning activities that take place over a four-day period. The lesson illustrates the usefulness of combining and blending different teaching techniques (e.g., didactic discussion, guided discovery, demonstration) across complementary learning activities. It also identifies a range of classroom activities that can be used to promote collaborative learning (e.g., the class discussion, the small-group slinky manipulation, the group poster presentations). Finally it emphasizes the important role of physical interactions with equipment, especially within this age group.

*Box 5.2* Classroom context scenario, a lesson on waves

> - In Ms. Gould's middle-school science class, each student describes in his/her science journal the waves he/she knows about, along with related facts or ideas. The students then share their individual work in a discussion guided by the teacher.
> - Groups of four to five students experiment with a large wire slinky. Their manipulations are guided by an assignment sheet that tells them how to
>
> *(Continued)*

*Box 5.2    (Continued)*

> generate different kinds of waves, as well as questions aimed at guiding their exploration of the waves' characteristics. Each group collects observations on the waves it generates, with the teacher circulating among groups to guide students' manipulations of the slinky and attention to interesting aspects of the resulting waves.
>
> • Each group develops a short poster presentation using large sheets of paper and felt-tip markers. They describe the waves they generated and the wave characteristics they noted. The groups then deliver their poster presentations to the rest of the class, with the teacher taking an active role in critiquing each group's findings and in directing class discussion.
> • After sharing their presentations, students read material from their science textbook that introduces formal terminology for waves and wave properties. They are also given homework in which they write down definitions for various terms. This homework is submitted and discussed in class.
> • The final element of the lesson is a demonstration of how sound waves are transmitted through different media (e.g., solids, liquids, gases). The teacher uses an assortment of musical tuning forks in combination with objects and surfaces in the classroom (e.g., air, the floor, a table).

The results of the initial ethnographic study challenged some of our original assumptions. For example, we found that classroom space was very congested; rooms were filled with tables, equipment, and other materials. In developing our proposal, we assumed that each student would have his or her own computer; the teachers and school administrators had supported this, and our project budget provided funds for it. However, there just did not seem to be enough space for one computer per student. We found that teachers employed a variety of instructional styles, from traditional didactic to unstructured discovery. They seemed to blend these dynamically and idiosyncratically. Of course, on reflection it is not surprising that a task as complex as teaching entails an eclectic blend of strategies, but the literature on school reform focuses strongly on project-based explorations. Our Marissa scenario was all about student-driven discovery learning, but the classroom ethnography showed that whatever we developed would need to accommodate or at least coordinate with other instructional styles as well.

We observed that students frequently work on laboratory exercises in groups. Indeed, this organization was highly over-determined: The schools did not have enough equipment or space for each student to have her or his own set-up, teachers would not have had time enough to manage personal set-ups, and collaborative learning is valued by teachers and motivating for students. We saw that students collaborated on many kinds of tasks: Students organized themselves into groups and organized coordination among those groups, they manipulated equipment together, they gathered and recorded data, they discussed interpretations, they created and delivered presentations, and they coached one another as necessary. We observed several kinds of collaborative interaction – for example, consensus-building during group conflicts, impromptu mentoring by the more prepared students of those less prepared, and initiative-taking in making and executing experimental plans. These observations made salient to us that different kinds of collaborative tasks and interactions might need to be supported differently. They also suggested potential contrasts between roles of co-present collaborators and remote collaborators; our initial vision had focused only on the latter.

The classroom observations also validated and refined aspects of our project vision. For example, we had emphasized the role that simulations could play in easing the overheads of equipment handling. We found that students worked with a variety of physical materials, such as carts on tracks to study inelastic collisions in high school and slinkies to study wave motion in middle school. Particularly in high school, students used standalone sensors-and-calculator ensembles, for example, to measure and graph velocities of moving bodies. The first time or two students carried out equipment set-up activity, it was clearly productive learning; however, routinized scripts of set-up, calibration, and manipulation to obtain data sets, carried out through many classes, became a significant tax on class time. Box 5.3 summarizes some of our classroom observations.

*Box 5.3* Example classroom observations

- Classrooms are filled with tables, equipment, and other materials.
- Teachers idiosyncratically recruit and blend different teaching styles (e.g., didactic and discovery).
- Students collaborate on a variety of tasks (e.g., manipulating apparatus together, coaching one another).
- Students use various collaborative techniques (e.g., consensus-building, mentoring, initiative-taking).
- Teachers employ many exercises; much time and attention is spent on manipulation (middle school) and laboratory technique (high school).

Studying the classrooms made vivid the great variety in classroom contexts among the four teachers with whom we worked. By design, our team was made up of two high-school physics teachers and two middle-school physical science teachers; one in each pair was from Blacksburg, the major town in Montgomery county, and one was from a rural school. There were sharp disparities between the town and rural contexts. The high school in Blacksburg was listed among the top 100 high schools in the United States by *Newsweek* magazine in March 2000. Blacksburg High School offered several sections of physics each year, including college advanced placement physics, to students who were largely college bound. In contrast, the rural high school only offered physics every other year, and to classes of only three to five students. Indeed, we were surprised to learn that the two high-school physics teachers in our project team were *all* of the county's high-school physics teachers: There were only the two of them, and one taught only part-time. This was daunting, but of course it also was part of the motivation for our project objective to give students in this diverse and dispersed community direct access to peers through networked collaboration.

We initiated a series of bi-weekly project meetings involving the teachers, university faculty, and graduate-student researchers and rotated the meetings among the four school sites, as well as at Virginia Tech. This allowed the university people to experience all of the classroom spaces, as we discussed the teaching and learning activity that went on there. Meeting occasionally at our university laboratory was convenient for demonstrating and discussing candidate technologies and prototypes to support collaboration and data visualization. This series of meetings went on for more than four years. Throughout that first spring the focal topic was the ongoing collection of materials and observations from the classrooms.

We needed to learn about the teachers' classroom practices and to have them help us interpret things we observed in the classrooms. We needed to build working relationships and mutual trust. The teachers were all easy to engage in such discussions and quite articulate about what they did in the classroom and why. We were surprised to find that the teachers were at the same time also developing working relationships with one another. Most of them had not worked closely before and knew one another only casually. This was good for us. The four teachers had distinct perspectives and values, as well as teaching styles and activities. We learned a huge amount as, in coming to understand one another, they compared and contrasted their approaches and experience. Indeed, this exchange further emphasized that our software would have to support a variety of teaching strategies. The teachers had differing perspectives specifically about collaboration among teachers and among their classes. All were skeptical that such cross-classroom collaborations would be sufficiently easy for them to manage or beneficial enough to their students so as to be immediately self-justifying.

This skepticism was positive and constructive. The teachers were not being stodgy or uncooperative. Rather, they were projecting the emerging visions of the project onto their classroom practices and reflecting on the implications for effectively coordinating their own teaching with another teacher, perhaps miles away, and for coordinating the learning activity of their students with that of other students, similarly remote. Practitioners appropriate a design by projecting it onto their situated activity. This was the first time that the teachers asserted their domain expertise to draw a strategically formative implication for the project. In that sense, this is where the teachers' participation in our project really started. Their skepticism challenged all of us to think more concretely and more critically about collaborative learning activities. Most importantly, it made the core challenge of our project into a shared problem.

Appropriation is not like flipping a switch, however. Also in the spring of 1996, George Chin – a Virginia Tech graduate student at the time – conducted a series of structured interviews focused on the teachers' practices regarding collaborative activities and their initial attitudes towards the project. Box 5.4 presents responses of four teachers to one of the interview items that specifically queried their expectations about their project roles. Two of these teachers had worked with us for a year to develop the NSF proposal, which centrally emphasized teachers as designers and the need for participatory approaches to the design of educational technology, and had also worked with Laughton for a year, participating directly in the design, and not merely testing, of new educational technology. The other two were recruited by the school system much later. However, the four all seem to have had the same initial expectation that their role would be chiefly to test or to facilitate testing with students. They thought that someone else would be deciding what was designed and implemented for them to test.

*Box 5.4*  Responses of four teachers to an interview question

---

Prior to the start of the project, what role did you anticipate for yourself on the LiNC project?

*T1*: I think I was expecting to be more of a guinea pig – you build it and I test it – you pick my brain and leave.

*T2*: I did not truly understand the LiNC project, but thought I would be asked to try out programs with my students written by Tech people.

*T3*: I thought the programs would be developed and we would test them with the students and evaluate them – make suggestions for changes if need be.

*T4*: Initial expectations were to function as contact with students. I thought we'd be involved mostly with trial runs of software and possibly some data collection. The possibility that this was a double blind experiment was also present.

---

Indeed, T4 is even suspicious about possible deception in the project's true goals. This reaction is extreme, but perhaps what is most significant is that T4 was willing to say out loud what others might have felt and repressed. As discussed above, technology has had an awkward history in the culture of schools. Teachers are not in a good position to judge whether a technologist is inspired or crazy, but they do know that the odds are biased strongly against very much coming out of a classroom technology project, particularly one that seems radical or ambitious. So they remain wary. Through the course of working together, trust can be built and wariness can subside. But this is a journey and requires a process.

## Appropriating the Virtual School

We were feeling successful toward the end of spring 1996. We had set out to explore participatory design with teachers, and we had reached a point where the teachers had clearly taken some ownership in the project. But in fact we were still only at the beginning of our participatory design interaction.

In July, we held a two-week workshop for all project members. One of the central objectives was to analyze the ethnographic data that had been collected during the preceding spring. We made a detailed analysis of several videotaped classroom interactions. As a group (four teachers, four human–computer interaction designers, four software developers) we used claims analysis, as described in chapter 2, to identify salient features in these scenarios and the desirable and undesirable consequences of these features for learning. This kind of work is exciting but demanding. It is directed brainstorming in which lines of causal reasoning are rapidly improvised, questioned, and refined. The teachers regularly analyzed and designed classroom activities in their work practice. However, they were not used to being explicit and public in identifying tradeoffs in classroom situations. They were not used to other people asking them why something would or would not work, or how it might contrast with something else. As one teacher commented: "It intruded on the way I design activities – I like to brainstorm and think out loud, [but] every time you say something, it gets analyzed."

Nevertheless, the teachers were remarkably effective in these participatory design rationale sessions. Figure 5.2 shows the proportion of design features (e.g., equipment set-up activity) and claim consequences (e.g., teaches laboratory technique, limits class time available for gathering data) identified in the workshops by the teachers, the computer technologists, and the human–computer interaction designers (Chin, Rosson, and Carroll 1997). In this analysis, the teachers were the project team's leaders at identifying teaching and learning issues, key situational features, and tradeoff relations in consequences for students. And, more importantly, the teachers and everyone else on the project team saw that this was the case.

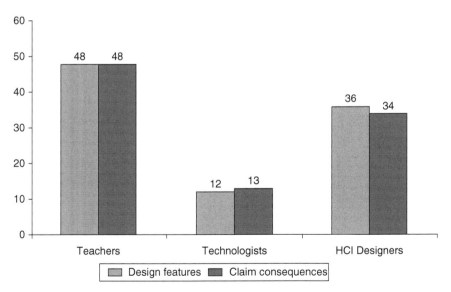

*Figure 5.2*  Proportion of contributions to claims analyses by teachers, technologists, and human–computer interaction designers.

An example is a discussion we had about student leadership in groups. We analyzed a group activity in which students measured kinetic energy for collisions involving model trains. One issue we identified was leadership style. We contrasted a consensus-building style, in which the leader ensures that all ideas are considered and enhances group dynamics and the self-esteem of members, with an individual initiative-taking style, which is efficient, challenging, and provides opportunities for group members to play leadership and supporting roles. Our discussion identified upsides and downsides of each style, but was focused on the efficiency of initiative-taking for group leadership. At this point, the teachers emphasized that, while task-oriented productivity is important, a more critical consideration is that all group members have the opportunity to hypothesize and test their individual ideas and to participate fully in the group activity. This led to a more complete tradeoff analysis of student leadership, and had specific ramifications for issues of floor control and group formation in the virtual school environment (Carroll *et al.* 1998).

Through the workshops, the teachers came to recognize how important understanding classroom situations was to everyone else in the project, and how critical their own expertise was to achieving that understanding. After the workshops, the teachers continued to lead the team with respect to understanding classroom activity. The teachers were even affected *as teachers* by this analytic work. Thus, during the workshop, the teachers articulated some rationale for assigning students to groups – students with complementary skills and leadership styles can be grouped together, known personality conflicts can be avoided, natural mentoring relationships can be facilitated. Prior to this analytic work, the teachers had been quite relaxed about group formation, allowing students to choose their own partners (generally friends). However, in the year following the workshop, the teachers became much more proactive in creating groups, helping to design and using online tools for group assignment.

In the fall of 1996, we began a three-year phase of iterative development. We designed and carried out a series of classroom collaborative activities, supported by various software prototypes that we called the Virtual School (Carroll and Rosson 1998; Isenhour *et al.* 2000; Koenemann *et al.* 1999; Rosson and Carroll 2002). For example, middle-school students at different schools used text chat, synchronous audio, and video teleconferencing to collaborate on a melting/freezing point experiment. Each group was given one of two possible substances, and collaborating groups compared measurements from their lab experiments in an attempt to determine which group had received which substance. The teachers played a central role in conceiving of and analyzing these activities. They identified the opportunity of pooling data as an appropriate and intrinsically motivating application of networking among classrooms in the Virtual School, and they led the analysis of how student groups might use various networking mechanisms to collaborate in these activities. This was a process of reflection in action (Schön 1983): The teachers analyzed the technology by "auditioning" it in classroom activities. They tried to predict educational benefits and assess them by formulating activities involving sharing of data, equipment, and expertise.

Each set of activities evoked a new draft of requirements for our evolving suite of software tools. Initially, the Virtual School was a loosely integrated ensemble of software tools, some we created and some we adapted. Through the iterative process of refining the Virtual School, we redesigned and more closely integrated the various tools, particularly session management (Figure 5.3 below) and the collaborative notebook (Figure 5.5 below). Eventually, the Virtual School became an application implemented with a comprehensive collaborative software platform called CORK (Content Object Replication Kit; Isenhour *et al.* 2001). This is described in chapter 7. The description here focuses on what the Virtual School was like for students and teachers toward the end of its development process.

Students launched the Virtual School by double-clicking an icon on the desktop and entering their user name and password. They could select names from a list of the authenticating user's project group, co-located and remote, to indicate who was present. This "group logon" approach, designed directly with the teachers, provided presence awareness for team members without requiring each team member to log in separately. Security was not compromised, because only those

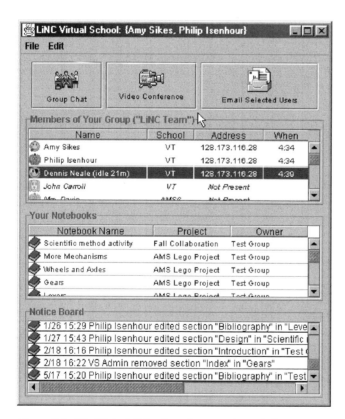

*Figure 5.3*   The Virtual School session overview window.

operations available to the authenticating user and *all* other users who claim to be present could be performed.

After login, the session overview window appeared (Figure 5.3). This window contained a user list showing the name, icon, and school for each team member. Team members not currently logged into the system were shown in italic with gray icons. For members who were present, the user list also included the address of the machine from which they had logged in, the time at which they logged in, and the length of time that they had been idle. This was to give students a quick snapshot of their team's current status. While the user list encouraged students to focus on their own team members, and especially those who were remote, the Virtual School also provided an option to view a list of all users currently logged into the system. The name, icon, project group, school, machine address, login time, and idle time were shown. Students used this overall view to locate and contact system developers for immediate assistance or to report problems, as well as to check the status of other students and groups to form an overall impression of activity in the system. For example, students in one class can see if any of their remote team members' classmates are online, and then use the chat tools (described below) to inquire about absent collaborators or the status of possible computer problems.

The lower portion of the session overview window displayed a list a list of project notebooks the user could access, and a Notice Board presenting a log of team member editing activity for various sections of project notebooks. Above the user list in the session overview window were buttons for accessing the three primary communication channels used in the Virtual School. For synchronous communication, the Group Chat button opened a text chat tool (see Figure 5.4). This tool, like Internet Relay Chat and instant messaging products used on the Internet, allowed an arbitrary number of users to communicate synchronously by sending text messages.

Unlike many other text chat systems, the Virtual School chat tool supported content persistence. All messages were saved and restored when the chat tool was opened. This feature proved to be a significant enhancement, allowing team members to review past discussions of task decomposition and delegation and generally to reinstantiate work context. Providing automatic persistence offers a significant advantage over systems that require chat sessions be explicitly saved to the local disk, since users often do not recognize the importance of a conversation until later. Finally, persistence supported late joiners, students who log into the system after their partners, allowing them to catch up on missed conversation without interrupting the ongoing group interaction. Indeed, this proved to be a critical feature, as different team members' class period schedules often overlapped only partially.

Private chat functionality was also available. In the Virtual School, the content of private chat sessions was preserved as long as at least one participant in the chat remained logged in, but it was discarded once both parties left. Given the structure of the collaborative exercises that were undertaken using the Virtual School, essentially all project-relevant chat conversation occurred within the group chat. If, however, users felt that the content of a private chat should be

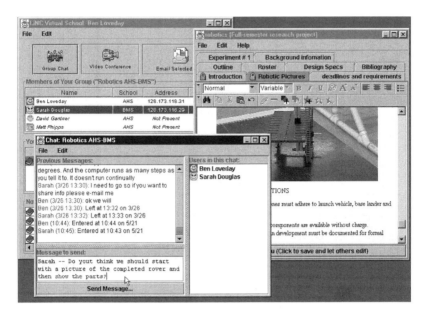

*Figure 5.4*  The group chat window (session overview and robotics notebook windows are in the background); note that messages from a previous day's conversation are still accessible.

preserved, they could copy it out of the private chat window and save it manually in a notebook (described below).

Where video cameras were available and network bandwidth allowed, the Video Conference button launched a third-party conferencing package, directing it to a user selected in the user list. This select-and-click approach to launching video conferencing saved considerable startup time, particularly in the classroom environment, where users at both ends of the conference tend to use different machines for each session. We used primarily Microsoft's NetMeeting conferencing software, which provided synchronous application-sharing in addition to video and audio conferencing.

Given the unpredictable nature of synchronous collaboration in the classroom, email remained a critical communication channel. The Virtual School included an email client for sending and receiving mail and attachments. As with video conferencing, students could select one or more users from the user list and then click the Email button to send a message. The email client also had address book functionality to simplify the composition of messages directed to individual team members or to the entire team. The integration of the email client was another attempt to reduce overhead for users, by eliminating the need to launch and log into a separate email program.

Notebooks were the central component of the Virtual School, serving as containers for content created either by individuals or collaboratively by teams. Each notebook was divided into sections (see Figure 5.5), and each section could contain a different type of data. The most commonly used section type supported basic HTML-style formatting of text and images. Other section types provided structured editors for specific kinds of content. Bibliography sections allowed users to build reference lists collaboratively. Project planning sections supported hierarchical decomposition of project tasks with start and end dates, descriptions, and status information. Outline and Gantt chart visualizations of the tasks were provided to allow both students and teachers an overview of progress on a project. Whiteboard sections supported collaborative drawing and image annotation. The notebook architecture was extensible, allowing section types to be added as new viewer or editor components were written or adapted for collaborative use.

Virtual School notebooks supported both synchronous and asynchronous modes of interaction. Any number of users could view a notebook simultaneously, and any one user (or any group of users working at a single machine) could take control of a section for editing by clicking a button on the notebook page. Other users with the notebook open would see a small red lock icon on the section tab, and could also see who was editing the section. Changes made to notebooks were pushed to other users, allowing remote team members to discuss

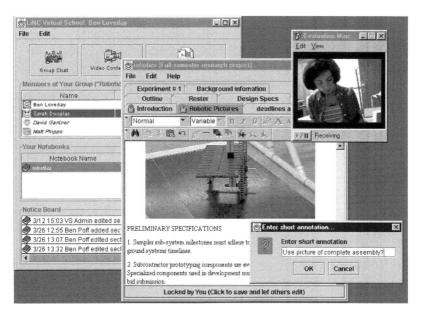

*Figure 5.5*   The Virtual School collaborative notebook (the session overview window is in the background, and a video conference window is at the top right). The robotics project notebook had twelve sections. In this figure, the currently opened section ("Robotics Pictures") is locked for editing, as indicated by the lock icon (which appears on the screen as green). An annotation is being added to the section through the prompt at the lower right.

changes as they were being made. This approach to synchronizing notebooks was employed because it is robust even when collaborators are working together with relatively slow network connections, because it produces a fluid transition between synchronous and asynchronous collaboration, and because it makes clear to users where editing is occurring and who is doing the editing (Isenhour, Rosson, and Carroll 2001; Stefik *et al.* 1987).

Probably because the notebooks present joint work, we found that student teams engaged in substantial discussions about past, present, and future changes to shared content through email, chat, and video conferencing. The notebook also supported explicit annotations describing changed content and included automatic tracking of contributions. Teachers or team members may insert annotations anywhere in the notebook. Annotations appear as small star icons, with color used to differentiate teacher and student annotations (not visible in Figure 5.5). Moving the mouse over an annotation icon caused a small "tool tip" window to appear, showing who added the annotation and when it was created. The icon could be double-clicked to reveal the full annotation text. The notebook's "Show authorship" feature allowed each contributor's text to be displayed in a different color. We observed that authorship coding was sometimes used to code contributions by school instead of by individual student – for example, when multiple team members were working together at a single computer and taking quick turns at the keyboard.

Authorship coding provided detailed information about who contributed what within a given notebook section. To provide higher-level, coarse-grained information on recent modifications, the session overview window included a Notice Board that logs recent changes to shared data (Figure 5.3). Students could use the Notice Board to find out which notebooks and sections had been changed recently by other team members. Double-clicking on a Notice Board entry opened the changed section, and the authorship-coding feature could be used to find specific changes and contributions.

When users logged into the Virtual School alone, they had access to the notebooks of all their project groups, along with any private notebooks they might have created. When several users logged onto a single machine, they had access only to notebooks common to all members present. Teachers had access to all student notebooks. Notebook content was stored on a central server and retrieved on demand: Thus students could access their Virtual School content from any machine, including from home, without having to transfer data.

While students had the ability to create new, blank notebooks for themselves or for their groups, we provided project-specific scaffolding for project notebooks – those notebooks that would eventually present the project deliverables. The Virtual School included a notebook help function that could be configured by the teacher. Our original intent for help content was to provide assistance targeted on the features of the notebook itself, but in practice the help function was appropriated as a means for distributing assignment descriptions, model illustrations, and other immutable project material that traditionally would have been photocopied and distributed physically.

Teachers could also create templates to define initial structure and content for the project notebooks, providing implicit guidance to students. Template notebooks could simply contain the pre-defined sections corresponding to required parts of the project report, or more detailed content such as instructions, outlines, lessons, and challenges. The content originally added by the teacher could be distinguished using the "Show authorship" button, but was not protected. This approach carried some risk of tampering, but it also allowed students to extend the original content. This feature proved to be useful in community mentoring activities (see below), where mentors added new questions and refined lessons and instructions based on knowledge of their remote partners.

The Virtual School server integrated an http (Hypertext Transfer Protocol) server to which any standard web browser could connect. This interface supported secure, automatic publishing of notebook content. Students and teachers could use a web browser to log in and securely view all of their notebooks from anywhere on the Web. For notebooks representing finished work, students could assign a public URL to the notebook, allowing unrestricted viewing by anyone. The server generated web versions of notebook content dynamically, so notebook sections retrieved through the Web always reflected the latest work. The automatic web publishing capabilities were used by the teachers to review student work from machines with slower network connections or without the full Virtual School client, such as their home computers.

The Virtual School was a complex software system that required a substantial amount of technological understanding and skill to create. However, that skill would have guaranteed only a complex software system, not an effective tool for collaboration between classrooms. The teachers worked through the design, contributing many key ideas, and then closely evaluated the system in use and offered many more ideas for refinements and redesign. For example, they contributed the key idea of including template data in notebook sections to model their intended use by students. They suggested the inclusion of a project information button to access teacher-generated support materials, which later evolved into the help button described above. They designed a milestone-tracking capability to help student groups manage themselves, which was incorporated in the project planning tools (e.g., in the "deadlines and requirements" section in Figure 5.5). And they proposed a "message tool" to attach teacher comments to notebook sections, which later was embodied in the commenting function, described above.

Box 5.5 summarizes design rationale associated with collaborative science learning scenarios in the Virtual School (Chin and Carroll 2000). Connecting classrooms leveraged unique strengths, such as a 25-foot high pendulum one school had constructed in their shop facility. All the schools were able to gather data from and investigate the motion of this unusual pendulum. The Virtual School provided richer discussions and peer-collaboration experiences for the relatively small number of physics students from the rural school. It also provided meaningful content for the students to encounter, learn about, and use information technology that many had not used before, such as video conferencing and collaborative editing software. Finally, by integrating across teachers and classrooms, the Virtual School provided students with a more diverse classroom context and with opportunities to learn and practice skills that arise in such contexts. For example, high-school physics students strengthened their own understandings of physics concepts by explaining those concepts to middle-school students.

*Box 5.5*    Claims pertaining to collaborative science learning in the Virtual School

---

Using the Virtual School to support collaborative science projects carried out across classrooms and school sites

+ leverages unique resources through the school system (like one school's giant pendulum)
+ allows science classes to be offered in rural schools where not enough students may register
+ integrates acquisition of and practice with broader technology and collaboration skills with science learning
+ provides a rich computer-mediated communication experience to students, incorporating text and video chat and a collaborative notebook
+ exposes students to a variety of collaborative interactions (mentoring, brainstorming, dividing up work, replicating results, also face to face as well as computer-mediated), evoked by project-based activities and a diversity of students (with respect to grade level and school, as well as teacher preparation styles)
+ entrains interactions with students from other grade levels, classrooms, and even school sites; students learn more about their school, their school system, and their county
+ provides an authentic and creative joint endeavor for teacher collaboration.

− But partially overlapping class periods in different schools entails that asynchronous collaboration must supplement synchronous interaction.
− But ambient noise in classrooms, from other students' talking, voice chats, and video conferences, is distracting and entails a need for local sound-damping (headphones, etc.).
− But group interactions entail technology bottlenecks, such as that only one student can operate the mouse.
− But managing cross-school site networking infrastructures is a new and significant technology maintenance responsibility (and expense) for school systems.

---

Different teachers prioritized aspects of their students' preparation differently. When students from two (or more) classes worked together, they learned to integrate this diverse preparation in order to enhance the overall performance of their distributed group. And because this distributed group spans the grade levels, classrooms, and even schools of the local community, students inadvertently learn about their community in ways they would not if they worked only in a single classroom context.

There were of course also potential downsides associated with this scenario. We found that, even in our small collection of schools, class periods started and ended at very different times; moreover, "last minute" schedule changes always seemed to occur. At best, students had a few minutes overlap to coordinate synchronously. Also, classrooms always seemed noisy; Virtual School video and audio interactions added to the din, but the general classroom din of face-to-face student conversations was a constant distraction to others trying to collaborate, especially when they were relying on audio. Finally, although it was good in some ways that groups had to coordinate their input through whatever member was holding the mouse and/or operating the keyboard, this also was a bottleneck for getting ideas into the shared spaces of the Virtual School.

## Bigger projects and community mentoring

In late spring 1997, the teachers proposed a focus they called "projects." They had concluded that the pedagogical value of the relatively brief classroom activities we had been investigating was too limited, that the overhead of initiating these activities was too high relative to their value. They urged a different approach for the 1997–8 school year, one involving activities that extended over several weeks, even months. This was another turning point in their appropriation of the project and in the basic parameters of the team's collaboration. Other members of the team immediately supported the proposal. More realistic, more ambitious classroom activities would drive our software ideas more vigorously and were more consistent with our original visions of transforming education. However, this episode was still a turning point: Most of the *costs* of developing and managing longer-term projects would fall upon the teachers themselves. It is very significant that the teachers took the initiative to develop and articulate a new focal design concept to the group as a whole, and that this design concept entailed more responsibility and more work *for them*. That is a huge step for anyone to take. The teachers embraced the Virtual School as a major tool in their own pedagogical planning, in contrast to their earlier principle of cooperating as long as the project did not diminish learning opportunities for their students.

The teachers' projects proposal was another punctuation in their developing role in our project. After this point, they regularly met as a subgroup within the larger project. Their efforts to understand one another's teaching styles and pedagogical objectives became more focused as they tried to develop an integrated curriculum with common objectives, timing, scale, and grading. It became understood in the project team that the design of the classroom activities belonged to them. And the classroom activities were the primary source of requirements for the software design efforts. Thus, to a great extent, the teachers' planning drove all other aspects of project activity.

During the 1997–8 school year, the teachers introduced various complex and innovative classroom activities. In one activity, high-school and middle-school students collaborated on the design of a robot; the middle-school students designed a grasping arm, and the high-school students designed a mobile base (the Virtual School screen shots in Figures 5.4 and 5.5 are from the robot project). Many of these longer-term projects involved the development of mentoring relationships with community members, thus directly leveraging the BEV and integrating community participation and social ties with science projects. The teachers developed mentored projects in areas such as the optics of photography, mechanics in the context of amusement parks, the astrophysics of black holes, the engineering principles of bridge-building, and the aerodynamics of kites and model planes. Several of the teachers had worked with community mentors in the past, and were eager to explore this kind of teaching and learning interaction with the virtual school software.

The mentoring projects in 1997–8 focused on the middle schools. In many cases, one of the teachers already had, or had initiated, a community contact, which students then followed up and developed. Examples of community contacts are spouses of other teachers, parents of former students, and friends from church. We also mined our own contacts and Virginia Tech departmental web pages to identify university faculty with relevant expertise. Community members with the relevant backgrounds who agreed to participate were invited to an informational meeting where the goals of the project, the initial expectations, and the software to be used were reviewed. The teacher at the in-town middle school encouraged students to find their own mentors, and mentors interacted with both groups and individual students. The teacher in the rural community worked through established personal relationships and community contacts, and assigned groups in advance to mentors with appropriate backgrounds. The teacher in the town setting, who had access to a larger community, including faculty at Virginia Tech, had approximately 90 percent of her 80-some projects employ mentors. The teacher in the rural community chose to focus mentoring activities on a single class, with a mentor assigned to each of six project groups.

In subsequent years, the teachers made the projects even more challenging. Thus, in the second year (1998–9), there were only five mentoring projects, but each one included a group of middle-school students, a group of high-school students, and a community mentor (Gibson *et al.* 1999). The pedagogical rationale for incorporating mentors from the real world is to enhance validity, relevance, and context of the classroom projects (Glasgow 1996). We found that the students were very positively disposed towards mentoring, as well as towards collaborative learning interactions with students from other schools and grade levels. Curiously, we found some evidence that students from the rural middle school and from the in-town high school were especially positive about working with community mentors (Carroll and Neale 1998; Gibson *et al.* 1999).

The mentors played a variety of roles. They were sources of information, fielding specialized questions that teachers might not be able to address. They helped students anticipate and avoid pursuing unproductive strategies. They helped students focus on project objectives – students often did not narrow their approaches enough to make progress. In these ways, the mentors provided cognitive scaffolding for the students, guiding them in managing the scientific inquiry process (Ritchie and Rigano 1996). In our study, one mentor coaching a project on the physics of bridge designs encouraged pursuing just two design alternatives in depth; this proved to be a turning point in the students' project. The mentors were also role models, showing the students that mathematics and physics are relevant to real problems and can potentially offer careers.

In an interview, one mentor refused to cite a principal role, enthusiastically describing the range of roles he played. The community mentors did not want to be limited to the role of "expert," as we discovered by casually using this term. They felt that "expert" implied having extensive and specific knowledge of the particular project, rather than having relevant knowledge and experience and a willingness to apply it. The mentors wanted to act as more than mere sources of knowledge: They wanted to coach and encourage and to share in the small discoveries that occurred in the projects – as one put it, to have "fun" while "showing the value of experiential learning."

The teachers gave the mentors a relatively free hand with respect to curricular goals, offering only implicit guidance through the particular resources they suggested and provided – for example, a particular book or access to a project page. The mentors seemed to like having the freedom to explore interactions and approaches. However, the lack of definition of the mentor role also had some downsides. Mentors felt some uncertainty about how much control they could or should assume in the planning and execution of projects, how much support they could expect from the teachers, and how much project involvement the teachers expected; also some were not comfortable with the Virtual School tools, especially desktop video conferencing. The teachers felt they lost touch with some project activities through distributing responsibility to mentors. But they were also reluctant to ask the mentors for additional check pointing or assistance – for example, with grading – feeling that this would have entailed paperwork the mentors had not agreed to in advance.

In subsequent years (Gibson *et al.* 1999) mentors asked for explicit feedback from students on suggestions and mini-assignments they gave, and teachers monitored the mentoring relationships more closely. In the second year, 1998–9, the school system implemented a firewall to exert more control over Internet access in the schools. The firewall also prevented video conferencing interactions with community mentors for several months. We were able to work directly with the school's technology coordinator to reconfigure the firewall to eventually permit our video conferencing, a nice consequence of working in a small community setting.

Some of the uncertainties regarding mentors were manifest in student–mentor interactions; students initially seemed to need extra guidance. Some students took this openness as an opportunity, spontaneously defining and adopting roles to facilitate mentor interactions. For example, one boy managed video conferencing sessions for his group, while one girl managed email contacts with the mentor. The email channel was used to provide persistent structure, integrating group activity across video conferencing sessions. Many of the female student's messages documented decisions made in one session regarding plans about what to do in the next session. In many cases, students jumped right into the project, posing direct questions at various levels – for example, "How is the angle of the first hill determined so that the train (roller coaster) has enough energy to make it through the ride?" and "We were wondering if you had any information on websites on (stereo) speakers." The students surprised the mentors with the level of their engagement and communication skills, which was experienced as highly rewarding to the mentors.

The teachers were also impressed. They felt that a greater range of interaction channels stimulated a greater range of learning styles and cognitive orientations of particular students. A teacher noted the improvement in the female student's writing skills through the project, presumably due in part to her email role. Another teacher commented, "Students really feel good about finding something they're good at." Students acquire a sense of empowerment from mastering skills that enable their specific niche in the project. The teachers felt that the most unique skills developed by the mentoring interactions were in time-management and prioritization. The video conferencing sessions were brief. Students needed to bring the mentor up to date on their activities since the last session, engage in joint activities, discuss courses of action, get feedback, and decide what would be accomplished off-line during the next week.

We found that the rich collaborative tools of the Virtual School – video conferencing and shared whiteboards – definitely did support mentoring interactions beyond what was possible with email only. The aerodynamics mentor in 1997–8, for example, felt it was extremely important to be able to see what the students were working on and to give them immediate feedback; he felt that shared whiteboard drawing was particularly useful (O'Neill and Gomez 1998). He regarded video as less important than shared drawing, but described the importance of seeing what the students were doing as he explained things to them in order to make adjustments. Overall, mentors used the Virtual School tools to interact with students and their projects about 40 times each on average.

However, we also found that face-to-face interaction is critical, particularly in launching successful mentoring relationships. Students who initiated contact with mentors themselves through email had more limited interactions with the mentor and fewer requests for information or clarification of a particular issue. Students who established a relationship with a mentor through personal face-to-face communication, through a family member or some other personal contact, tended to develop more sustained interchanges with that mentor throughout the course of the academic year. This also seemed important from the mentors' perspective. The aerodynamics mentor felt that his initial face-to-face meeting helped make subsequent email interactions effective by allowing him and the students to imagine more vividly the real other people with whom they were communicating.

One of the most successful mentoring relationships we observed in the first year of mentoring projects, however, was initiated via email, but became rich and successful through direct face-to-face interaction. A boy working on a bridge project contacted a mentor at Virginia Tech, and, through discussions about the project, they discovered they lived in the same neighborhood. They developed a friendship, and the student visited the mentor many times through the course of the project. They actually built model bridges together at the mentor's house. The boy's teacher commented that she had rarely seen the level of enthusiasm and knowledge this boy developed for his science project, and it was a result of the mentoring process. Although one could imagine being able to do similar activities with video conferencing, the experience would not have been as rewarding for the student or the mentor; nor would the relationship likely have progressed to this level. But, notably, email enabled this relationship, and subsequently helped facilitate face-to-face communication as the project proceeded.

Curiously, this same mentor, in some ways the most successful we observed in the first year, had difficult interactions in the second year (Gibson *et al.* 1999). He began working with his two new groups in an extremely proactive manner, not only explaining the physics concepts to the students but also suggesting specific ways in which they could explore these concepts in the classroom. However, he felt that his new cohort of students did not engage enough, that they did not respond to suggestions. He complained that he was "without feedback from either bridge group" and that "an email on their progress would be nice." This mentor replied completely on email; he did not have access to his students' work through the Virtual School. His very successful interaction in the first year had involved much face-to-face interaction, augmented by email. It could also be that his expectations were too high, based on the previous year's experience, and/or that the reduced novelty of mentoring interactions diminished his satisfaction. Sadly, this mentoring relationship did not regain momentum.

Early in the second year (1998–9), video conferencing occurred primarily among the students, and mentoring interactions were relegated to email and chat within the Virtual School. The lack of video seemed to motivate the mentors to visit the school sites more than they had in the first year. Indeed, in follow-up interviews, the mentors stated that they believed the ability to video conference from their offices would have lessened the need for face-to-face interactions; however, they did not believe it would have removed it entirely.

The acoustics project group initially communicated with their mentor only through email. However, a few weeks into the project, the mentor made a trip to the students' classroom and gave a lecture on the physics of acoustics. Although the students expressed concern that the content of the lecture was too difficult, this meeting was often referred to in subsequent electronic meetings. The mentor made a second trip to the school in which project plans and goals were discussed, and physics concepts were revisited in the project context. This mentoring relationship produced the most chat and email traffic of the six 1998–9 mentoring projects. The mentor for the robotics project regularly visited the middle-school classroom of his group, sitting with the students as they interacted with their remote high-school counterparts. The remote group members could see and speak with the mentor through video conferencing and chat with him through text. Indeed, the mentor brought working robots to the classroom and demonstrated them through video conferencing. This group also visited their mentor in his robotics lab at Virginia Tech. Emails to the mentor played a smaller role in this project than in the acoustics project, perhaps because the use of Virtual School conferencing was so frequent.

The acoustics and robotics projects in 1998–9 – the two groups that had face-to-face interaction with their mentors – exchanged two to five times as many emails and made the heaviest use of the Virtual School. Content analysis of these interactions showed that they addressed issues beyond information exchange, schedule coordination, and project status, such as providing support and reassurance and requesting and providing specific feedback on the project work (Gibson *et al.* 1999). The mentors who were completely reliant upon computer-mediated communication had significantly less impact in focusing the groups' work and the final outcomes of the science projects.

Box 5.6 summarizes claims pertaining to the use of the Virtual School to support community mentor scenarios. We found that it was important in facilitating the mentoring relationships, though it was more effective when combined with face-to-face interactions, especially early in mentoring projects. The software helped to maintain continuity in mentoring relationships, making it easier for mentors to interact with the students more often. Students liked visiting mentors in their labs and offices, and in some cases were able to experience the use of special equipment, such as a wind tunnel at Virginia Tech, through video conferencing tools. Mentoring interactions provided new roles for students to play in project-based learning, particularly with respect to managing mentor communications.

*Box 5.6*  Claims pertaining to community mentoring scenarios

---

Using the Virtual School to collaborate with community mentors

+ provides students access to community experts who might not be able to travel regularly to school sites (especially sites remote to them)
+ provides students access to specialized equipment located in the community (for example, the wind tunnel in a lab at Virginia Tech)
+ exposes students to teaching and learning interactions that are grounded in the community beyond the school and also helps them learn more about their own community
+ provides new roles for students to play in learning interactions, such as managing mentor email or video conferences
+ engages community participation directly and persistently in school activities.

− But students, mentors, and teachers might have difficulty coordinating enough or effectively.
− But firewalls and other protective measures may limit access of school computers to community mentors.

---

The Virtual School facilitated teaching and learning interactions grounded in the community beyond the school. It connected school learning to people and activity in the community and placed students in the role of partner, challenging them to organize themselves to manage these interactions. Reciprocally, these interactions engaged community mentors in school activity more directly and more persistently, opening up the black box of school practices. The mentoring projects were a particularly inspiring example of a possible direction for community networks beyond asynchronous posting and reading of community information.

Some challenges remained. Students, mentors and teachers sometimes felt they were not aware enough of what was going on; students and mentors sometimes failed to coordinate or otherwise to meet one another's expectations. And there were technology issues, in this case chiefly having to do with firewalls, but more generally with the abiding tension between protecting children in their school uses of the Internet and supporting new teaching and learning opportunities that employ the Internet.

The long-term mentoring projects in a sense closed the loop of Virtual School development. We had worked our way back to the BEV, and to consideration of how community network infrastructures could create new opportunities for the school and the community to collaborate in public education. Indeed, the long-term projects, including the mentoring, were targeted at the springtime academic/science fairs and other events that involve presenting school work to parents and other community members, further promoting more comprehensive and action-oriented relationships among parents, communities, and schools (Krasnow 1990; Shields 1994; Wadsworth 1997). One of the BEV projects on which we worked later with these same teachers was a virtual science fair, presenting the long-term projects to the community through the BEV (chapter 7; Rosson and Carroll 2002).

## Participation as developmental

Participation is inherently problematic. Reaching a point in human relationships of honest and reciprocal engagement is not easy. Differences in profession and practice, in knowledge and skill, and in goals and motivations all can undermine participatory commitments and interactions. Our approach in the Virtual School project was to work together along many fronts for a very long time and to identify areas where different member constituencies could make unique contributions to the collective effort. This approach led to a project that was highly inefficient with respect to producing a software system, though we did ultimately produce an innovative system to support distributed project-based science collaborations. However, our approach also led to a project that provoked a huge amount of learning, not only in students, but also in the teachers, in the community mentors, in the university researchers, and in the larger Blacksburg and Montgomery County community.

The strong commitment we made to participatory design was facilitated significantly by the fact that everyone on the project team resided in the same community. The teachers taught in the schools that our children attended. We regularly saw one another when we shopped in town. One of the teachers lived four houses down the street from me. It is just easier to reach across the chasms of profession and practice, knowledge and skill, and goals and motivations when one's partners are real people, neighbors.

More than merely being residents of the same community, the members of our project team were all residents of the very community that had appropriated the Blacksburg Electronic Village. And, analogously to the BEV project itself, we came to see our explorations of collaborative learning possibilities in a networked community as emblematic of the whole community's vision and ambition. This definitely helped us all to expect more of ourselves and more of one another with respect to cooperation, mutual understanding, and continual learning.

One of our primary objectives in this work was to better understand how to engage our neighbors in the design of relatively advanced collaborative systems. We wanted eventually to create and investigate collaborative software. But, in part because systems like the Virtual School had not been built before, and because we were not part of a commercial venture, we were concerned more with what we could learn than we were with how quickly we could produce a working result. Community networking might be just the right place to explore how far participation can be pushed, and with what consequences. After all, participation is fundamental to what a community is, but it is one option among others for the relationship of users to system developers, as evidenced by how superficially it is sometimes pursued.

Three top-level lessons about participation emerged from this project. First, we learned that participation is possible, that it can produce results, but that it takes a lot of time and effort, far more that one would expect by extrapolating from examples of limited participation in the technical literature. In 1999, one of the teachers said:

> Actually, my role in LiNC has been much more than I expected. I like feeling like I am an expert at something and that my experience is valued. I like feeling comfortable talking to all other players as equals. I like to truly collaborate and I like to be treated with respect. Finally, I like honesty even if I disagree.

Taken in the context of school technology in general, and even in the context of where our project started (Figure 5.1), this is a remarkable result. It is plausible that the process we went through could be accelerated (Carroll *et al.* 2000). But we do not know that.

Second, we identified some of the key skills, insights, and achievements that comprise participation. Looking back, there were three critical points that allowed the participatory relationship we achieved:

1   Our domain experts were able substantively and creatively to problematize fundamental project concepts and assumptions. In doing this, they became

co-owners of the project. It is critical to appreciate how different this is than the "buy-in" that superficial versions of participatory design seek from their domain experts. Buy-in alone makes one, at most, a consultant, and more likely just a customer, but in no way an owner.

2   Our domain experts were able to identify specific areas in the project where they could be the key contributors, where they could take responsibility for producing designs or other information artifacts. They were not assigned project roles; assigning roles merely affirms that someone other than them is "in charge." In our case, the domain experts claimed both their roles and the project responsibilities those roles entailed.

3   Our domain experts were able to produce design results and present them to the overall project team. It is critical to appreciate how much more this is than merely sharing expert domain knowledge: Participatory design actually does involve design!

Third, we were led to reconceptualize participation as developmental in the sense of psychologists such as Vygotsky (1978). That is, we were led to regard participation not just as mutual learning, but as mutual transformation. Participation is a two-way street: The teachers were growing and developing; the university research was growing and developing too. In the latter phases of the Virtual School project, we created a Collaborative Critical Incident Tool (CCIT), an online forum in which all the members of our entire project team could present and discuss significant events that occurred throughout the Virtual School. Just as the teachers had come to see that their perspectives could be critical to the design of effective technology to support collaborative learning activities, other team members came to see that they could contribute to reporting and making sense of classroom episodes. In analyzing these forums, we found that contributions to the CCIT discussions were very diverse across the member constituencies of our team (Carroll, Neale, and Isenhour 2003, 2005).

By the early 2000s, the teachers with whom we worked were not only innovative designers of computer-mediated collaborative learning activities, they had become coaches for other teachers in the school system who wanted to employ networking and collaboration in their classrooms (Carroll *et al.* 2000). They had presented papers at professional teacher meetings and at education research meetings; they had written proposals for further training and research programs. Eventually, these teachers helped to frame the vision for a regional teacher professional development project, a collaborative system that spanned two county school divisions in Virginia and involved dozens of teachers (Carroll, Choo *et al.* 2003; Rosson *et al.* 2007). Consistent with Vygotsky, but difficult to prove of course, we were led to see participation as a path to human development that has no upper bounds.

In this project we set a high bar for participation. We did not want to inhabit the fool's paradise of merely labeling user acquiescence as active participation. Going into the project, we believed that a deeper and longer-term commitment to participation would be essential to developing a successful Virtual School. As mentioned above, this commitment was both more obvious to make and more easy to achieve in our case, because all of us were residents of Blacksburg and Montgomery County. However, as it turned out, this embedding in the community also allowed us to benefit much more from adopting a participatory approach.

Our work with the teachers was quite visible to the larger community – much more visible than we had anticipated. In retrospect, however, it is easy to see why. The project was immediately visible to the families of hundreds of middle-school and high-school science students; after all, the parents had to give consent in order for their children to participate in the research, and we sent home periodic updates on the project. It was also immediately visible to science teachers, and other teachers, throughout the Montgomery County system; they were interested in new initiatives in which their colleagues were involved. During several presentations I made at local school board meetings and teacher professional development workshops, I was always surprised at how much everyone already knew about what we were doing.

The effect of this visibility was that our efforts to establish a true participatory relationship with the teachers continued to pay off in every other community partnership we forged. The Virtual School project became a model for how we, as university researchers, could engage over relatively long spans of time with community actors to jointly address their concerns, needs, interests, and ambitions. We followed this model through a series of other BEV community-based projects. Our subsequent community partners all knew something of the Virtual School project, and they expected to participate. Our original commitment to participatory design made every subsequent project easier.

# 6 Reaching across generations

School is an obvious potential nexus for community innovation. The core function of a community's public schools is to evoke and guide learning and to prepare for the future. But there are many other anchor institutions in communities, including municipal government, downtown businesses, and a wide variety of nonprofit organizations. In the United States, local nonprofit groups address many public functions that in other countries are administered by government, among them public libraries, social services (such as food banks, clothing donation, homeless shelters, housing for the poor, and meal delivery to the homebound), fire companies, rescue and emergency medical services, community heritage and historical societies, local arts groups, animal rescue and adoption, and senior centers. Participation in these organizations is vital to the success and sustainability of American communities.

Through the course of our work in the Blacksburg community we came to realize that community nonprofit groups rely heavily on older community members who disproportionately volunteer to serve in these groups. Indeed, one of the first grassroots groups to appropriate the BEV called itself the BEV Seniors. The group is hosted by the Blacksburg Seniors Center, and is concerned broadly with active retirement, and specifically with community service relating to and employing the Internet and the BEV. When we started working with the BEV Seniors group, the core was about a dozen persons and the membership was about 100. Main activities were training and information seminars offered free to the community and community-oriented projects carried out through various Internet tools, including email lists and web pages. As described in chapter 3, the seniors also took initiative in hosting after-school Internet activities for students at Blacksburg High School. The group quite explicitly articulated its goal as leading the Blacksburg community in developing and making use of the BEV.

## Web forums: Participatory community information

In March 1995, our team created one of the first web forums, the Web Storybase (Rosson, Carroll, and Messner 1996; Rosson 1999). Our research interest was to explore how users of the then still new World-Wide Web would appropriate the

HTML forms technology that had transformed the Web from a strictly browsing environment to one that was potentially interactive. In chapter 2 we described the central role of community information exchange, and especially discussion, in community networks, going right back to the Berkeley Community Memory project. We designed the Web Storybase site as a place to contribute and to comment on personal stories about using the Web (Figure 6.1). Visitors to the site were able to type their contributions directly into form fields in the web pages. The stories and comments we gathered provide a fascinating snapshot of why and how people were using the Web in 1995, as that use was still emerging and evolving. As the Storybase grew, we added a capability for authors to categorize their stories, allowing visitors to browse more specifically, for example, stories about Cyber-relationships, Web Culture, etc.

Some contributions to the Storybase described particular websites, but most were more personal than this, and some disclosed quite personal experiences (one early story was entitled "I found my love on the Web"). More than half of comments were positive and supportive, consistent with the principle that self-disclosure is a powerful technique to evoke responses from others (Archer 1980). The personal and supportive nature of many of the Storybase interactions contrasts with reports of other Internet interactions at about the same time. For example, Shirky (1995) described a combative culture of newsgroups in which people posted comments primarily to disagree with earlier postings.

The project continued for nearly five years and collected nearly 400 stories. An example is "Grandma at the keys," one categorized as "making connections":

> After over seventeen years on and off with a computer in my real estate business I am still often mystified by all the tricks of the trade. One of the self-taught, I tend to read mystery stories instead of computer books. Nevertheless I find it not only a necessity in my business but a pleasure. One of my grandchildren decided I should get into the internet. Right! I could see the phone bill after he got through playing around with it. What's really irritating is the little dweebs are so darn quick with anything new. But this is one time they are not going to be ahead of grandma. When I get finished I'm going to be the best realtor in cyberspace! As for the kids, the last time they got into the computer where they weren't supposed to be they locked up the machine, quietly closed it down and left me high and dry. Now you just know they're going to get another go round!

A few years later, people would take these experiences for granted. But when this was posted in 1995, people were still discovering such transformational social affordances of the Web. This story evoked sixteen comments; most were from other grandmothers! Two examples were these:

> I'm a grandma too, and my 71-year-old husband and I want to be in on all the excitement. The more you stretch your mind muscles, the younger you

## Welcome!

We are researchers at Virginia Tech exploring the use of the World Wide Web and the Internet. As part of our research, we are collecting usage stories...almost everyone finds this new medium exciting, though often elusive; fun, though sometimes frustrating and even frightening.

We feel confident that YOU too have a story to tell. Maybe it's one you've already shared with friends or colleagues; maybe it's something that just happened and is fresh in your mind. Or, maybe something in the stories below will cause a reaction, or make you remember a related experience. Browse or search the stories we have now; when you're ready to contribute your own story, follow the link below.

Thanks in advance for your stories! Please also feel free to send us comments about this page, especially those of you who have been here before (we have recently reorganized).

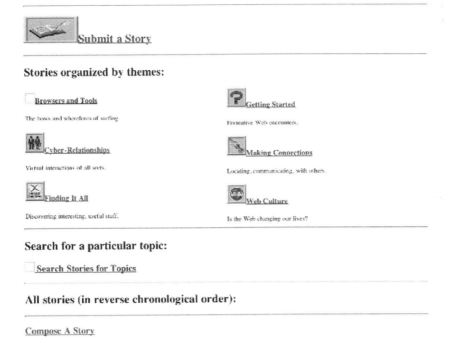

Submit a Story

## Stories organized by themes:

**Browsers and Tools**
The hows and wherefores of surfing.

**Getting Started**
Formative Web encounters.

**Cyber-Relationships**
Virtual interactions of all sorts.

**Making Connections**
Locating, communicating, with others.

**Finding It All**
Discovering interesting, useful stuff.

**Web Culture**
Is the Web changing our lives?

## Search for a particular topic:

**Search Stories for Topics**

## All stories (in reverse chronological order):

Compose A Story

*Figure 6.1*   The welcome page (homepage) for A Web Storybase.

stay and we are both planning on participating as long as we can. We are starting a new hobby of digitalizing pictures and are having a ball. There's so much on the Net, a second lifetime won't be long enough.

How wonderful to see all the grandmoms on the Net. I'm a brand new user and accidently landed on this website and read your great stories. I'm a grandma also, and need advice on using the Net. Where are the best chat sites? Are there support groups I can get into? I'm a professional watercolorist and have been searching for an artist group to chat with. Any suggestions?

One of the outcomes of the Storybase project was to suggest many further community applications for web forums. For example, the Collaborative Critical Incident Tool (CCIT), discussed briefly in chapter 5, was developed to help identify and analyze data episodes across the LiNC classrooms (Carroll, Neale, and Isenhour 2003, 2005). As we were still developing the Storybase in late 1994 and early 1995, we also developed the BEV HistoryBase (Carroll *et al.* 1995). The HistoryBase was primarily a repository of documents comprising the history of the BEV, such as the early planning document "Enhanced communications in the town of Blacksburg" from October 1990, the initial vision statement for the project "The Blacksburg Community Network" from April 1991, the video clips from NBC *Nightly News* and CNN from February 1994, meeting minutes through the years from the Blacksburg Telecommunication Advisory Committee, and project proposals and descriptions of projects carried out within the BEV, such as the Virtual School project and the HistoryBase project. It included message-of-the-day items, brochures and user guides, issues of the BEV online newsletter, reports of visits, demos, and community social events, and talks and papers describing BEV research. Initially, it consisted of more than 350 documents.

We included personal stories and accounts of the BEV. For example, in the preface to this book, I related the story of how a garage mechanic contacted me to help him respond to complaints he had heard were posted in one of the early BEV newsgroups. I wrote an account of this episode for the HistoryBase, in part to serve as a model and a prompt to motivate other residents to contribute their stories to the history of the BEV. We created a version of the Storybase forms page to allow users to directly contribute stories about the BEV or to comment on stories already posted. We also directly gathered interviews with Blacksburg community members.

We presented the HistoryBase through a simple timeline user interface with clickable regions corresponding to quarters (Figure 6.2). Clicking in a quarter resulted in a temporally ordered list of BEV documents of all types that were produced in that quarter. Documents submitted to the HistoryBase were also characterized by a fairly elaborate keyword scheme and by the dates of events to which they referred. For example, selecting the second quarter of 1995 displayed a list of 69 documents; one was a CNN video clip describing how Blacksburg residents could shop online at a local grocery store. This document was submitted to the HistoryBase on April 16, 1996 (the submit date), but was created by CNN on May 27, 1995 (document date), and referred to events in Blacksburg around the date it was created (event date). The clip was classified with the keywords "Media coverage: TV." The keywords enabled views of the documents filtered by attributes other than date. For example, one could view all of the media coverage documents, or all of the minutes of the Blacksburg Telecommunications Advisory Committee, in a homogeneous list of minutes documents. The default view was to browse HistoryBase documents in the temporal context of all the other BEV documents from a given quarter.

We wanted the HistoryBase to be largely self-maintaining and owned by the BEV community; we did not want to overtly moderate it. On the other hand, we

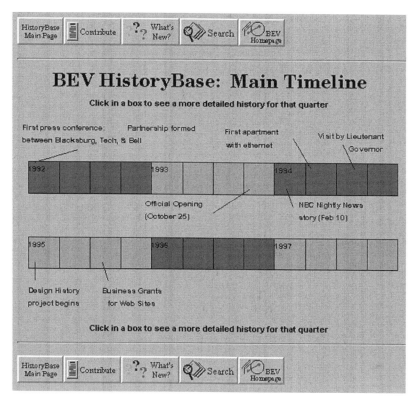

*Figure 6.2* The BEV HistoryBase main timeline.

did not want a totally open forum like the Web Storybase. We implemented pass-word security, using the BEV name server. Thus, *only* people with BEV accounts could make HistoryBase contributions. Our goal was that this community archive should incorporate all and only the documents, opinions, and accounts of the BEV community. Contributors could not be anonymous – also a contrast with the approach we had taken in the Web Storybase. This approach, however, depended on all members of the BEV community having their network accounts through a single service provider, which they did in the early days of the BEV. However, as described in chapter 3, the BEV decentralized the management of user accounts in 1996. Members without formal ties to Virginia Tech were asked to obtain their networking through commercial service providers (aka the "kicked off the BEV"). Unfortunately, this turn of events had the side effect of *excluding* much of the BEV community from actively participating in the HistoryBase proj-ect. The overwhelming preponderance of documents in the end was contributed by the BEV management team. The BEV HistoryBase did not become a lively discussion forum, perhaps also because, unlike the Storybase, it was not primarily about the self-disclosure of personal experiences and perspectives. However, it was used by academic researchers who studied the BEV (e.g., Silver 2004).

## Blacksburg Nostalgia

In the fall of 1995, we heard through a friend of an interesting discussion thread in the BEV Seniors' mailing list consisting of recollections and discussions about what Blacksburg was like in the 1950s and 1960s. This thread apparently had generated some interest among the members. We were still working on improvements to the Web Storybase, and thought that a similar approach might better support the seniors in gathering, organizing, and publishing their recollections. In May, we met with Keith Furr, who had started the "nostalgia" thread on the Seniors' email list and was a leader in the seniors group. There were several further planning discussions with Furr and with Connie Anderson, another leader in the seniors group who had extensive interests in email and the BEV.

Late in May, we – along with Anderson and Furr – presented the proposal for a "NostalgiaBase," as we called it, to an open meeting of seniors (Carroll *et al.* 1999). We were quickly caught up in another community participatory design research project (Carroll and Rosson 2007). There were no online interactive community history projects to serve as models. We were guided chiefly by the exploratory work we had done with web forums and by the objectives and continuous feedback from our partners in the BEV Seniors. We explored the concept of community history and of a web-based community history forum by creating an instance of it.

The seniors were generally receptive to the idea. Their chief concerns pertained to privacy and spamming: in our Web Storybase, stories could be contributed, viewed, and annotated by any Internet user. Some of the seniors did not want their contributions to be accessible publicly; some did not want their contributions to be freely annotated; some, indeed, wanted all access to the Nostalgia materials to be limited to members of the BEV Seniors' email list. However, others specifically wanted more visibility for the project, suggesting, for example, that this forum could be a way of reaching "lost Hokies" (i.e., former residents of Blacksburg and/or alumni of Virginia Tech).

There was consensus to go ahead with the project. At first, it was announced only *within* the seniors group, hoping to allay their concerns about unwanted access and contributions (in the pre-Google Web, limiting the explicit sharing of a URL was an effective way to restrict access). The forum was moderated by the seniors, who could review and reject contributions that were deemed inappropriate. It was subsequently advertised and used more broadly, though the primary story initiators remained the senior citizens, with others providing commentary or asking for further elaboration of postings.

There was particular enthusiasm for posting old photographs of Blacksburg as a means of evoking stories; this was seen by the seniors as a specially attractive affordance of the Web over their original email list. The project concept was differentiated from an official history project sponsored by the town of Blacksburg, as indicated in this excerpt from the seniors' email newsletter:

> We will be emphasizing contributions of individuals built around their memories and interviews of a number of individuals, not currently in the group. It appears that we will be able to use old photos. This will not be a formal history. The town already has a group working on that but this will be much more personal and I believe much more friendly to those accessing it. The persons there today seemed very pleased with the concept.

The Blacksburg Nostalgia forum attracted a variety of interesting stories and reflections, most quite personal and informal. In some ways the stories emerged as a series of associations from a collective community memory. For example, one story begins by saying that other people's contributions helped bring to mind memories. The author recalls some details about a meat market, and then turns to memories of a big snowstorm 30 years before, referring to specific places in Blacksburg and depths of snow, particular winter activities (sitting on top of a telephone pole, tunneling in snow drifts), and specific events (pipes bursting in Virginia Tech buildings). Finally, the story turns to memories of the origins of computing at Virginia Tech – connecting to an earlier discussion thread. It recalls the model number of the university's first computer, the location of the old wooden building in which it was housed, and its memory capacities and programming languages.

The story attracted annotations on the snowstorm theme, including another recollection of people tunneling through drifts (in this case to get out of their houses). Another annotation described wintertime life for female undergraduates at Virginia Tech during those cold winters in the 1960s. And another pushed the "first computer" memories back to the 1950s. Subsequent annotations introduced facts about where on campus that very first computer was eventually located, how the US Navy had once occupied some of the wooden buildings, and how the Navy had built a firing range that was shared with local Boy Scouts. (This story is presented and discussed below.)

This simple web information system – though innovative at this time, when interactive web applications were rare – highlights an important role played by senior citizens in a diverse community. They are the ones with the many years of memories, as well perhaps with time and motivation for sharing those memories. By doing so, they can evoke commentary, community bonding, and reinforcement of community identity in others. The community's history is part of its present and its future, and living witnesses can tell that history in the most engaging way.

As illustrated in Figure 6.3, the Nostalgia website presented an old black and white photograph of downtown Blacksburg (clicking on the photograph displayed a full-sized image). There was a brief introduction, including a "Compose Your Story" link (to contribute a story by means of a web form) and a "hear from you" link (to send email comments to the site developers). Below this header was the default view of the index of submitted stories, a reverse-chronological enumeration of stories submitted. The index entries consisted of a story's title

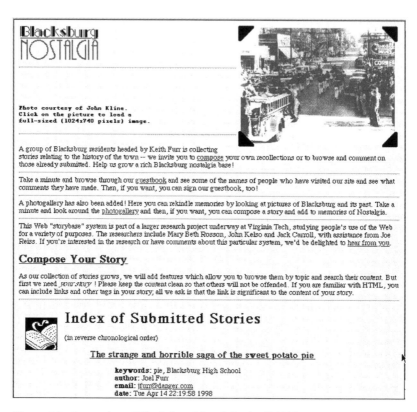

*Figure 6.3*   Screenshot of Blacksburg Nostalgia, April 1998.

(which was the link anchor to its content and annotations, if any), keywords suggested by the author when the story was originally submitted (e.g., weather, stores, downtown, roads, unusual incidents), its author's name, an email link to the author, the story's date of submission, and a summary of its annotation status (total number of annotations made and the date of the most recent annotation).

The brief introduction encouraged visitors to browse the stories, to comment on stories already there, and to contribute stories of their own. Selecting a story title in the index displayed a new web page with the story title, author, and content, followed by its annotations (if any) in chronological order. Annotations did not have titles, but were date and time stamped when they were submitted. Both stories and annotations had email links to their authors to facilitate one-on-one follow-up interactions between Nostalgia authors and visitors to the site. At the end of each story listing was a link to "add an annotation to this story" (and, of course, a "go back" link).

If the user selected "add annotation," the current story page was redisplayed along with a web form for entering an annotation. Thus the most recent annotation was displayed immediately above the form, reminding the author of the context in which the new annotation would be published. The annotation author was prompted for the text of the annotation, as well as for his or her name and email address. Selecting the "submit annotation" button added the annotation immediately; reloading the story's page would display the updated listing. The annotation also generated two email notifications: one was sent to the system administrators, who periodically reviewed stories and annotations to ensure that they were consistent with community standards and with the content concept of the Nostalgia project. The second notification was sent to the author of the story that was annotated.

Visitors to the Nostalgia site could also add a new story; "compose your story" links appeared at the beginning and the end of the story index. The story composition page included another black and white photograph of old Blacksburg (even older than the one on the homepage). The title of this page was "Tell us YOUR story ..." and it had a blatantly motivational header: "We appreciate your contributions to the Blacksburg Nostalgia project. Your contribution now will help to preserve your memories for others to enjoy and elaborate – years from now, your loved ones and friends will be able to return to this base of stories and revisit Blacksburg as you and your friends knew it!" Below this material, a web form was displayed with prompts for story title, story text, author's name and email, and suggested keywords.

Authors were given an opportunity to preview their formatted stories and annotations (Hypertext Markup Language – HTML – tags were processed if included in the submission) and to make editing changes before they confirmed submission of the story to the database. They were sent a confirmation email message when the contribution was submission was finalized. The Nostalgia project directly reused the Practical Extraction and Report Language (PERL) programs and database design we employed in implementing the Web Storybase project (see Carroll *et al.* 1999).

All contributions to Nostalgia were reviewed by a system administrator, who was notified when new stories and annotations were posted, and who regularly visited the site to review submissions. If an inappropriate story was contributed, the administrator deleted the relevant line in the story index; if an inappropriate annotation was submitted, the story file itself would have had to be edited. As it turned out, only one contribution was ever deleted – a story whose text consisted almost entirely of "blah blah blah." This relatively benign intrusion contrasted sharply with our experiences with the Web Storybase, where almost as many stories were removed as were posted, and where the unacceptable stories were sometimes offensive (Rosson, Carroll, and Messner 1996). We attribute this to the strong association of Nostalgia content with the local Blacksburg community, to the submission protocol of identifying author information, and to the smaller and more intimate core group of story contributors – namely, the 100 or so members of the BEV Seniors group.

The design vision of Nostalgia was recollection and discussion of community history by and for the community itself, including its diaspora. One might call this everyday history and heritage. This goal contrasts with other heritage-oriented information systems, which often tend to focus on history in a grander context of conventionally famous places and events. Thus, Campiello (Agostini *et al.* 2002) was directed toward visitors, tourists, and Internet browsers interested in Venice, Italy. The local community was involved in creating some content, largely through school projects, but the focus was on conventional history, not on personal and everyday history. Palaver Tree Online (Ellis and Bruckman 2001) involved guiding schoolchildren to gather recollections from elderly community members as part of a lesson on civil rights. Such recollections and interactions could have been quite personal, but in fact they tended to be rather school-oriented, evoking rather generic questions such as "What is a sit-in?" and "How was a march organized?" Klaebe and Foth (2007) describe a project in which stories were actively elicited and curated by researchers as a proactive technique to engender sense of community among members of a newly forming community.

## Making community history

The Blacksburg Nostalgia system was open as of the last week of May 1996. Our overall objective was to create an accessible forum for community discussion of local history. An example is a story entitled "Nostalgic Musings" and its annotations, shown in Box 6.1.

*Box 6.1* "Nostalgic Musings" and its annotations

---

### Nostalgic Musings

**Author:** Keith Furr
  **Email:** furr1@vt.edu
  The responses of others' email reminded me of a few additional things. Yes, the dirty meat market was where many of us bought meat. It was in a building not much better than the fruit stands you see beside rural roads and it sure wouldn't pass state health standards now for cleanliness. However the meat was inexpensive and very good. I believe it cost something less than a dollar a pound for T-bone steaks.
  The big snow in 1965–66 (I think) piled up drifts such as I have never seen before or since. We had just had Elizabeth & Julie and lived about a mile out on Glade Road in a small house. The drift in our driveway was over eight feet deep and the road into Prices Fork Road was impassable. The County had plowed the latter road so some friends of ours (Webb and Sara Richardson) offered to bring some milk and other groceries to the intersection of Glade and Prices Fork Road. I hiked out but with the deep snow it was hard going. Just behind where Krogers is now, the drifts were

*(Continued)*

*Box 6.1*  (*Continued*)

over 20 feet deep. I sat down and rested on the top of a telephone pole there! In a similar snow, five years earlier, 1959–60, the men who lived on the road got together and dug a tunnel through a drift at that same location.

That same winter it seemed to snow every Wednesday and Friday starting in Late January and continuing until March. From 1960 until 1966, if my memory serves me correctly, the weather seemed to be much colder in the winter than it was for many years afterwards with the summers being very dry. Lawns were typically brown by July and August. Since then until recently, it seems to me that we have had more moderate weather for the most part except for, I believe, 1979, when we had an extreme cold spell during Christmas break when it got to 12 below zero and stayed below zero for about a week. Pipes burst in 68 buildings on campus and many persons who left for the break came home to find a lot of water damage. There were additional cold snaps later on when it got to − 18 in Blacksburg and − 26 up at Mountain Lake. I hope our current weather trend is not a sign of returning to the "good old days."

By the way, in the context of computer interests, I remember Tech's first official computer. It was an IBM 1620 and it had an amazing 32 kb of memory. It was located in a wooden building located where Derring is now. This was an immense improvement over the one I had access to at Duke. It had 2 km of memory on a rotating magnetic drum. We had to use either of two languages on punched cards, SOAP or Bell. Anyone else remember those two primitive computing languages?

**Annotation by:** David Mize
**Email:** dave.mize@tcr.com
**Date:** Fri Jul 26 23:34:28 1996

I remember being 8 or 9 years old during the heavy snow storm in the early 60's. I was able to walk up a snow drift to the porch roof of our farmhouse. My grandfather pushed out the back door, then went around front and spent two days digging a tunnel to the front door.

**Annotation by:** Elaine Hunter
**Email:** Hunter_Lane@hq.navsea.navy.mil
**Date:** Sat Feb 08 22:35:35 1997

I was a student at Tech that winter, and yes, I was female. We girls were not allowed to wear slacks to class, nor were we allowed to wear them to the dining hall. The small group of us who did not live in Hillcrest were taking our meals in the main dining hall. As the temperature dropped to 15 below, we were finally permitted to wear slacks to meals as long as we kept long coats on and buttoned until we were seated at the table! I guess they were afraid the guys would discover that our legs went all the way up. But it was a fine group of men who went to Tech. They always allowed us at the front of the very long line. Jim Sheeler was among them. Where are the rest now?

**Annotation by:** Barbara Harrell Holdren
**Email:** BarbH1193@AOL.com
**Date:** Thu Jun 12 21:12:35 1997

I grew up in Blacksburg where my father was a professor in the Accounting Department for 40 years. When I read your comment about the first official computer, I remembered something he wrote in his autobiography (he realized he was dying and wrote 75 pages on a yellow legal pad). He mentioned the IBM 650 and the fact that in 1957 and again in 1959, IBM sent him to Endicott, NY to train in data processing. For a while he used this information as part of the "Auditing" course in accounting, and then in 1963–1964 it became a course. I remember visiting the building where the computer filled a good-sized room – I think it may have been in Burrus Hall or a nearby building. Pamplin Hall wasn't there then. Was this the same computer you're remembering?

**Annotation by:** Ted Shelton
**Email:** tcsiii@bev.net
**Date:** Mon Sep 08 01:40:49 1997

Speaking of wooden buildings in the area where Derring is now located: there was a building that contained a firing range. I remember sighting-in my first rifle, a Marlin 22, there. And I remember being taken on a tour of the computer room in a wooden building back in that same area/era. I think it was much later when the computer was moved to Burruss. I remember when 460 all the way thru blacksburg was 2 lanes, with that marvelous 3-lane section south of town going up the hill where the Forest Service is now located. Anybody remember the old Navy barracks at the Tech Airport?

**Annotation by:** David Moser
**Email:** dmoser@mail.telis.org
**Date:** Tue Sep 09 23:50:57 1997

During the 50's that firing range was made available to Boy Scout Troop 56 when my father was scoutmaster. Many of us scouts earned our marksmanship merit badge there. There was nothing unusual about 11–13 year olds carrying rifles WAY back then!

**Annotation by:** Shannon Bennett
**Email:** shbennet@vt.edu
**Date:** Tue Oct 14 22:31:13 1997

I've been in Blacksburg for only three years now, so I don't really have any true stories. However, I am interested in you who do remember Blacksburg in the pre-suburban era to please e-mail me with your opinions of Blacksburg today and how it needs to change to become a more prosperous place.

**Annotation by:** Wendell Hensley

*(Continued)*

Box 6.1   (*Continued*)

**Email:** wendelltsi@aol.com
**Date:** Sat Nov 08 10:07:06 1997
Yes, Ted Shelton, I remember the Navy barracks at Tech airport, as well as the "Sandy Airfield" next to it (basically the site of the now present main runway) where we used to play cowboys and indians in the 1940's. There was an accessible steam tunnel under this desert-looking area where we little kids could stand and walk through, scaring ourselves in the damp darkness complete with creepy things.

The story itself is implicitly a continuation of a broader discussion. For example, the author begins by saying that other people's contributions helped bring to mind additional memories. He goes on to address one of these with some details about a meat market. He then turns to his memories of big snow storms from 30 years ago, referring to specific places in Blacksburg and depths of snow, particular winter activities (sitting on top of a telephone pole, tunneling in snow drifts), and specific events (pipes bursting in Virginia Tech buildings). Finally, the story turns to memories of the origins of computing at Virginia Tech – again apparently continuing an earlier discussion thread. It recalls the model number of the university's first computer, the location of the old wooden building in which it was housed, and its memory capacities and programming languages.

This is a very informal story – the kind of thing you might expect to hear around someone's electronic kitchen table. It casually visits several topics – starting with "yes, I remember the dirty meat market" and ending with "does anyone else remember the SOAP or Bell programming languages?" It vividly sketches an assortment of images. The annotations it evoked are an interesting set; they continue to spin out the historical themes in similar style.

The first annotation points back to the snowstorm theme, offering another recollection of people tunneling through drifts (in this case to get out of their houses). The second (seemingly from a "lost Hokie") paints a few images of wintertime life for female undergraduates at Virginia Tech during those cold winters in the 1960s. The next pushes the "first computer" memories back to the 1950s barracks located at the Tech Airport.

The fourth annotation continues the topic of wooden buildings, but remembers one with a firing range. It also points to the immediately preceding annotation, agreeing that the university's early computer was moved to Burruss Hall. It concludes with a new topic of wooden buildings, asking about a Navy barracks located at the Tech Airport.

The fifth annotation responds to the fourth, introducing the fact that the firing range was made available to a local Boy Scout troop. The sixth annotation is a meta-comment by a relative newcomer to Blacksburg, thanking the authors for their contributions and asking about the future of the town. The seventh annotation skips back to the Navy barracks subtopic, recalling games of cowboys and indians from the 1940s played near there, and an underground steam tunnel that was accessible. This story has had a fairly rich lifecycle. It was contributed on June 25, 1996, and annotated over a period of sixteen months (through November 1997).

We tracked the usage the of Nostalgia site for the first two and a half years. During this period, sixteen stories were contributed, with stories getting about three annotations each on average. The site was accessed about 300 times per month through this period. (For more detailed discussion of the use of Nostalgia, see Carroll *et al.* 1999).

For each story, we attempted to identify the main focus of the contribution; in some cases we coded several distinct points for a single story. The majority of the stories contributed included discussion of a place or places. These stories often named a colorful store or restaurant that no longer exists (e.g., the "dirty meat market") or some other historical landmark (the Huckleberry train station). The next most common story theme, involving nearly half of the stories contributed, was a memorable event of some sort (e.g., a particularly severe snowstorm). Nearly half of the stories tried to convey what everyday life was like at a certain time (e.g., what it was like to be a teenager in Blacksburg in the 1960s). Other themes were discussions of specific people (e.g., the owner of a business and his wife) or of singular objects (e.g., the first computer at Virginia Tech) and generally occurred in concert with memories of places or events.

Most of the stories provoked annotations by other users. More than three-quarters of the annotations provided additional details or added details to an earlier annotation. In some cases, stories or annotations raised questions that subsequent annotations attempted to answer or clarify, creating a sort of discussion. Several annotations conveyed a reaction of some sort, generally an appreciation of a specific detail or of the overall contribution.

The use of annotations to provide further detail is precisely the sort of thing that we had hoped to observe in the Nostalgia site – essentially threaded discussions, but with the implicit goal of creating an extended description of specific shared places, events, or perspectives. It was notable that many of these details were contributed by former Blacksburg residents. The seniors' original interest in involving "lost Hokies" was clearly achieved, and demonstrated that one affordance of the Internet and the Web is to make it possible for people to stay informed more easily about and even participate in communities with which they still identify, but from which they have become physically removed.

The Nostalgia content was submitted by 30 distinct contributors; about one-half made a single annotation. Eleven different individuals wrote the sixteen stories. We classified the contributors (based on email addresses, personal knowledge, and comments made in their stories) into three groups: BEV Seniors (eleven), "lost Hokies" (twelve), and others (seven).

As we expected, the core population of authors were members of the BEV Seniors group: one senior submitted four stories, and another contributed two. The seniors often also annotated one another's stories. As one reads through the full set, there is very much a sense that these are community members who are longtime friends and are collaborating to produce rich descriptions of the "old days" in Blacksburg. In several cases it appears that an older couple who share an account jointly authored a story or annotation. During the first few weeks, when stories and annotations were being produced rapidly (22 in under 30 days), the annotations often had a conversational character, beginning with a personal salutation (e.g., "Earl, do I remember correctly ..."), and a similarly personal response as few minutes later (e.g., "Yes, Connie, there was a Kroger where Tech Bookstore is now located and ...). This sort of back-and-forth conversation is similar to what one would expect in an email exchange among friends.

However, in the second half of the 26-month period the contributing users gradually seemed to become a less homogeneous group. The seniors were still contributing on occasion, but there was more evidence of "lost Hokies" – the Blacksburg diaspora community that the seniors had hoped to reach with a broadly accessible web forum. For example, one story presented a wealth of detail about life as a child and teenager during the 1960s and 1970s – memories of the main highways surrounding the town, open land being developed into apartment buildings, development fiascoes resulting in legal suits, a high-school friend who died in an auto accident, what the "in" things were for high-school students at that time. The author of the story was a former resident of Blacksburg, who at that time lived in Colorado. Also common were annotations from these former residents, some simply appreciative of the good memories being shared (in one case from an adopted child seeking background and history concerning her birth father), others contributing their own details or seeking information about their pasts.

In October 1997 and March 1998, we surveyed the Blacksburg Seniors by email regarding their knowledge about, use of, and reactions to Blacksburg Nostalgia. In the October survey, we contacted people who had contributed stories or annotations. For the March survey we used the seniors' mailing list. Each surveys attracted only a half-dozen respondents. Also in October and March we visited meetings of the Blacksburg Seniors to discuss the Nostalgia project in person; each meeting was attended by 35 to 40 members of the group.

Based on these sources, most seniors learned of Blacksburg Nostalgia through the seniors' email list, though a significant minority discovered it while browsing BEV web pages. Lost Hokies played a role here too: In one case, a former resident, who stayed in touch with Blacksburg by regularly browsing local web pages, alerted other members of his family, who were still residents, about the existence of Nostalgia; two of those family members subsequently contributed. Of the seniors who had visited the Nostalgia site, about half had done so ten or more times, and half had done so four or fewer times.

User comments were fairly positive. Many comments emphasized the fun of reminiscence: "It is so much fun to be with people and recollect old times." Some users indicated that Nostalgia confirmed specific memories they had; others said it confirmed that their memories were still accurate (i.e., "My memory is pretty good"). A few comments suggested that Nostalgia could be a community information resource: "It provides a source of information of a historical nature and may be valuable to those doing historical research."

Some users felt that the simple sequential organization of the stories and the lack of embellishment in the presentation were strengths of the design. However, others suggested the inclusion of more photographs and the provision of a guest-book as improvements. A topic list of place names, events, etc., that might also help trigger memories was another suggestion. Several users expressed the hope that more seniors would contribute stories. One thought that the project should be incorporated into the town of Blacksburg's bicentennial commemoration.

In response to our 1997–8 user surveys and workshops, we designed and implemented two enhancements to Nostalgia: a guestbook and a photo gallery. The guestbook permitted visitors to record their comments and contact information in a web form and browse the entries made by other guests. Our idea was to make "mere" browsing more active, more visible, and perhaps more rewarding by providing those who do not contribute a story or annotation a way to express overall impressions of the project. We also thought that the guestbook might facilitate the development of social ties among residents interested in informal community history, on the one hand, and lost Hokies who visited the site but had not posted a story or annotation, on the other. However, these possible benefits entailed some increased complexity in the Nostalgia site. We in effect incorporated a parallel forum into the system to support lightweight discussions about discussions, and that seems inherently confusing.

From the start of the project there was always great enthusiasm among the seniors for old photographs. The two photographs we had originally incorporated into the Nostalgia pages to create atmosphere attracted considerable interest and discussion. This interest motivated us to work with a local collector of old photographs to create a page specifically for digitized photographs. Users could browse the Nostalgia photo gallery page and, from there, contribute a story pointing to a particular photo. They could also upload their own photographs to the photo gallery. The photograph collector with whom we worked saw this as an opportunity to engage the broader community in helping him to clarify the dates, locations, and identities of people pictured in the photographs, an early example of community-based crowd sourcing.

Design projects often wind up suggesting new design directions, and our experience with Nostalgia suggested further directions for this type of community information system. We felt that more stories and comments could have been evoked if the Nostalgia site had been enhanced with maps, descriptions of recent and ongoing development projects around the town, and links to other community news and information, such as blogs. We particularly wanted to include a graphical timeline of the history of the town. The timeline was a simple and, as far as we could tell, effective interface widget for the HistoryBase. For Nostalgia, a timeline view emphasizing landmark community events of the past several decades, as well as events already described in Nostalgia, might help to evoke personal memories by providing a richer temporal context. For example, it might trigger memories of incidents that occurred between other incidents previously recalled and described, or related to other events already positioned on the timeline (Trabasso and Stein 1997).

In chapter 2, we discussed claims associated with posting and accessing community information online. Online discussion was a foundation activity in the first-generation community networks of the late 1970s and 1980s, when it was implemented through electronic bulletin boards, email lists, and newsgroups. The BEV and the web paradigm for online information made community forum discussions more accessible. It allowed community forums greater visibility both within and beyond the community itself, and better integrated them with the broader community information infrastructure. Web forums allowed contributions to be more integral and object-like – pages in a website instead of lines in an endless news stream.

Making lived community history into a focal topic of community discussion elaborates the claims analysis of chapter 2. Discussion of any community information can be affirmative with respect to community identity and activity. Such discussion ineluctably reminds members of the social embedding of all that happens, and of the community values and identity commitments that local activities enact and promote. But community history, and particularly the relatively recent history that living members can corroborate, is in many respects the strongest and purest case. People remember episodes and events for reasons, and many of those reasons are the larger meanings that resonate through the particular episodes and events. Accordingly, discussion of lived community history may be especially effective in embodying community identity.

The Nostalgia project suggested additional design claims pertaining specifically to codifying community history in community networks, corresponding to three aspects of how community members interacted with Nostalgia. The scenarios and claims in Box 6.2 elaborate those presented and discussed in chapter 2. Most simply, the stories and comments could be browsed and read. Reading these stories helped bring to life the Blacksburg of the 1960s for people who were there, for people too young to have been there, for people who had since moved on from Blacksburg, and for everyone else on the Web.

*Box 6.2* Claims associated with Nostalgia interaction scenarios

Reading stories about the recent past decades of one's community

+ makes the community's unique heritage of people, places, and events more visible to all
+ helps younger community members understand and appreciate community heritage
+ vicariously connects current community members to past people, places, and events
+ enriches community identity for members and for people outside the community
− But could make the community seem quirky or parochial.

*(Continued)*

Box 6.2  (*Continued*)

Recalling, posting, and discussing community history online

+ makes the community network more participatory
+ makes the process of codifying community history more participatory
+ includes community members who might have relocated outside the
   community
− But could distract attention from concerns about the present and future
− But contributing text to a web forum is more complex, both technically and
   socially, than merely browsing and reading.

Integrating explicit referents (such as digital photographs of people, places, and
events) with online community history information and discussion

+ more vividly evokes personal memories in community members
+ makes community history more engaging for others
− But uploading images to a website is more complex, both technically and
   socially, than merely contributing text.

A more active participation in the Nostalgia activity was recalling, posting and discussing stories and comments, described in the second claim in Box 6.2. These interactions make the community network more participatory than the original static web page paradigm of the BEV. More specifically, they make community history a participatory and collaborative endeavor, something one does as much as something one merely reads. A distinctive feature of the Nostalgia forum was the inclusion of digital photographs depicting people, places, and/or events in stories, described in the third claim in Box 6.2. Photographs more vividly evoked memories and reflections about Blacksburg and also made the stories more engaging for people to read.

As is typical in design rationale analysis, we have identified potential downsides in these claims. One obvious potential downside is that reading and writing about the community's past could distract attention from its present and future. Of course, one could argue that ignorance about the community's past jeopardizes it future all the more. The stories posted in Nostalgia describe a time when Blacksburg was much smaller and more isolated than it was in 1995, when it was hosting one of the most advanced community networks of the time. To a harsh outsider, the stories and comments could seem the naive ramblings of bumpkins. Sharing anything of significance always entails the risk of being ridiculed for one's values and beliefs; sharing personal recollections on the Web could magnify that risk.

Every new technology-based activity entrains potential complexities. Contributing memories, comments on memories shared by others, or old photographic images entrains technical complexities of just doing new things. Thus, circa 1996, few people had digital photographs or were routinely uploading such images. And these activities also entrained new social complexities: Contributing one's images or texts to a web forum instantly makes them accessible to the entire world. Even if the contents are perfectly acceptable and entirely relevant to the forum, one might have second thoughts. Again, in 1996 few people had been able to share their personal photographs and recollections so widely at the push of a button.

## CommunitySims

Several years after the Nostalgia project, we initiated a project in which elderly community members and middle-school students collaborated to design and build visual simulation programming projects illustrating current community issues. Our vision in this project, CommunitySims, was to mutually leverage the complementary strengths of the young and old with respect to community issues and information technology: We hypothesized that elders would have more knowledge about, experience with, perspective on, and interest in community issues, but relatively little experience with visual simulation programming. In contrast, we expected that middle-school children might be comfortable with, curious about, and perhaps even experienced with programming and visual simulations (Lenhart, Hitlin, and Madden 2005; Mayer *et al.* 1997) but have comparatively little experience with community issues.

The old and the young in contemporary communities are isolated from one another in ways they were not in the arrangements of several generations ago. It is no longer typical for three (or more) generations of a family to reside in the same community. Indeed, when we started the CommunitySims project we knew no family in Blacksburg with that degree of cross-generational continuity. On the other hand, the community included plenty of elderly members and many children; they just were not related to one another. We wondered if cross-generational community-based activities could be designed that might engage and benefit both the old and the young, and perhaps bring them together.

We wanted to explore the possible synergies that could result if complementary, cross-generational energies and experiences were combined, ideally with the older and younger partners mutually serving as models and guides (Bandura 1977, 1986) while reciprocally expanding their own understandings (Lave and Wenger 1991). We wanted to engage diverse members of our community in a shared learning and discussion process that would enhance appreciation of community issues, in part because diversity in collaborative learning can promote socio-cognitive conflict and discussion of alternative solutions (Foot, Morgan, and Shute 1990). We wanted to promote new and creative ways for community members to think about and employ computing technology in raising and discussing these concerns (see also Arias *et al.* 2000), and thereby to create an authentic learning task, connecting information technology and everyday community life, that might engage both the older and younger partners (Brown and Campione 1996). Our ultimate objective was to share the visual simulations with the larger community through a web forum to provoke a broader discussion about the issues depicted.

Our approach was to host a series of full-day workshops in which pairs of elderly persons and middle-school children worked together. In the early workshops, the focus was on brainstorming and refining simulation ideas and learning about the visual simulation tool (Stagecast Creator). Subsequent workshops shifted focus to actually implementing simulation models. My colleagues and I were active facilitators for these collaborative activities: We designed quick-start instructional materials for Stagecast Creator (Smith and Cypher 1999), and we implemented example simulations based on some of the best ideas from the early workshops to serve as models for the pairs in the later workshops (Lewis *et al.* 2002; Rosson and Carroll 2003; Rosson *et al.* 2002; Seals *et al.* 2002). In the discussion below, we focus on a workshop involving three cross-generational groups, who extended simulations and then designed and implemented new ones. The older people in these groups were all females, and one of the groups included two middle-school students; the other two groups were pairs (Rosson and Carroll 2003).

The Stagecast Creator visual programming environment was designed to support programming by example (Smith and Cypher 1999). One builds a program by combining visual "characters" on a rectangular grid, called a "stage." The user creates visual appearances for each character, along with rules that describe how the characters will move, change appearance, and interact with other characters during the simulation. Thus the effects of a simulation program are experienced as visual animations in which characters appear, move, encounter one another, change shape or color, and so on. Figure 6.4 shows one of the CommunitySims projects – a schoolyard fight.

In this simulation, the students, the teacher, and the door are all characters whose interactions are described by visual before/after rules. For example, as shown at the right in Figure 6.4, anytime two boys are adjacent and facing forward, the "schoolyard tension" variable is increased. If the variable reaches a threshold value, adjacent boys will begin yelling at one another and eventually pushing and hitting one another. At that point in the simulation, the teacher character emerges from the door and stops the fight.

The challenge in this activity is to identify meaningful and interesting community situations that can be visualized and specified as characters and interactions. Based on ideas generated in the workshops, we came up with a set of Creator simulations, including Smoking Kids, in which two kids smoke at school, get sick, and collapse, Flirting or Hurting, in which a boy is rebuffed by a girl and then tries to force his attentions on another girl, Noise Pollution, in which college students have a party with loud music, an older resident comes out to complain, and police arrive, Cliques, in which kids on a school playground form groups based on their "coolness" or "sports" interests and exclude others, and Classroom Bully, in which a boy picks on others in class and a teacher punishes him with detention.

Our participants were self-selected in the sense that they had had prior experience with Creator programming that was engaging enough to make them continue to volunteer to work with us. All the participants in the design workshop

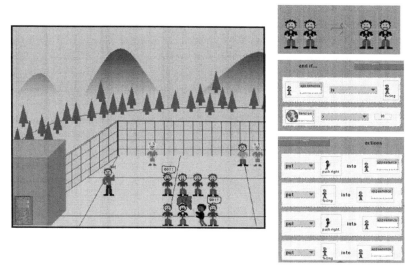

*Figure 6.4* A schoolyard fight simulation built in Stagecast Creator (left) and a rule visually specifying when the pushing is to begin.

had been part of earlier workshops focused on the efficacy of different training approaches for Creator (Seals *et al.* 2002; Wissman 2002). We expected that there would be difference in prior experience with computing between the older and younger participants, and this was in fact the case. However, the older people had on average more than five years of computing experience, and most were regular users of word processing software. There were substantial differences in the use of spreadsheets, graphics and drawing editors, and web programming: Most of the younger participants had experience in these areas; most of the older participants did not.

In the workshops, older–younger pairs first were reminded of Creator basics and the concept of community simulations. They then experimented with and extended one or two simulations that we had already created based on ideas generated at previous workshops. Then they brainstormed further ideas for community simulations, and selected one or two ideas to implement in Creator. Even in the initial activity of revisiting Creator basics, there were clear generational differences. The younger members related to the review very actively trying functions, enhancing examples, and calling back and forth to one another with ideas and tips, instead of following the self-instruction sequence. The older members reacted more directly to the community issues that the simulations were designed to raise. For instance, one older woman reacted to the Noise Pollution simulation by saying: "I agree that courtesy demands speaking to the neighbors first before calling police. Also, where is a responsible adult?" In contrast, the students tended to focus on animation realism and usability issues – for example, "OK ... I don't see what is happening here," or "This one is too short to understand."

In part because the younger members were quick to suggest things to do, they assumed the role of programmer in all of the pairs. Their ideas were often fairly low-level, such as adding a dive-bombing bird or having a car slide off the road. The older members tended to react gently but also to articulate ideas at a more thematic level. For example, when a younger member suggested adding more police cars to the Noise Pollution simulation, her older partner remarked that they would also have to move the other characters around to make space ("We probably need to get our people off the road before they get run over"). This resulted in a much more elaborate interaction in the simulation.

The groups brainstormed ideas for new simulation projects that reflected their different community stakes. Among ideas that seemed to originate with the older members were sewing club activities, managing a library bookmobile, and participation in the annual downtown festival. The students' ideas included getting lost on the first day of school, town rules for using skateboards downtown, and reactions to substitute teachers.

Interestingly, all of the three cross-generational groups chose to build new simulations involving aspects of traffic management, perhaps a common denominator of community life, and easily visualized. Driving is governed by familiar laws and conventions; this may make it an especially evocative context for surfacing and discussing community values. Finally, the public nature of traffic laws may cause the underlying values to seem uncontroversial, with the result that traffic issues are a "safe" topic for collaboration by dissimilar individuals.

We examined the content of the interactions between older and younger partners. We were interested to see if we could identify distinctive age-related roles or perspectives in the contributions. We expected that the elderly participants might adopt a community perspective, leveraging their knowledge and experience, but also their greater interest in and commitment to the community. Thus, we thought that the elderly members might take more responsibility for articulating the community meaning of the simulations. In contrast, we thought the younger participants might adopt a perspective more immediately focused on the technology interactions and the graphic content of the simulations. We were interested to see if there could be a possibility of mutual learning among the participants, through a productive dynamic between their different perspectives on community simulations.

We saw some evidence of this during the simulation programming activity. For example, one team worked on traffic accidents at difficult local intersections, and the older member provided the real-world context:

*Woman:*  Do you want the cars to have an accident?
*Girl:*   Yeah ... where's there an intersection in Blacksburg where they could have an accident?
*Woman:*  Alright, Tom's Creek [a busy intersection near the university].

Another team was working on the traffic congestion the town experiences when Virginia Tech students arrive in the fall. They first wanted to create an appropriate background for their road and cars. The boys were quickly able to open and begin using a paint program to draw storefronts:

*First boy:*   We're just gonna write down "building" on a little square.
*Second boy:*   Yes, like, there are signs that tell you what the shop is. We can call it a "shop building."
*Woman:*   Are you going to call it "building"? Oh, come on, you could call it something creative, like Kroger's!
*Second boy:*   This is downtown, though. We just choose a random spot to do it … the place by Rocket Music and Souvlaki's, where the old middle school is.
*First boy:*   Souvlaki and Dairy Queen, where there's always concerts, the pizza place.

Here, a modest suggestion by the older team member prompted the boys to remember and share specific downtown experiences and to position their simulation at a familiar downtown location. This made the simulation project more concrete, tying it more firmly to the otherwise generic notion of "downtown." Concretizing "downtown" also helped the boys generate more details concerning the look and behavior of the simulated world. Nonetheless, as can be seen in Figure 6.5, this project ended up as an interesting mix between the "realism"

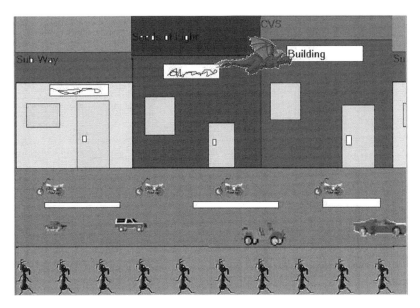

*Figure 6.5*   Downtown traffic congestion simulation.

that one might expect of an adult simulation developer (e.g., actual store names) and the "fantasy" that seems to be engaging to boys of this age (marching ants, a tank driving down the street, a flying dragon).

In some cases, it seemed the elders assumed a "designer" role where the students assumed a "programmer" role. In the snippet of interaction below, the older woman states a simulation goal and proposes that they need "variables" for different aspects of their scenario; the girl responds with options she knows can be implemented in this simulation environment, in this case suggesting that simulation characters might represent "types" of people – a person's clothing could convey something about him/her, church buildings can be decorated with expressive symbols, and so on. In this case, the pair was working on a simulation of a town newcomer who needs to learn about the many places of worship that she or he can choose to visit.

*Woman:*  Now the problem is we gotta do this! So what are gonna be the variables? We got somebody who's gonna come in. The question mark – we got a new person coming in, and it's gonna be a question mark – 1, 2, 3, 4 – red, green, blue, yellow, and the …
*Girl:*  We can make four different people.
*Woman:*  And the decision-making would be depending upon …
*Girl:*  What they're wearing, or …?
*Woman:*  Well, we said music, charities …
*Girl:*  So, we could have something over the churches, like, something that symbolizes music and charities. Jewish churches? I don't know. We could have one that focuses more on art? I don't know, like, that has a pretty church, because some people might want to go to a church that has pretty stained-glass windows.

After the activities, we asked participants to complete 21 Likert items rating the extent to which various characteristics would make a hypothetical simulation feature more "fun." The rating included characteristics like action, artistic detail, cute, educational, fast, funny, manipulate, matches the real world, moral lesson, randomness, and silly. The older and younger participants agreed on the importance of some characteristics – for example, everyone felt that more "action" and "artistic detail" would make a simulation more fun. They also seemed to agree that some features were less likely to increase the fun of using a simulation – for example, both age groups gave relatively low ratings to the features "educational" and "moral lesson." However, we also observed some differences. The younger participants, but not the older ones, felt that "silliness" and "real world," and to a somewhat lesser extent "randomness" and "manipulate," were important characteristics for a simulation to be fun.

At the end of the workshop, participants were interviewed about their experiences and rated their possible interest in working with simulation activities in the future. Likert items asked whether Creator simulations can help to build community; whether participants wanted to build or to extend simulations; and how well the participant understood Creator. The younger participants rated their understanding of Creator much higher than did the older women – 4.0 versus 2.5 on a 5-point scale. Conversely, the older participants were more optimistic than the students that working on community simulation could help to build community – 3.3 versus 2.7. All participants answered "yes" to a question asking whether they would want to continue working on CommunitySims. But they emphasized different aspects of future plans. The younger participants were intrigued by social simulation (e.g., "I thought it was really fun when we got to make our own world," or "I'd like to make games out of existing sims"), the older participants were more cautious regarding simulations ("Yes, but I need to have more knowledge about creating a simulation project").

It seemed that all members of the CommunitySims intergenerational teams were engaged in the process of creation and felt rewarded. The participants were moderately positive about their overall collaboration experience (averaging 3.73 on a 5-point scale). The older women took the simulations, and the concept of CommunitySims in general, more seriously as discussion prompts for community issues, and felt that they were able to provide guidance about community issues and interactions in the design activity. The younger members were eager and able to take on the somewhat complementary role of Creator programming, and were able to help their older partners learn and apply simple programming interactions (Rosson and Carroll 2003; Rosson *et al.* 2002).

One of the pairings especially seemed to encourage the possibility of mutually productive community learning reaching across the generations. In this group, the younger member clearly became a "mentor" for his older partner with respect to simulation programming. This particular young person spontaneously adopted the practice of narrating what he was doing as he programmed the pair's simulation. This "thinking aloud" narration (Ericsson and Simon 1984) had the effect of evoking a stream of elaboration questions from his partner, which clearly seemed to enhance learning about how Creator worked for both of them. Of course, it was more typical for the older members to relate to their younger partners as "mentors," but this was with respect to the community issues and meanings of the simulations. The possibility of mutuality in cross-generational mentor/mentee relationships is less obvious and quite interesting as a community-learning paradigm.

We created a website for CommunitySims to which we posted the simulation examples we had created, based on the early workshops, and the simulations created by our community participants. Figure 6.6 displays a screenshot of the welcome page the users encountered when first logging in (guests could also visit, but were not permitted to upload or download projects). We used the website in the workshop described above to present example simulations to the participants, but we also wanted to use it to make the project visible to the larger Blacksburg community.

One lesson from the CommunitySims project is that it seems possible to engage cross-generational teams in a community simulation activity, but it is not an easy thing to do. We did see episodes in which the generations played

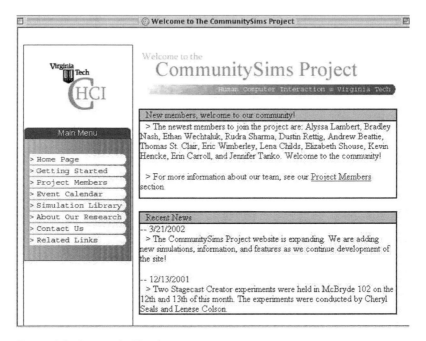

*Figure 6.6*   CommunitySims homepage.

complementary learning roles to the benefit of both, but we also saw cases where the members were talking past one another and not engaging. For example, younger members valued silliness in the simulations, but the older members did not. A challenge, then, might be to design simulation themes that incorporate some silly elements but still make a community-oriented or values-based point. An example might be a simulation of smoking kids in which the kids pass out or even "die," but then recover and start puffing again. The older and younger participants actually agreed that the simulations needed to avoid being heavy-handed morality lessons.

Our starting assumption was that somewhat controversial topics would generate more excitement and interest among the participants. Thus, we were encouraging of simulation themes such as the Classroom Bully, Flirting and Hurting, and the schoolyard fight. However, we observed that the cross-generational pairs all were attracted to traffic management themes – far less controversial, but a category of community interaction that might have been common ground for both the older and the younger members. This caused us to hypothesize that controversial topics might evoke too much affect and expose personal values that people might find awkward to share with partners they didn't know well, and who were far from their own age cohort. Perhaps more generic issues, such as traffic management, are just better themes for this kind of project, or perhaps they are better initial project themes – that is, better projects to bootstrap interactions among diverse community members.

Box 6.3 summarizes some design claims specifically pertaining to the CommunitySims project. One interaction scenario is the design activity of our workshops, and the other is a scenario in which community members not involved with the CommunitySims activity encountered the simulations on the website. The design consequence we were pursuing in this project was that the Sims activity could be a prop for conversations about community issues and events as well as about visual simulation programming. We hoped that such interactions might be feasible, and that they might create opportunities for mutual learning in which older people could share their knowledge and values about community issues and events with younger people, who could reciprocally share their knowledge and skill regarding information technology.

*Box 6.3*  Claims associated with CommunitySims interaction scenarios

Collaborative and cross-generational design of visual community simulations

  + could facilitate cross-generation discussions of community issues and events
  + could evoke mutual learning in which older partners share knowledge about community issues and events and younger partners share knowledge about information technology.

  − But they could be unsatisfying to the extent that the interests and values of older and younger partners are distinct and difficult to reconcile in a coordinated activity.

Encountering community simulations online (through the CommunitySims website)

  + could inspire other community members to think more about the depicted issues and events
  + could inspire other community members to think about visual simulations as a medium for personal expression
  + could inspire other community members to engage in cross-generational collaborative projects.

  − But they could mystify people who do not know what a visual simulation is, have never tried to run a visual simulation from a web browser, or who cannot see the point of the simulation activity.

The second claim pertains to an interaction scenario in which a community member who had not been part of the Sims workshops encounters the projects through the website. The various projects might inspire other community members to think more about the issues and events depicted in the simulations. More broadly, the projects could inspire people to think further about the premise of the Sims project that visual simulations could be employed as a medium for exploring and expressing interpretations of social and community issues and events. Most broadly, the projects could suggest the feasibility of cross-generational collaborative activities to leverage the different strengths of each constituency of the community in thinking about, discussing, and addressing community issues and events.

A potential downside for the claims about the Sims activity is that the collaborative activity might not be sufficiently rewarding, that the differences in knowledge, interests, and values between the old and the young might be too great to afford a meaningful collaborative activity. A downside for the second scenario, about other community members encountering the Sims website, is that such community members might not know enough or be experienced at all with visual simulations or with running visual simulations from a web browser. They might also be able to manage the mechanics of viewing the Sims projects but not appreciate the point of the projects as considerations of community issues and events.

## The fire keepers

Our experiences with Nostalgia and CommunitySims illustrate how elderly members of a community can play active leadership roles in new kinds of technology-mediated community activities, such as transforming oral history into digital forums or discussing community issues through visual simulation props. In both of these design projects, elderly citizens made critical, creative, and unique contributions to an activity that benefited all members of the broader community. In the Nostalgia project, the BEV Seniors enriched the whole community by sharing glimpses of their everyday memories. The CommunitySims project illustrates the rich give and take that can emerge when community members of different ages and with different knowledge and skill bases are offered complementary roles in a shared endeavor. Both efforts were rather small-scale design projects – Nostalgia was active for five to six years with a few thousand accesses per year, while the elders' contributions to CommunitySims took place over a two-year period. However, the community impacts were novel and affirmative, even if modest in a global perspective. These systems provided new means for the seniors to strengthen the kind of strong contribution that elderly members have always made to their communities.

Much research and other writing about the elderly and information technology tends to emphasize deficits – the special challenges older people face in learning and using new technologies (e.g., Czaja and Lee 2003). This emphasis on ameliorating deficits is of course important, and there surely is a need to help older people stay effectively connected to our rapidly evolving digital society. However, the deficits-and-challenges perspective on the elderly has the downside of validating what is in many respects an inaccurate stereotype – namely, that being elderly is a kind of disability *tout court*.

The truth of the matter is more nuanced. The elderly are a major source of volunteers for all community nonprofit groups, including many social service organizations that primarily support younger community members. Indeed, a study of webmasters for community groups found that about half of people adopting this relatively new civic role were elderly (Rosson, Ballin, and Nash 2004). These older webmasters tended to regard the role as more than merely one of tech support – for example, seeing it as a way to leverage their knowledge about the community in a new way, or as a means to directly support their broader interests in the community, such as increasing the visibility of regional art. A larger web-based survey study of people who classified themselves as "informal web developers" also revealed a significant group of older participants who were motivated relatively more by interpersonal and community goals than by technology skills development (Rosson, Ballin, and Rode 2005).

The elderly are not merely a vulnerable segment of the population that needs looking after. Indeed, as the BEV Seniors declared, the elderly are also a segment of the population that is disproportionately *looking after the rest of us*, both by organizing and staffing traditional social services as essential as food banks, low income housing, and water quality, and by filling new civic roles in society, such as serving as community webmasters. Because they take on these roles as interested volunteers, there is rarely a pre-existing support structure for them to pursue the full range of goals they bring to their group activities. Thus some of the most effective "help" that can be provided to the elderly in this context is to find ways to better empower them to achieve their community-oriented goals (Carroll, Convertino *et al.* 2011; Rosson and Carroll 2009).

Mitigating the negative aspects of growing old is valuable and worthwhile. However, from the broader standpoint of human development and activity, it is tragically self-limiting. Even a little fieldwork shows that elders have already adapted in creative and constructive ways to contemporary social realities. They have appropriated roles, including new roles with respect to management of information technology. In the design experiments described above, elders have been able rapidly to assimilate and control new roles, using information technology to create social and material goods. As a consequence, a radical rethinking of workplaces has been proposed that would more deliberately try to leverage the wisdom and the patience of older workers to the benefit of all workers (Convertino, Farooq *et al.* 2005; Convertino *et al.* 2007).

The elderly are the fire keepers of human organizations. They maintain community memory. They pass on community practices to younger members. They ensure the continuity of the community. Somewhat paradoxically, it is important to support the elderly both in the obvious sense of compensating for their weaknesses and in the perhaps less obvious sense of facilitating their leadership in groups, communities, and organizations.

# 7  Designing our town

Appropriately, most of our BEV design research projects were initiated to address needs and concerns of particular citizen groups in Blacksburg, to leverage and support the interests and initiatives of such groups that were already underway, or both. The teachers with whom we worked on the Virtual School were already collaborating, though generally with just one other teacher apiece, and were already using computers and networking in their teaching. Some were already inviting community mentors to visit their classrooms periodically to work with their students. The software we developed enabled a more ambitious and comprehensive version of what they were already doing. Similarly, the BEV Seniors were already circulating stories of Blacksburg as it was in the 1960s through their email list when we proposed to work with them on the Nostalgia site.

These projects are examples of a strong form of participatory action research (Carroll and Rosson 2007; Kindon, Pain, and Kesby 2007; Schuler and Namioka 1993). The ultimate users were involved from the start and throughout, and they exercised real power in making decisions about what to do and how to do it. This style of community network design research ineluctably contributes to community development: The very process of engaging in such projects is itself active community participation, irrespective of immediate external outcomes or the ultimate sustainability of the outcomes in community institutions.

Participatory action research is typically, perhaps necessarily, application specific. That is, it begins with and springs from real and concrete needs, concerns, interests, and initiatives of stakeholders. This is a good thing; it engages with particular lived experience in the community, ensuring the validity of the design problem, and enhancing the relevance of the design outcome. But it is also a limitation. The narrow focus on effectively addressing concrete needs, concerns, interests, and initiatives of specific stakeholders, particular individuals, and their groups and institutions entails some conservatism with respect to technology. It tends to circumscribe design palettes to existing technology infrastructures and best practices, and to investigate how those infrastructures and practices can be marshaled to needs, concerns, interests, and initiatives that have been identified. Accordingly, participatory action research is unlikely to produce design outcomes that broadly challenge established paradigms.

A contrasting design strategy is to problematize the existing paradigms and infrastructures, to rethink not only current designs but also the current palette for design, and to directly investigate new possibilities for infrastructures and practices. This approach, perhaps necessarily, takes a broader and shallower view of particular contexts – that is, of the concrete needs, concerns, interests, and initiatives of stakeholders. It addresses classes or categories of design problems rather than particular instances.

This distinction is useful, but it is more nuanced than a simple matter of black and white. Our Nostalgia project was participatory design. The stakeholders, in this case the BEV Seniors, originated and "owned" the design problem; the initiative was theirs. The design activity involved all of us thinking about how the current web technology could be effectively applied to realize their specific vision. In the end, the project wound up slightly pushing the paradigm for web forums by supporting user-contributed photographs, but fundamentally the project was not about questioning and enhancing the Web or web forums as an infrastructure. It was about realizing a particular design vision of how to apply the then emerging paradigm of web forums to a community-centered purpose.

The design research project we consider in this chapter, MOOsburg, was an effort to rethink computing infrastructures for community networks in a broader manner. It specifically questioned the second-generation web paradigm of community networking that had been inaugurated by the BEV. MOOsburg was an extended investigation of three key paradigmatic challenges and possibilities for community networks.

The first issue is the dominance of the publication/browsing paradigm for interaction and the possibility of offering richer interaction experiences to users. As remarked in chapter 2, it was ironic that web-based second-generation community networks typically afforded *less* interaction for their users than the first-generation community networks. Community discussion was the centerpiece of first-generation systems like the Berkeley Community Memory and the Cleveland Free-Net. The centerpiece of the early BEV was a set of flat HTML pages that could only be browsed by users; the listservs, newsgroups, and email lists that were the social core of the BEV were relegated to the background. Easy access to rich information sources is important, and providing access to community information is without question a central function for community networks. But providing access to other community members is desirable. Indeed, referring to the distinction we investigated in chapter 4, merely being aware and informed of community activity is a passive form of community participation, important but distinguishable from active participation such as engaging in public discussion and working on community initiatives. One design goal of MOOsburg was to explore technological approaches to enhancing *interaction* in community networks.

The second issue is the dominance of information hierarchies and the possibility of other approaches to organizing information (and interaction) in a community network. Digital data are often organized hierarchically in file systems. For example, a folder for "BEV" documents might include an HTML document for the "BEV homepage" as well as folders for document categories such as "Neighborhoods," "Government," "Village Mall," and so forth. Each of these folders would contain specific kinds of documents and perhaps, further, more specific folders. The underlying structure of all community networks in the first and second generation is like this – as an information hierarchy. Hierarchies are a simple and general rubric for organizing information. However, it is also desirable to organize information in a way that specifically suits that information. Community networks are distinctively about specific places and physical locales. Thus, community information might be presented *spatially instead of hierarchically*: For example, the school is *next to* the town hall, the senior center is *down the street from* the Presbyterian church, and so forth. A second design goal of MOOsburg was to explore technological approaches to presenting community networks to their users as *places*.

The third issue is the dominance of individual interactions and experiences in how we think about community networks and the possibility of helping individual users to be more aware of the larger context and dynamics of what is going on within the community and the community network. People throughout the community have a current status; they are somewhere in the community, doing something, often with others involved. Beyond that, they are formulating plans, pursuing goals, and making sense of what they have been doing and what they have experienced. They are persistently connected to community organizations and places and to other community members through a wide array of affiliations, ongoing activities, and other relationships. When community members act, they are acting within this expansive network of activities and entities, including other actors; their actions have meaning and effect within this larger social context. A third design goal of MOOsburg was to explore technological approaches to enhancing *awareness* of community activity.

Our vision for MOOsburg was of better-integrated second-generation community networks, networks that provide a more coherent and meaningful experience of the community and its activity, and that directly afford and support community action and social interaction. The MOOsburg design research project cross-cuts the projects described in previous chapters, and in a few cases it spawned more focused projects, which we undertook as a reality check on our developing ideas about community computing infrastructures. We never imagined that MOOsburg would emerge directly as a comprehensive infrastructure solution, and we certainly never intended it to be seen as an alternative to the BEV. Rather, we framed it as an open-ended test-bed project, an infrastructure design research project within the context of the BEV (Carroll and Isenhour 2011; Carroll, Rosson, Isenhour, Ganoe *et al.* 2001; Carroll, Rosson, Isenhour, Van Metre *et al.* 2001).

## MOOsburg

In the fall of 1995, I led a graduate seminar on the topic of community in the Internet. Eventually, the seminar came to focus on the tradeoffs between publication and interaction. The director of Virginia Tech's BEV group visited the seminar and explained that making the BEV more interactive would require too much bandwidth. This was an energizing thing to say to a roomful of computer science graduate students! They immediately tried to prove him wrong. Some of the students experimented with early web-based virtual communities like AlphaWorld (1995). Others implemented a traditional text-based MOO (Multi-user domain, Object-Oriented; Curtis 1992), modeling the geography of downtown Blacksburg and the Virginia Tech campus, called MOOsburg (Kies *et al.* 1996). Within a few weeks, these interactive community network prototypes were available to members of the BEV community. Later that year, the BEV group itself reconsidered their initial position and created a BEV Chat service.

MUDs (Multi-User Domains) and MOOs offer an interesting combination of synchronous and asynchronous communication mechanisms. Users in a MOO can chat with one another, but the database that underlies it is persistent: users can create, modify, and manipulate objects, changing the state of the MOO for subsequent users. For example, users can leave messages posted on bulletin board objects; the messages remain until they are deleted. MOOs are fundamentally spatial – their content is organized into "rooms," and users navigate the information structure with directional commands (for example, "go north"). This evokes an experience of spatial immersion and co-presence with other participants (Benford *et al.* 1996). These environments are most often used for fantasy-oriented entertainment and informal social activity (Cherny 1995; Curtis 1992), but they have also been used for professional meetings (Bruckman and Resnick 1995; Glusman *et al.* 1999), as learning environments (Bruckman 1998; Haynes and Holmevik 1998), and as general navigation tools (Dieberger 1996). Our MOOsburg project investigated the creation and use of a MOO in the context of community and home activities.

Figure 7.1 is a very early screen shot from MOOsburg. This is the default "place" where users entered the system. The place has a name, Squires Information Desk, and there is a short description associated with it, meant to help people imagine the place. Objects are mentioned that the user can operate. For example, the information panel provides direct links to some important destinations in the system, such as the town hall, the pamphlet can be read to get user orientation information about the system, and one can pick up the penny and play the slot machine (and lose). There are also two footballs here; these are examples of user-created objects. They can be picked up and carried away to other places in MOOsburg. Users can move directly from Squires Information Desk to three other locations using "obvious exits": Front Steps, Off-Campus Housing Room, and Squires Game Room.

MOO commands are simple. To move to an adjacent room, one types the direction – in this case "south," "northwest" or "north." One can display the pamphlet by typing "look pamphlet" or "look at pamphlet." At this point in the interaction, visitors had already given informed consent to be part of the MOOsburg experiment, but they could always review what they had consented to by typing "help consent." Part of the fun in a MOO is to see which commands do what. Thus, the user can "take" the football, but not the slot machine or the trash can, and one can only "play" the slot machine if one is holding the penny. One can "go" south, northwest, or north, but not east, northeast, or west. And so on.

MOOsburg directly associated information about places in Blacksburg with isomorphic locations in the MOO. We were inspired by contemporaneous projects such as Jupiter (Curtis and Nichols 1994) and MediaMOO (Bruckman and Resnick 1995), and by proposals and analyses suggested by Dieberger and Frank (1998), Erickson (1993), and Harrison and Dourish (1996). We wanted to evoke and leverage the local knowledge, place-specific interactions, and emotional identification that residents of Blacksburg have for their town. For example, people rendezvous at Squires Information Desk (Figure 7.1) to go out for lunch. They know that very different kinds of information and conversation are available at the Library, at Town Hall, and at Bolo's Café, even though the three are just a few blocks apart. And so forth.

If other people are in the same MOO room, one can type messages to them, as in a chat. But one can do more than in a chat: One can manipulate and discuss the objects in the MOO room with a partner or create additional objects to be manipulated and discussed. Early MOOsburg users started up many activities that attracted the cooperation and participation of others, inspiring further initiatives. For example, members of the Science Fiction and Fantasy Club had a regular

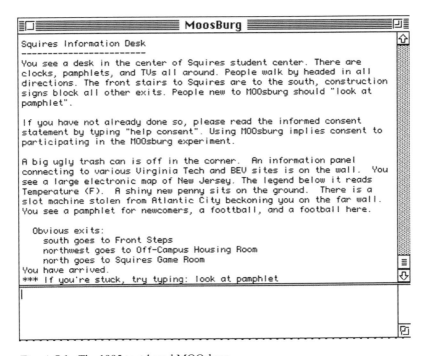

*Figure 7.1*   The 1995 text-based MOOsburg.

meeting in a MOOsburg pub. Residents of several Blacksburg neighborhoods built their own homes in the MOO – so much so that a community steering committee was formed to manage MOOsburg real estate.

Several teachers became interested in MOOs. They appreciated the austerity of the text-only interface and its encouragement of writing and imagination. The public library worked with us on a book review forum. They were also interested in developing a collaborative story-writing tool for the children's reading room in their MOO site. Users created novel objects and behaviors, such as a Cowbot that roamed the MOO, lowing at people, and a self-serve souvlaki machine for the local Greek restaurant. As we had experienced in the Nostalgia project, members of the Blacksburg diaspora from as far away as Australia participated in MOOsburg.

MOO software dates from the late 1970s (Bartle 2003) and was standardized by the early 1990s (Curtis 1992; Curtis and Nichols 1994). The MOOsburg project began at a time when MOOs were being integrated with web browsers. By 1996 we were using a web-accessible, Java applet-based interface to MOOsburg. Though it still used text-based input and output for all interaction, the applet was generally more accessible than a standalone MOO client. It also provided the opportunity for minimal forms of linking to web-based content outside of the MOO. A student project took advantage of this opportunity and added a clickable image-based map to the web interface. This represented a significant usability improvement, as novice users could simply click on map locations rather than type navigation commands. We also integrated MOOsburg with other tools. For example, the town of Blacksburg approached us about running their bi-monthly forum using MOOsburg instead of a chat. They were particularly interested in the MOO slide projector object, which they saw as a convenient display for maps and plans under discussion by committees and residents. The MOO allowed users to chat about something they all could see.

Early work on the MOOsburg client focused on adapting Web and Java components to hide as much of the text-based interface as possible. These components attempted to split the incoming stream of text into separate graphical representations of location, co-located users, and chat conversation content. These were then presented in separate frames in a web page. Similarly, buttons and menus provided shortcuts for common navigation commands. This effort succeeded in providing a web-based, graphical interface to the MOO that was more accessible to the novice user than a traditional MOO interface. An early example is shown in Figure 7.2. At the bottom of the frame is the MOO's underlying text stream. The location has a text description in its web presentation but a slightly different version in the MOO description. Direct exits from this location are rendered as web links in the main panel, and also indicated in a compass widget in the left border. At the top center of the main panel is a weather widget with a Java script for getting the current temperature.

The development of effective content for MOOsburg required significant and ongoing input from community members. As was true in all of our design projects, we did not have people and resources enough to design and implement a

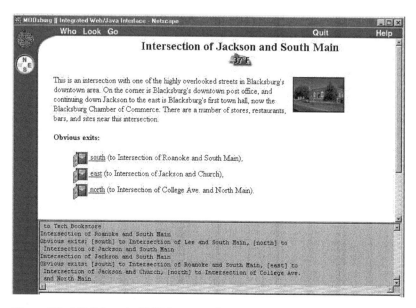

*Figure 7.2*   MOOsburg in 1997, incorporating Web and Java components.

MOOsburg location for every community group wanting to participate. Our strategy was to populate a few key locations as examples and to scaffold a distributed development effort. Ultimately, as is true with any community network infrastructure, local groups must be able to take control, in this case to create and manage their own specialized MOOsburg locations and objects. This led us to focus specifically on enabling end-user programming and design (Lieberman, Paterno, and Wulf 2006). For example, in courses at Virginia Tech during the spring of 1999, students experimented with a number of MOOsburg extensions, including a virtual science fair, an online auction, an event publicity system, a project collaboration room, a rental office and online fair, a sign-up calendar for sports and games, and a collaborative storybook editor for children. Each student team worked closely with community members in designing their online activities. For example, the storybook team began by meeting with children and observing them working together on paper-based story-writing activities; the rental office project team visited and gathered interviews at an actual housing fair; and the science fair team talked to teachers, students, and community members about their science fair activities.

Through our early experiments with MOOsburg we learned some important lessons. First, we did see that providing a platform for community interaction could be very positive. More than this, we were encouraged that users could make relatively permanent contributions – that they could be designers of their own community space. We observed that interaction in BEV Chat tended to be brief and superficial, perhaps due to the fact that the chat itself was ephemeral: Contributions persisted only until the chat session ended, usually just a few minutes. In MOOsburg, visitors could make permanent contributions, such as the Cowbot and the children's stories. We were excited by the possibility of an advanced community network infrastructure in which participants could appropriate the roles of author and developer.

We also concluded that the spatial community model seemed to work well. Hierarchical information spaces, like websites, ineluctably emphasize categorical membership and obscure other relationships. Thus, all schools are part of the school system, and all community non-profits are part of another category. A conceptual information hierarchy implicitly suppresses spatial relations, such as the fact that the Seniors Center is across the street from the High School, which shops are adjacent to one another on Main Street, or which dry cleaner is easy to make a stop at when you are traveling between your home and the grocery store. Yet such place-based relationships are constitutive of everyday community knowledge and activity. We found that it was easy to evoke the knowledge and emotion about places in the physical community, even with our text-only interface. It seemed that users appreciated this, and that place could indeed be an effective rubric for community network information and interaction.

Knowing where the library, the middle school, and the dry cleaners were in Blacksburg directly oriented a user to MOOsburg. People rather quickly engaged their social and geographical knowledge and appropriated MOOsburg for their own purposes. However, there were also problems with the MOO place model. The underlying data model for a MOO is not very constrained. A MOO is a directed graph of rooms; a room's position in the graph is determined solely by the rooms to which it is *adjacent* – that is, the set of rooms to which or from which one can move directly. There are no further constraints, which makes geospatial nonsense a routine MOO experience. For example, I can place my house next to yours, even if you already have neighbors, just by linking my room in the MOO directly to yours. There is no underlying coordinate system like latitude and longitude; a user can "go east" and then "go north," and end up in a different location than if they first "go north" and then "go east." This sort of thing can be great fun if one is playing in a MOO, but it undermines the objective of felicitously modeling the community as a place. We saw evidence of both fun and puzzlement.

We also saw that, for many users, the fact that most of their computer interactions were with graphical user interfaces and web browsers made the MOO seem a quaint, austere, even arcane user experience. We concluded that this would eventually be a significant obstacle to broad acceptance of a community MOO. Our system could display a message that you had arrived at the public library, but, except for the words "public library" and the text of the location description, it seemed just the same to arrive at the Greek restaurant, or anywhere else. As mentioned above, one approach we took to this was to employ a web-accessible, Java applet-based interface to MOOsburg. This allowed us, for example, to add a clickable image-based map to the web interface and permit users to navigate directly through the map rather than through MOO commands. Such piecemeal enhancements ultimately served to bring the fundamental problems with the MOO's spatial model into sharper focus. Thus, the map component could not resolve conflicts in the underlying MOO model, and it had to be updated separately from (and could therefore easily get out of sync with) the MOO database. Because of the loose coupling between the map component and the underlying MOO data, the map component could not integrate or visualize information about user activity occurring throughout the MOO. Thus, we were not able to support awareness for users.

## MOOsburg 2

We had initially viewed the availability of widely used MOO infrastructure as an advantage that would allow us to concentrate our efforts on supporting application development. However, our experiences with the text-based MOOsburg, or what we later thought of as MOOsburg 1, especially with respect to adapting graphical and interactive components to coordinate with the legacy MOO infrastructure, led us to create our own software platform. This rethinking and redesign coincided with a consolidation of our Virtual School software (chapter 5). Before 1999, the two projects had proceeded in parallel, but from this point forward they leveraged a common underlying software infrastructure that we named CORK (Content Object Replication Kit; Isenhour *et al.* 2001).

CORK synchronized clients through object replication – that is, changes made to any object, location, or bit of text in any client view of the MOO were "pushed" to the server and to every other client through lightweight change messages. As illustrated in Figure 7.3, a user interaction, such as annotating a map, in a given client is pushed to the server and to the other clients though a change message. This keeps all copies closely synchronized and minimizes the amount of data that must be transferred to describe the consequences of user interactions.

This approach to supporting collaborative interaction is entirely different from that of MOOs. The state of a MOO is maintained in a single database that resides on a server. Users interact directly with that underlying database through MOO commands that change the state of the database, and these changes are reflected in changes to what is displayed in the user's session. This approach is elegant for small amounts of data transfer, which is indeed the case for traditional text-only MOOs. Problems arise when MOOs are extended to coordinate with graphical and interactive user interface widgets that reside in the user's client, such as the map widget and slide projector we developed. As user interfaces become more graphical and more interactive, the state of the server's database must be updated more often, and the updates involve transferring much more data to and from the user sessions or clients. This makes system performance sluggish and also causes complications for the software, such as the manual coordination we had to orchestrate to synchronize the map component and the MOO database.

Our new MOOsburg client allowed us to incorporate Java user interface components to provide a more dynamic user experience. Since we were freed from

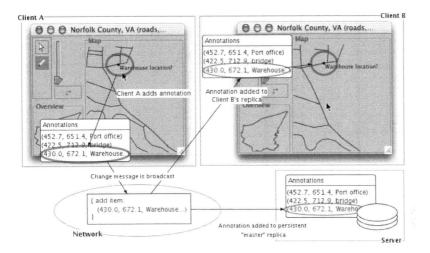

*Figure 7.3* Content Object Replication Kit (CORK) synchronizes clients during a collaborative interaction.

the limitation of client–server data exchange through a single input/output text stream, distinct user interface components could be provided for interacting with different types of objects in MOOsburg – for example, maps, whiteboards, shared notebooks, planners, and shared files. Changes made to any object are visible in real time to others currently viewing or editing the object, and are preserved for users who access the object at a later time. Since both client and server were written in Java, both were compatible with a wide range of platforms and operating systems, including Windows, MacOS, Linux and Unix, making MOOsburg accessible to most potential users. CORK also allowed a more flexible authentication scheme, checking user identifiers and passwords.

In MOOsburg 2, the navigational map component directly accessed and coordinated with the underlying MOO database, allowing dynamic interaction and awareness features. For example, the map views of a particular building could indicate visually MOO locations with many objects, many users, locations visited most often, and so forth. Where in MOOsburg 1 users could be aware of who was doing what at a particular location only by being there, in MOOsburg 2 we were able to provide awareness of what was going on throughout the community system (see Schafer, Bowman, and Carroll 2002).

We discarded the MOO's directed graph model of space. In our new model, locations had fixed Cartesian coordinates. This approach allowed us to use detailed vector maps of Blacksburg to depict MOOsburg. Vector maps allow smooth zooming, panning, and other visual transformations, as well as selectively hiding and showing various layers of map detail (e.g., topography, roads and buildings, etc.). This was a big step beyond the map widget of MOOsburg 1, which was just a flat map image with fixed regions defined to be link anchors. The new map was a powerful interactive element that could display many layout views of Blacksburg (Schafer, Bowman, and Carroll 2002).

In MOOburg 2, locations were presented graphically. Each location consisted of a signature view, as well as a place-based chat and other collaborative tools and objects left by the creator of and previous visitors to that location. The graphical view associated with a location was often a panoramic photograph, allowing the user to "look around" the location (as in Figure 7.4). We also used two-dimensional photographs of the corresponding place in Blacksburg (e.g., Figure 7.2), diagrams sketched using whiteboard tools, or other signature graphics. In addition, the view displayed avatars for users who were at that location and icons for objects in use at that location.

Figure 7.4 shows the Corner of College and Main, a major intersection in Blacksburg. The widget in the upper left of the photograph allows the user to pan 360 degrees to view the location from any angle; this was an early application of what are now often called street views. The map widget in the lower right shows a buildings and roads level view of Blacksburg. The larger dot (which appears as green on the screen) indicates where the user currently is, and the smaller dots

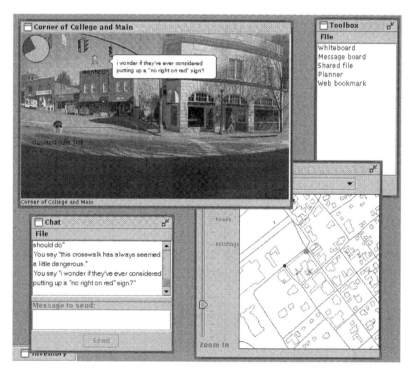

*Figure 7.4*   MOOsburg 2 organized locations in a coordinate space that was navigated by pointing in an interactive map.

(blue) indicate other locations; color was used to code level of activity at locations. The user could click on a blue dot to move instantly to another location. The map could be scrolled and zoomed – the figure shows the zooming control; it is just possible to see the labels for the zoom levels where roads appear and where buildings appear.

Figure 7.4 shows the place-specific chat tool. Chat content in MOOsburg 2 was persistent, as in MOOsburg 1. At this stage in the project we were experimenting with chat bubbles for depicting conversation. The figure shows the user's most recent chat contribution both in a list view, on the lower left, and in a chat bubble overlaying the panorama. Also overlaying the panorama is another user's avatar (shown on the screen as a greenish face wearing a purple beret). The other user has been idle for one minute, presumably why there has been no response to the user's statements about traffic safety. On the upper right is the Toolbox of objects that could be added to the location, in this case containing a whiteboard, a message board, a shared file, a planner, and a web bookmark. Anyone at this location can manipulate these tools. A menu of actions for any object can be accessed by clicking on the object's name in the Toolbox or an icon in the location view. MOOsburg 2's content objects included formatted text editors and drawing tools that were not only interactive but also collaborative. They allowed roughly the same kind of expressiveness as web content of the day (circa 2000), with the added benefit of being collaboratively editable. Users engaged in a discussion could translate their ideas immediately into published content.

Users enter MOOsburg by navigating their web browser to the MOOsburg page and typing in their user identifier and password. After login, the MOOsburg client window opens and displays a graphical view of the current location, as in Figure 7.4. For public users, we have implemented a self-service, email-based account maintenance system for obtaining user IDs and resetting passwords.

Our design allowed locations to contain subspaces as an approach to managing the distinction between locations like the Corner of College and Main, which may be important but are nonetheless simple in their structure, and locations like the library, the middle school, and the town hall, each of which contain other locations. Thus, one might go to the location of the library (by pointing in the Blacksburg map), but, once there, one could also *enter* the library's subspace, at which point one would see the floor plan of the library as the current map. Location creators could construct multiple floors within a building, each with its own floor plan map and content locations.

This model is obviously a compromise: Cartesian coordinates of latitude and longitude render geographical space in a familiar and constrained manner. But they do not capture the architectural containment relationship between a building and its rooms and other spaces, and they break down entirely for multi-story buildings, in which distinct places often have identical latitude and longitude. Nevertheless, our hybrid model of place resolves two of the key limitations of traditional MOOs, including MOOsburg 1: Directed graphs are too weak to model physical geography in general, and they have no way of representing complex spatial structures like buildings.

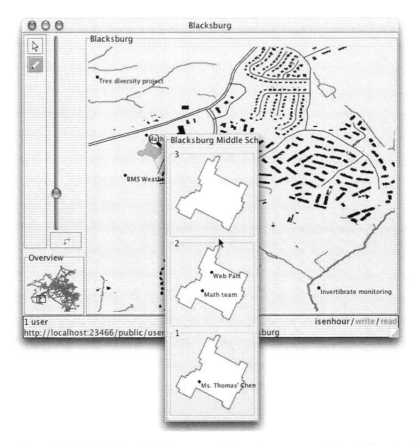

*Figure 7.5*  Detail of the Blacksburg map with a subspace map of the middle school.

Figure 7.5 shows a refined iteration of the locations and subspaces approach. In this image, the floor plan of the local middle school has been opened from the Blacksburg map. The school is a three-story building. Several locations have been mapped in this particular subspace (the Web Pals project and the Math Team activity).

Participants could create new locations within MOOsburg, or within any subspace, by pointing and clicking in the map. By default, newly created locations contain a text chat object, as well as a toolbox that allows users to instantiate other generally useful objects. For example, a user creating a location for the scene of a story from Nostalgia could include a web bookmark to the story and its annotations in the Nostalgia forum. Users could populate a new location with new objects, or with objects brought from elsewhere in MOOsburg. For example, a user might add a new library room to the library building and put notebooks within it.

More advanced users could implement new types of objects. For example, a book object might be created to present online reference materials. Standalone versions of some simulations created in the CommunitySims project (chapter 6) were placed at locations corresponding to the community issues – for example, at the dangerous traffic intersection. People having a conversation about traffic safety at a particular intersection, as in Figure 7.4, are perfect candidates to view the simulations. The mechanism for building and deploying user-defined MOO objects is similar to creating Java applets: Developers implement a new kind of MOO object in Java and put the compiled object code on the Web. They then create and configure a *machine* object within MOOsburg that describes the new kind of object; this connects their code to the MOO so that instances of the new kind of object can be created in MOOsburg. When other MOO users create or use an instance of this object type in MOOsburg, the code that defines the object's behavior is automatically downloaded as needed. We have also implemented a developer's kit containing libraries and utilities for quickly building, refining, and testing MOOsburg objects outside of the MOO.

MOOsburg seamlessly integrated synchronous and asynchronous interactions. Thus, a user could immediately see the effects of other users' actions at a location in real time, but could also see the preserved effects of past actions. Chat interactions were of course synchronous, but permanent chat logs were associated with every chat and could be revisited, for example, by collaborators who missed a meeting or discussion and needed to catch up. In this respect, we expanded the notion of awareness support beyond mere awareness of ongoing activity to awareness of activity extending through time and perhaps space.

## Experiences with place-based community interaction

New technologies, especially those that are infrastructural, are only revealed as they are used and extended. MOOsburg 2 enabled a variety of interesting applications that helped us identify new ways to utilize and support place-based information, interaction, and awareness, as well as new design challenges for achieving this. Each application project raised new issues and led to new features and tools in MOOsburg. Some of these were quite general. The machine concept emerged from the need for a mechanism to allow independent groups throughout the community to contribute new objects and to be able to integrate their code into the overall system. Each project also promoted the development of user documentation, including a basic "how-to-extend" example (a sign object that simply displays a text message).

Many extensions suggested through application projects were relatively specific to particular contexts. The project collaboration room demonstrated how to use a MOOsburg object to access useful external services (e.g., a hierarchical file browser), as well as how a pre-existing MOOsburg object (the shared whiteboard) could be specialized to create a new kind of object that is better suited to a room's needs (a multi-page "easel"). The storybook project raised customization and integration issues that are likely to arise for many user-developed extensions: The children working together on the stories needed a persistent communication channel. The team decided to include a chat tool specific to each storybook, while recognizing that, in the long run, the children might be confused by having two chat options (i.e., the story-specific chat and the standard MOOsburg chat).

One concrete and very useful product from the demonstration projects was a set of Java objects that can now be recruited by other MOOsburg end users. Among these were a science simulation, a storybook, a calendar, the easel, a question–answer board, a bid processor, and an event reminder. Current student projects are exploring the reuse and/or specialization of these objects, as well as building additional extensions. All of the demonstration projects combined HTML screen and graphics development with the programming of one or more Java classes (thus defining new objects for the MOO). The Java programming was a relatively ambitious level of user extension, but an important one to support early in MOOsburg development, when the number and variety of interactive objects and services was small. Clearly we do not expect that the average community member will be able to write Java classes in creating their own content. However, they may well be able to specify simple extensions to such classes using more high-level languages.

One project that allowed us to bring together the Virtual School and MOOsburg quite broadly was the Virtual Science Fair, a collaboration with Montgomery County Public Schools. Like the physical display of school science projects arrayed on tables in the gymnasium or cafeteria, projects in the Virtual Science Fair were accessed from the high-school gym. However, parents and community members could view the projects, learn about them, and discuss them at any time and from anywhere (see Carroll, Rosson, Isenhour, Ganoe *et al.* 2001).

Figure 7.6 shows a screenshot from the Virtual Science Fair. We located the fair in the gymnasium of Blacksburg High School. On the panorama for the gym are icons for a user named Isenhour, a projector tool, a comment board, a Venturi simulation science project, and another project on the effects of light on plan growth. The Diamonds science project web page has been opened in front of the MOOsburg window.

The panorama images we employed as signature views for many locations proved to be quite popular. People liked them especially for open locations, such as the outdoor amphitheater or downtown intersections – for example, the Corner of College and Main in Figure 7.4. One apartment complex created a fairly extensive virtual tour of their facilities; in modeling their subspace, they included panorama views for every room in several apartments, plus views from balconies and a few from outside the buildings. The Virginia Museum of Natural History employed panoramas for representing large exhibit rooms within their subspace, as illustrated in Figure 7.7.

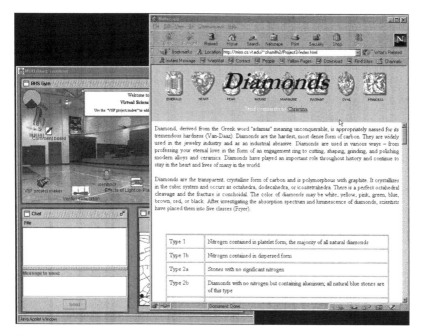

*Figure 7.6*    A Virtual Science Fair project web page opened from within MOOsburg.

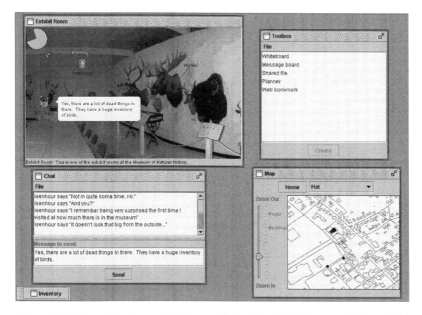

*Figure 7.7*    One of the large exhibit rooms in the Virginia Museum of Natural History.

In the museum project, our partners were interested in using MOOsburg activities as an enhancement to activities in the physical museum. They did not want to create virtual museum experience separate from the physical museum. This led us to devise a specimen database that could be carried around; specimen instances and invitations to join interest-based groups could be deposited in locations throughout MOOsburg, where they would be incidentally encountered, reminding people of the museum and of particular specimens in the museum, and perhaps inducing them to interact with others about the museum or about that specimen. Thus, instead of a virtual museum duplicating the physical museum and an online database accessible at one Internet address, the museum created a distributed presence in MOOsburg, pervasively engaging people about the region's natural history.

Distributed activities raised the challenges of composing and coordinating tools and resources *across* locations in MOOsburg. For example, one might want to take an action whenever a museum specimen was opened. The obvious, albeit tedious, way to do this would be to observe activity at the location of the specimen. We developed the concept of avatar proxies, simple scripted agents, that could be dispatched to wait in specified locations or search for specified objects or users in order to carry out tasks that could not be executed from a single location (Farooq *et al.* 2003). Thus, to continue the example, an avatar proxy could be posted along with a museum specimen to invite whoever opened the specimen to join the specimen discussion group. Admittedly this was a somewhat exotic extension; the concept of software agents was still quite novel in the early 2000s. Programming the agents was supported by a forms interface, but was still an unfamiliar task.

For several years, we worked with the Save Our Streams group in Blacksburg. One of the group's ongoing projects was monitoring water quality and other characteristics of Stroubles Creek, a distressed stream that runs through the center of Blacksburg and the Virginia Tech campus through a variety of underground storm drains, crawl spaces, and pipes, resurfacing at the western edge of the campus. In this project, results are gathered at various points along the stream. We created a place-based discussion forum tool for the group, integrating a forum discussion with the MOOsburg map. Contributions to the forum could be geo-tagged by clicking on a map location – in this case a location along Stroubles Creek – indicating to what place the forum post pertained (Figure 7.8; see Schafer 2004). This tool allowed them to associate stream quality data directly with specific locations. (Another approach, one we did not implement, would have been to deploy avatar proxies to the various stream monitoring sites to report on data and discussions from each separate site.)

The possibility of, and the need for, distributed places was a further interesting elaboration of MOOsburg's concept of place. As mentioned earlier, we elaborated the latitude/longitude coordinate model of geography to incorporate subspaces so that we could both describe buildings and other complex locations as integrated places and articulate their substructures. The Natural History Museum and Save Our Streams had locations in the town, and thus in

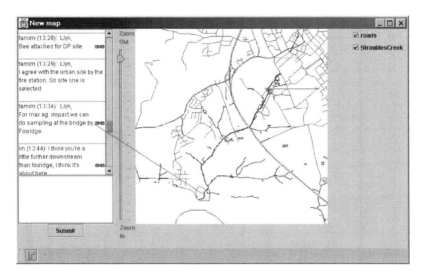

*Figure 7.8*   Place-based chat about Stroubles Creek water quality.

MOOsburg, but their activity was distributed throughout the community space. These groups identified with their locations, but they did not want their influence to be limited to a single place. They wanted tools that could be used throughout MOOsburg in order to facilitate interaction and awareness among the wider community. This concept significantly challenged even our elaborated model of place, but we were able to support it with the map-based forum, virtual specimens and specimen discussion groups, avatar proxies, and other specialized tools to allow the community to explore the possibilities of extending the spatial metaphor of a virtual town through activities that leverage space in ways not available in the physical world.

The various application projects on which we collaborated helped to develop a strong example of place-based community information, interaction, and awareness. Indeed, creating a place-based alternative to hierarchical web information and a collaborative alternative to static community websites seemed to make it possible for us to observe awareness interests and concerns that could never even arise in more primitive community systems. For example, presenting the science fair as an activity, as opposed to a collection of static web pages, would not have been possible in the BEV. Similarly, the interests of the museum in distributing specimens throughout the community system, and thereby raising awareness of the museum and its collection and programs, would not have been a possible ambition in the BEV itself.

A community network of static web pages allows community members to be aware of the structure of the community – for example, of the fact that there is a local Save Our Streams group. People can read the group's description and perhaps see who belongs to it, and, if the web page has been updated recently, view reports of the group's activity. This level of community awareness is important; it corresponds to what we called informedness in chapter 3. There we associated informedness with a somewhat passive level of participation. A community system like MOOsburg takes informedness to an entirely different level. Community members could see activities as they transpired, view results of activities immediately as the results were obtained, and indeed interact with the results and with those gathering and reporting them.

But there were also fundamental issues that remained troublesome throughout the MOOsburg project. One was mere access. Text-based MOOs and static web pages are limited, but they were easy for people to access from home computers, even if they were depending upon telephone modem connections to the Internet. We struggled with bandwidth problems in the Virtual School project, where we automatically published all documents to the Web so that the teachers and students could access materials from home without having to download or run our rather substantial client software. We investigated a prototype we named MOOsburg-lite, a web-based client for MOOsburg 2 that would allow users with restricted bandwidth to do more than merely browse webified versions of CORK objects. This was a convoluted undertaking. One of the key areas of difficulty was rendering MOOsburg's interactive map in both a transactional http form and a fully interactive Java form. We made some progress, but maintaining a dual-client development strategy was more costly than we could bear as a small university group.

Another problem was that some of our partners seemed to remain confused about the very concept of MOOsburg. As usual, the BEV Seniors had been among our first partners in the MOOsburg project. Some of them saw it as a natural extension of the Nostalgia project, and they constructed their own meeting facility in MOOsburg. Nevertheless, even several years later, we encountered one member whose eyes seemed to glaze over at talk about "going to" a place in town by clicking on an interactive map: "Why would I ever want to do this when I can walk there?" The concept seemed paradoxical in a way that talk of "going to" a URL in a web browser was not. One possibility is that the vividness of panoramic depictions evoking real places backfired by creating a conceptual hall of mirrors effect, as suggested by Figure 7.9.

Our applications of the MOOsburg infrastructure produced a range of proof-of-concept and usability outcomes. We saw that residents of Blacksburg were able to envision and, in some cases, design and implement new kinds of collaborative interactions that exploited our strongly place-based community infrastructure. We developed and refined a set of general object prototypes for collaborative authoring, annotation, and discussion, and we demonstrated new ways to integrate community web resources with collaborative tools that provide additional and valuable collaborative functions beyond those of standard web

*Figure 7.9*  A vivid depiction of the physical town may create a conceptual hall of
mirrors.

pages. Our neighbors were able to creatively appropriate MOOsburg, as they had
the BEV itself.

Box 7.1 presents a summary of design rationale for MOOsburg (see also
Carroll and Rosson 2003). The first claim analyzes scenarios in which community members carry out activities like information-gathering and collaborative
interaction in a place-based community system. It emphasizes the desirable consequences of evoking and leveraging knowledge residents have about community
geography, institutions, heritage, and identity, and of introducing community
members to a richer community system experience building upon collaborative
virtual environment technologies. The design rationale also emphasizes potential
downsides, such as interacting with more sophisticated user interfaces and functionalities to engage in community network activities.

*Box 7.1*  Claims associated with MOOsburg

Place-based information-gathering and collaborative interaction in a community network

+ leverages knowledge that community members already have about where things are in the physical community, allowing that knowledge to generalize to the community system
+ pervasively reminds its users of the physical community as they interact with the online system, possibly strengthening community identity
+ may strengthen bond relationships between community members and the local shops, services, organizations, and other places that are modeled in the community system
+ can employ advanced graphical user interface techniques such as direct pointing in an interactive map surface or street view depictions of community places, making the community network a richer media experience
+ familiarizes community members with advanced collaborative environments, suggesting technology learning possibilities to them.

− But some community concerns or interests may not have an obvious or singular spatial location.
− But navigating and interacting in such a community system may be more difficult than using a simple website and, in any case, may be a new skill for many people.
− But navigating to and interacting in non-adjacent locations in the community system requires navigation shortcuts or would entail inconvenient "virtual" walking around.
− But being an active participant, such as authoring a new place, may be more technically difficult than creating and linking a new web page.

An integrated collaborative software environment as an infrastructure for a community system

+ allows comprehensive awareness support to inform users of who is doing what throughout the community network
+ helps to keep the community network design visually consistent and predictable for users, which could make it more attractive and more usable.

− But awareness of who is currently active in the community system may end up conveying that activity is quite low and raising concerns about critical mass.
− But it is less flexible to extend and more difficult to manage than a loosely integrated network of web pages.
− But it requires more extensive and highly skilled maintenance than does a simple website.

The second claim in Box 7.1 analyzes consequences of an integrated collaborative software environment as an infrastructure for a community system. It emphasizes the desirable consequences that such an approach makes it possible to support awareness, since there is an integrated system keeping track of events, and that it promotes a more consistent overall design. It also analyzes potential downsides, such as the greater technical complexity of maintaining and extending a collaborative virtual environment.

## Moving from MOOsburg

The MOOsburg project showed that place is indeed a general and powerful rubric for community information and interaction. But it also showed that place is not simple, certainly not as simple as the traditional MOO model, and still quite challenging even for MOOsburg. One thread of the MOOsburg project was a steady elaboration of the map functionality, but where should that stop? From an engineering standpoint, it is a question whether the benefits of the sophisticated MOOsburg map and its associated tools outweigh the costs of maintaining the integrated software system behind the map. Another way to structure a design investigation of place-based community systems is to ask how much benefit can be produced by very modest map technologies. For example, fairly crude community-level maps are employed in web-based systems – for example, the "nyc bloggers" site (www.nycbloggers.com/). This site uses the familiar New York subway map to provide a spatial index into blog content being generated in the city. Maps such as these are an engaging way to *discover* new blogs originating in one's neighborhood, though perhaps tedious as a primary interface to a collection of blogs one reads regularly. Jones *et al.* (2004) carried out a design space analysis for place-based community systems.

A more fundamental issue is that place as a singular organizing rubric might have inherent downsides – for example, in evoking a conceptual hall of mirrors effect. This issue converges with the observation that community information is not *only* place based, it also refers to the members of a community – that is, it is *person* based; it refers to the significant activities and projects of the community – it is *event* based; and it refers to the history and future of the community – it is *time* based. In other words, it is notable that community information and activity is often organized under concrete rubrics, and leveraging these in the design of a community system could be salutary. But place is not the only such rubric. Thus, the same content object might be viewed as a social network of people who have interacted with it, an affinity graph of other community objects to which it is related, and a timeline of events in which it played a role, as well as its location in a community map (see Carroll, Rosson, Dunlap, and Isenhour 2005). Perhaps the key point is that *multiple* concrete views of objects should be available, and the user should be able to choose one or more that suit a current task or interest (Convertino, Ganoe *et al.* 2005).

Figure 7.10 shows an example, depicting multiple views of a text document: as versions and deadlines in a timeline (top pane), as connected to other content

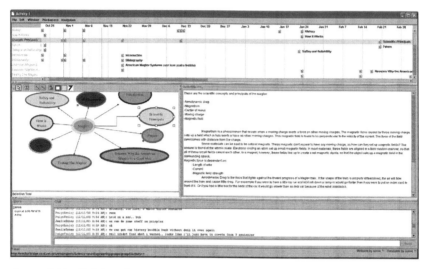

*Figure 7.10* Collaborative workspace incorporating a buddy list, chat, project timeline, concept map, and document editor.

objects in a concept graph (left pane), and as a text (right pane). (See Ganoe *et al.* 2003 for further discussion of this example.)

Finally, new technologies are continually suggesting new ways of incorporating place into community systems. A series of projects was carried out in Europe and Japan under the rubric of "digital cities" during the same period as MOOsburg was in operation (Besselaar and Koizumi 2005; Ishida and Isbister 2000). These projects employed virtual environment and ubiquitous computing technologies to produce high-fidelity, Internet-based simulacra of cities, updated continuously via cameras and other sensor data; an impressive example was Digital City Kyoto (Ishida 2005). These efforts addressed a wide range of goals, spanning technology development, new information services and applications, and support for community life. However, as Aurigi (2000) observes, they tended not to focus much attention on community participation.

The paradigm of mobile ubiquitous computing, based on location-sensitive devices such as smart phones, allows place to be directly exploited in the design of community systems. Consider interaction scenarios in which one walks around the physical community accessing location-specific information. For example, while standing in front of Annie Kay's Whole Foods in Blacksburg, one might access the history of that specific location, learning that the town's railroad station was located there during the period when the Huckleberry train ran between Blacksburg and Christiansburg. One might be able to contribute to a place-specific blog while at the location, leaving a Nostalgia-style remembrance of the Huckleberry train, or to access other tools and resources available at and pertaining to that place (Carroll and Ganoe 2008; Carroll and Rosson 2008). This is a vision of a successor to

MOOsburg in which the system navigation and depiction of places directly exploits places in the real world instead of vector maps and panoramas.

We set out in the MOOsburg project to design an infrastructure that could restore interaction among neighbors as a focal activity in community networks. Adopting the MOO software platform achieved this at one stroke, and more generally helped to focus more attention on chat and discussion in the development of the BEV itself. Initially, we were reacting to the contrast between user-to-user discussion that was so characteristic of first-generation community networks and the browsing and reading paradigm of early web-based community networks, which seemed to eliminate interaction. However, as with the issue of place, we found that interaction was not a simple design requirement. We implemented persistent chats in MOOsburg 2, instead of volatile chats that are deleted at the end of each session. We found that this approach seamlessly integrated synchronous and asynchronous interaction in MOOsburg, allowing greater continuity in interactions and also supporting better awareness of what was going on in various MOOsburg locations. However, persistent chats illustrate *both* real-time, synchronous interaction and publication. Thus, interaction and publication are not necessarily dichotomous.

Through the course of the project, our understanding of interaction, and of publication, broadened. In MOOsburg we developed threaded discussions, place-based discussions, comment boards, message boards, whiteboards, planners, shared files, and more. We supported the use of these tools, but also user customization of the tools. Indeed, we provided rudimentary support for users to create new kinds of content objects. Discussion, in this context, seems to transition into publication, which in turn transitions into *end-user design*, the integration of software design and programming activities into everyday life through tasks such as creating and maintaining personal spreadsheets and websites (Lieberman, Paterno, and Wulf 2006; Sutcliffe and Mehandjiev 2004). A better way to frame interaction is as participation in significant and personally meaningful activity. Communication channels are critical to this, but only part of it. Users of community networking infrastructures should control their own technology; they should be authors, maintainers, and designers. Ironically, this was precisely true of the earliest community networks, and became less true only as community networking became a broader and more diverse activity and came to depend on more sophisticated infrastructures. However, the sophistication of end-user design tools may be catching up and re-enabling a paradigm of end-user control.

From the start of the MOOsburg project we were interested in supporting a broad concept of awareness. People are aware of who else is in a MOO room because it is typed out in the place description. People are aware of who is in a collaborative environment, such as the Virtual School, because their names are enumerated in the buddy list. We felt we could support awareness in ways and to an extent that is normally not available in the physical world (Carroll, Rosson, Farooq, and Xiao 2009; Cooperrider and Avital 2004; Hollan and Stornetta 1992). For example, as mentioned above, persistent chat publishes an interaction at a location so that it can be reviewed and reused subsequently by the participants and by others; distributed museum specimens remind people of museum objects and activities even when they are far from the museum; map-based discussions link places and conversation turns by directly embodying places as referents in the discussion. Such interactions make participants more aware of their community – of the who, the what, and the where of community events.

These explorations of awareness suggest many other relatively simple ideas for using information technology to enhance community awareness. For example, the notion of specimen-based discussion groups could be generalized. The community library and other online resources could keep track of queries and other interactions and, without disclosing anyone's specific queries or other online behavior, both create a chat or discussion and invite users with similar interests and behaviors, facilitating new social connections (Farooq, Carroll, and Ganoe 2005). Recently, we have experimented with automatically aggregating RSS feeds from across a community's websites to create a single community information portal displaying all recently broadcast community information (Hoffman *et al.*, submitted). Each organization in a community may generate relatively sparse information, but aggregating the community's information could make all of it more visible, increasing community awareness for everyone.

Awareness both depends upon and is enhanced by participation in community activity. Being aware is knowing what other people know, what they expect, their attitudes and goals, the criteria they will use to evaluate collective outcomes, the kinds of things that get their attention and evoke action from them, and much more (Carroll, Neale, Isenhour *et al.* 2003; Carroll, Rosson, Convertino and Ganoe 2006; Schafer, Ganoe, and Carroll 2009). To be aware, community members must not only have effective data visualizations and reference frames, such as maps, they must also be able easily and effectively to build upon and customize existing rubrics in order to jointly construct and share data in ways that are appropriate for various circumstances. Communities and community networks are socially constructed and appropriated through human activity. A consequence of this is community awareness.

Finally, an obvious lesson in this project is that computing infrastructures is a costly and frustrating place to work. Throughout the MOOsburg project, our puny efforts were buffeted by the larger sweep of Internet and web technology. As the standard infrastructure evolved, everything we had done and planned to do was continuously reframed. The problem may have even been further exacerbated in our case since the infrastructures and applications were in the public and civic sector. Our partners in this work were public school teachers and community groups, constituencies with little clout or even visibility in the global marketplace.

In some ways, however, the MOOsburg project benefited uniquely from the community environment. Infrastructure development both occurs and has impact only through time and a variety of applications. We were able to work with community partners in a highly participatory and open-ended arrangement that might not have been possible in a business context with managers asking for quarterly reports. Indeed, we worked with the teachers almost continually for a decade, and nearly that long with the BEV Seniors. The value of the sustained and engaged cooperation of our community partners to the project was inestimable.

An interesting feature of really long-term infrastructure projects is that insurmountable problems can dissolve before they are solved. Throughout the MOOsburg 2 part of the project, and the latter phases of the Virtual School, we struggled with concerns about network bandwidth for our interactive clients. These concerns helped simplify and improve our software in many specific ways, but the overall issue was ultimately mooted as access to broadband network connections became pervasive.

One approach we took to mitigate the risk and expense of developing the MOOsburg infrastructure was to try to reuse standard software components. Our project began by adapting the traditional MOO platform. In MOOsburg 2, we reused Java components. During the ten years of this project, the open source software movement emerged and became a fairly mainstream alternative paradigm for software. Ultimately, BRIDGE (Basic Resources for Integrated Distributed Group Environments), the software layer that renders CORK objects as web and interactive views, became a SourceForge project (Isenhour and Ganoe 2004). Open sourcing is a very important facilitator of infrastructure continuity and may make longer-term, participative development projects more feasible in the civic sector.

We have moved from MOOsburg. Our recent work is focused on mobile/location-sensitive ubiquitous infrastructures for community networking and on feed aggregation in community information portals (Carroll, Horning *et al.* 2011). However, our work continues to be informed and enriched by the consideration of the strongly place-based design strategy of building a community system by constructing a virtual model of the community itself. The physical place evokes the community that inhabits it and, while we may not need to build a virtual doppelganger to achieve this, MOOsburg did evoke the community, and it still sets a level in that respect for future community systems.

# 8  Whither community networks?

People don't need technology to experience community. All they need is people. The impulse to identify with a group, to engage in collective activity, and to share bonds of attachment is as old as humanity, and a fundamental part of what humanity is.

Technology can support community, but its consequences are never simple and always involve tradeoffs. Neolithic villages entrained myriad technological innovations and strengthened human community, as analyzed and romanticized by Tönnies (2002) and many subsequent writers. But villages also spatially anchored communities, eliminating the random encounters of nomadic life and reducing the range of extra-community social interactions for members. And villages introduced role specializations that became divisions of labor and social class. Village life entrained property, trade and exchange protocols, and many other structures. Whatever else they did, these innovations strengthened the potentially oppressive downsides of social isolation and institutionalized inequity.

Through the past century, communications technologies, notably the telephone, were incorporated into community life. In the earliest implementations, one could chat with the operator at the telephone exchange to catch up with local news or join in a "party-line" discussion with neighbors. In the subsequent direct dialing era, one could speak intimately with busy friends and family, even when there did not seem to be time enough for a face-to-face visit (Fischer 1992). Such mediated interactions developed and strengthened community bonds throughout the local social network. One downside of the telephone is that its very ease could eventually cause the non-occurrence of visits among neighbors that might otherwise have occurred. Indeed, making it so easy to speak with friends and family might eventually have affected people's planning, reducing the amount of time they allocated for such interactions, and thereby "forcing" them to depend more on the telephone.

In this light, community networks are just another technological innovation that can support community, but not without their own complications and potential tradeoffs. In chapter 1 we posed three orienting questions, asking (1) how contemporary communities can appropriate new technologies, such as the Internet, for civic and social purposes, (2) how technologists and social scientists can collaborate with community members to envision and realize such innovations, and (3) what obstacles, challenges, early benefits, unintended consequences, and longer-term trajectories are entrained for communities, especially with respect to collective identity, local participation, and support networks.

These are core questions for community informatics. Our study of the Blacksburg Electronic Village (BEV) provides an example investigation into the questions and a programmatic answer. In this project, we adopted a participatory design research approach, working directly with community members and groups in relatively long-term mutual engagements focused on reciprocal learning about community and technology, and on creating and exploring new possibilities for community technology. Participatory design research is an action research method (Kindon, Pain, and Kesby 2007). It employs engaged action, participatory design of information technology, and applications as a method for achieving understanding and developing knowledge. It seeks to engage a wide range of stakeholders in a reflective design collaboration directed at producing, deploying, and evaluating new designs, and at the same time investigating and learning about the space of possible designs, including consequences for people and for concepts – as, in our case, community.

## Participatory design research

Our approach to design research emphasizes articulating design rationales through claims analysis of interaction scenarios. Thus, analyses such as those in Boxes 2.1 and 2.2 describe what human actors do and experience with a community discussion forum, and explicitly enumerate potential human consequences inhering in activities mediated by the discussion forum. Design activity must then try to mitigate potential undesirable consequences, such as the possibility that the forum will elicit flaming or polarize opposing factions in the community, and at the same time enhance potential desirable consequences, such as the possibility that forum interactions will entrain face-to-face interactions among neighbors or that they will help to remind community members how they can have constructive impact on local issues. Such descriptions support inclusive design participation: All stakeholders can understand and contribute to open-ended narrative analyses. As described in chapter 5, claims analysis can be particularly effective in engaging the domain expertise of non-technologists in participatory design discussions.

The original innovation that was the BEV – employing the World-Wide Web infrastructure in a community network – attracted, inspired, and energized the people of Blacksburg. The early external validation the project received in the form of media attention helped integrate the BEV into the Blacksburg community's identity almost immediately. As community members discovered and developed new roles in the project, they were able to contribute, and community interest grew. Innovation and community are both inherently engaging; their combination was quite attractive to the people of Blacksburg. But this was not without some irony. The "field of dreams" vision of the original institutional partners receded gradually as the community appropriated the project through wide-ranging local innovations. The appropriation was epitomized in the "kicked off the BEV" episode, in which the community was confronted with the opportunity and the necessity of taking ownership of the project. Working through the crisis was ultimately salutary for the community and for the BEV, but it entrained a mixture of immediate consequences that were both positive and negative (Box 3.4).

Our studies of the use and impacts of the BEV showed how community networks can modulate the use of the Internet. For example, our logging study showed that the BEV was a major Internet activity in Blacksburg. Our community survey showed that beliefs about community collective efficacy, civic and social use of the Internet, and a variety of community attitudes and behaviors, including community identification, community participation (both active engagement and passive participation through staying informed), and more extensive social networks in the community, were strongly interrelated.

We used path models to analyze factors associated with community identification, community participation (both active engagement and passive participation through staying informed), and more extensive social networks in the community. We found that community collective efficacy beliefs were associated with greater civic and social use of the Internet and, with and through that activity, greater community identification, community participation (both active engagement and passive participation through staying informed), and more extensive social networks in the community. Beliefs that the community can manage conflicts and dilemmas seemed to be an especially important aspect of collective efficacy with respect to strengthening sense of community, as analyzed in the conceptual model of chapter 1.

Interestingly, the path models showed that Internet use *not* mediated by civic and social purposes was associated with *diminished* community identification and participation. Like the telephone, the Internet can be used to engage with community activity, to facilitate community interactions, and to strengthen community identity, but it can also reduce interactions to anonymous lurking in a community portal or, indeed, provide an alternative to interactions. The Internet can be used for a vast and growing variety of human activities, many of them neither civic nor social. These latter uses are interesting and important in their own right, but our study indicates that they undermine local community.

Our surveys and follow-up interview studies suggested that highly engaged members of the community – those who were members or leaders of two or more community groups – made especially effective use of the Internet as a tool for community work (attending local meetings and events). We called these individuals *bridges*, as they span groups within a community.

Indeed, in our study, communities appear far from uniform across members. Bridges are critical people with respect to networks of groups. They can connect people to other people and to resources across groups. We also found that teachers and elders were important community actors. Teachers interact with large and diverse collections of community members through their teaching relationships with children. Even if they do not know each parent well, they are visible and important to the families of children currently in their classes, and often for years afterward. Elders frequently have relatively high knowledge about the community and discretionary time to become involved in community groups and activities. In Blacksburg, the Seniors Center was a hub of community activity, including after-school and other programs directed at information technology. Early in the project, a group of elderly community members named themselves the BEV Seniors and took on the mission of helping the whole community participate in the BEV.

Our Learning in a Networked Community project was a long-term participatory design engagement with a group of teachers. This project showed that such a long-term partnership was feasible and could be beneficial to all. It helped us identify some of the key challenges for long-term collaborations, including agreement on the surface that conceals deeper differences in values, goals, and expectations. It emphasized to us the importance of helping partners recognize their unique potential contributions. Once the teachers were convinced that their expert knowledge of classroom activity was critical to the design of effective classroom technology, they were able to contribute much more to every facet of the project. It is not enough to share power; partners have to convince themselves that they are full contributors.

With students, teachers, and administrators of the Montgomery County school system, we created a virtual school to enable collaboration among classrooms and across schools, as well as collaborations with community members beyond the schools. Student teams spanning classrooms and schools carried out projects and created multimedia reports in a collaborative environment, and later presented those projects in a virtual science fair accessible to the community. Student teams also worked with community mentors, who sometimes visited the schools in person but more typically carried out mentoring interactions mediated by the network. School–community collaborations open up the black box of classrooms and engage the community more actively in schooling.

Our collaboration with the teachers generalized to other community groups and institutions with whom we later worked, such as the BEV Seniors, the Virginia Museum of Natural History, and Save Our Streams. This was because we became more aware and skilled about establishing collaborative partnerships, but also because we developed a reputation in the community. The teachers in a local community are highly visible, and so are their research partners.

In this project, we quickly came to see the elderly as a powerful constituency of contemporary communities. Elderly people frequently know more about their local community than many of their neighbors, having lived there longer. They may also have more discretionary time than younger residents. While we definitely encountered elderly people who were challenged by aspects of information technology, we encountered many others who were intrigued, skilled, and creative with respect to technology. Indeed, when we first engaged with the BEV Seniors, we discovered that they already had the vision and plan for what eventually became the Nostalgia website.

We found that a variety of community members were interested in the stories, photographs, and reflections posted in the Nostalgia forum. Indeed, we were surprised to see that the Blacksburg diaspora, former residents who had moved to other locales, were also attracted to the forum. Later, we were able to recruit elderly partners who strengthened the community meanings in the simulation projects produced in the CommunitySims project. It was impressive how the elderly members of the CommunitySims teams patiently identified and articulated community themes in the animation ideas of their younger partners. It suggested to us a contemporary embodiment of a traditional role of the elderly in society – keeping the fire of the community.

In the MOOsburg project, we addressed a broader challenge. Instead of focusing on the needs and interests of a particular partner group or institution, we investigated a new paradigm and software infrastructure for community networks, a possible successor to second-generation community networks. Three key issues for web-based approaches in general were identified: the limited depiction of space, the limited interaction, and the limited support for awareness available in web-based community systems. We explored a series of alternative implementations that presented the community as a virtual place that could be navigated, and in which one could encounter and interact with other community members. Visitors could create and modify content objects, and move them around to locations in MOOsburg corresponding to locations in Blacksburg. They could keep abreast of where activity was occurring in MOOsburg and of who was doing what. The guiding intuition was to make MOOsburg seem more like a place in which one could engage in community activity and coordinate with the activity of others.

The project produced a series of interesting demonstrations and experiences for Blacksburg residents. It helped make the case for the inclusion of early web-chat services in the BEV, and later led to the development of place-based chat (Figure 7.8). It offered a framework for presenting the Virtual Science Fair activity (Figure 7.6). It provided, first, an easier way to visit the town's museum (Figure 7.7) and then, after the idea of distributing specimen instances, a way of pervasively engaging people about local natural history, at least throughout MOOsburg. By presenting a more integrated software system, we were able to support awareness of activity in the community system beyond what is possible with a more loosely integrated collection of linked web pages. We learned through this project that the community context, and specifically community networking, can still be a flexible and open context for exploring new technology ideas, as it was in the past for the Berkeley Community Memory, the Cleveland Free-Net, the Santa Monica Public Electronic Network, and the Big Sky Telegraph – all technologically innovative in their day.

However, we also learned from this project something about how difficult it is to question infrastructures. During the decade of work on the MOOsburg project, the web paradigm consolidated, even as it continued to evolve. In the end, we were outside the paradigm, and everything we did entailed effortful translation. This is a principle of technology ecology. The Cleveland Free-Net had to change drastically with the advent of the Web. And we can speculate that the mainframe-based Berkeley Community Memory might not have thrived in a context of personal computer adoption and that the closed network approach of the Santa Monica Public Electronic Network would have seemed confining in the context of the Internet.

## Reconstructing community networks

Questioning infrastructures is like questioning any other paradigm or orthodoxy. Change is not easy, and not quick. Nevertheless, infrastructures do change as questions pile up and new possibilities are envisioned and codified; indeed, they often change precipitously, as in Kuhn's (1962) analysis of scientific revolutions. In the case of the World-Wide Web, change has been continual. Indeed, so much has changed that the label "Web 2.0" has come into wide use, even though there never was a discrete release of a successor to what must have been Web 1.0 (Berners-Lee *et al.* 1992). Instead, a host of new capabilities were developed through many different initiatives over a span of years, culminating in the current Web.

Web 2.0 fundamentally reconceptualizes web pages as presenting and integrating interactions, instead of merely displaying static information. The early Web pages of the BEV were HTML files that were viewed in web browsers; the major innovations of Web 1.0 was that the pages had fonts and color, could embed images and graphics, and, of course, offered direct links to other pages. The content of Web 2.0 pages is typically not just a stored file; it is dynamically computed at the time it is accessed. For example, cnn.com updates its content throughout the day. Indeed, the content of Web 2.0 pages may continue to be updated while the page is viewed. Web 2.0 pages incorporate interactive experiences and applications; for example, users of cnn.com can view videos, participate in polls, and make comments on stories – all within web pages. Web 2.0 pages often incorporate awareness of where the user is; for example, cnn.com displays a summary weather report for the user's current location and links to news stories that are local for that user.

Perhaps even more important to the Web 2.0 paradigm is the integration of collaborative interactions. A rich and expanding variety of collaborative tools increasingly define what the Web is for and how it is used. In many important websites, such as Facebook, Flickr, YouTube, and Wikipedia, essentially *all* of the content is user-generated. Chats and forums are often embedded into contemporary web pages and web applications; people are discussing everything imaginable. Social media websites, such as Facebook, create interpersonal spaces where people inform and interact with their friends, though members often establish hundreds of friend relations. Some social sites specialize in sharing a particular media type, such as photographs (Flickr) or videos (YouTube). Sites like Digg have specialized in rating aggregated content such as news, videos, and pictures, though members can also make comments. Wikis emphasize collaborative content creation and editing and have made web pages and web sites into joint projects. For example, the English-language version of Wikipedia now consists of more than 3.6 million articles and has involved more than 40,000 authors/editors. Personal blogs have transformed commentary and opinion from the exclusive purview of newspaper editors and other media elites into a populist activity that anyone can pursue. Indeed, sharing has become real-time and full-time as people tweet reports on their daily activities to their Twitter followers.

The magnitude of collaborative Internet activity in the contemporary Web is staggering. The Swedish Internet monitoring firm Pingdom (2010) reported that, worldwide, there were 2 billion Internet users and 3 billion email accounts by the end of 2010; nearly 300 billion email messages were being sent each day. At the same time, there were 152 million blogs and 175 million Twitter users, who produced 25 billion tweets in 2010. Two hundred and fifty million people joined Facebook in 2010; by year end there were 600 million Facebook members, sharing an average of 30 billion pieces of content (links, notes, photos, etc.) per month. During 2010, 2 billion videos were viewed on YouTube per day, and an average of 35 hours of video were uploaded every minute. Slightly more than 2 billion videos were viewed per day on Facebook. Flickr hosted 5 billion photos by the end of 2010; more than 3000 photos were uploaded per minute throughout the year.

The role of collaboration in Web 2.0 is completely unlike the early Web, but, ironically, it is somewhat more like the early community network projects, albeit enhanced by more powerful tools and by its global scale. This contrast is more than just a matter of what is possible given Web 2.0 technology. For example, forums were available in the early web (e.g., Bentley *et al.* 1997; Rosson, Carroll, and Messner 1996; Suthers and Weiner 1995); indeed, several of our participatory design research projects – Web Storybase, Nostalgia, and the BEV HistoryBase – were explorations of multimedia web forums. However, in the early Web such projects were relatively rare; they were challenges to the paradigm, not examples of it. Many forums of that era were focused narrowly on gathering user comments about a particular website, where today forums are used as a general collaboration tool for discussion about common interests or activities (Serrano and Torres 2010). As analyzed in Box 2.2, this is precisely the role forums were playing before the Web in first-generation community networks.

A current focus of Web 2.0 is crowdsourcing (Howe 2009) – that is, activities in which the separate and often modest-scale efforts of large numbers of people are orchestrated toward accomplishing significant projects, such as labeling images to provide relevant retrieval tags (von Ahn and Dabbish 2004), digitizing books one word at a time (von Ahn *et al.* 2008), or translating all of Wikipedia from English to Spanish (Siegler 2011). Crowdsourcing has been analyzed as a new general paradigm for work. Howe (2009) cites anecdotes of crowds successfully performing work that is usually conceived of as requiring high levels of individual skill and attention – for example, providing corporate research in chemistry and designing tee-shirts.

An increasingly prominent facet of Web 2.0 is *cloud computing*, in which the Web hosts all user data and applications, replacing the desktop and operating system of one's personal computer as the platform for human–computer interaction. Google services are a good example of cloud computing; the user's Gmail and Google Docs data reside on Google servers. Similarly, the software that sends and receives Gmail, and that creates and edits Google documents, is accessed and used on Google servers. The user only has to have Internet access and a web browser. As is true of all aspects of the Web 2.0 paradigm, cloud computing is complex and involves many tradeoffs beyond the scope of this discussion. However, one obvious benefit is that users can make use of sophisticated software tools without having to install and maintain them – and, currently, without even having to purchase software or memory.

New infrastructures are opportunities to reconstruct technology solutions. The BEV reconstructed community networking as it had been developed and explored in the pre-Web Internet. Today, some of the functionalities explored in our participatory design research projects for the BEV have become pervasive in the Web itself. For example, thousands of web forums now exist addressing myriad topics, including history; many of these forums incorporate functionality for uploading photographs for discussion – for example, http://www.railroadforums.com. Indeed, sharing and discussing photographs is the core concept for Flickr, and discussing personal photographs with friends is a major activity in Facebook, as mentioned earlier. The consequence of this is that very little resourcing or technical expertise is required now to emulate projects like Blacksburg Nostalgia.

Even the more elaborate design projects we developed as part of the BEV can today be composed in a few moments with various generic web services. For example, the Virtual School enabled remote science collaborations among school students, including interactions with mentors and peers to plan and evaluate science activities, the coordination of experiments to leverage special equipment and to gather and pool data more efficiently, and the creation of collaborative notebook reports. Since that time hundreds of web-based science collaboratory projects have been developed to support analogous activities by students, teachers, and researchers (Kouzes, Myers, and Wulf 1996). The development of technology and support for collaboration is an active area of research (Olson, Zimmerman, and Bos 2008). Simple versions of the core functionalities of the virtual school, such as buddy lists, video conferencing, and collaborative writing, can be achieved (and for free) through cloud services such as Skype video, Google Talk, and Google Docs (this last supports collaborative writing and editing for several types of documents), although these generic services lack support for activity awareness across tools and sessions that are provided through the Notice Board and persistent chat.

MOOsburg was a deliberate effort to rethink infrastructure needs and goals for community networks. Our interests in providing richer interactions to users, in emphasizing the spatiality of the community, and in enhancing awareness of community activity drew us away from the Web platform and toward our own collaborative infrastructure. However, stepping back now, it is apparent that most of what we did in MOOsburg is quite consistent with what the Web has become. For example, navigating an information structure by pointing in a map that can be zoomed and scrolled was uncommon when we first implemented it in MOOsburg, but MapQuest, Google Maps, and similar services have made map-based interactions quite ordinary. Representing locations with panoramic photographic images was also a new idea in the late 1990s, but Google Street View has made this kind of depiction well known. Indeed, the core idea of organizing information geographically instead of categorically is being widely developed in geographical information systems and databases.

Even our earliest implementations of MOOsburg demonstrated that some community members were eager to build depictions of their own important places, chiefly their homes, businesses, and neighborhoods, as social places. This kind of activity was central to MOOsburg. It has more recently been implemented on a massive scale in Second Life and other virtual worlds. People indeed seem to want to depict and inhabit their own social places; a substantial proportion of user-created places in Second Life are built to correspond to places in the real world, including historical sites. At large scale, the city of Amsterdam is modeled quite extensively. Virtual social interactions in Second Life are spatially organized in ways similar to interactions in the real world (Friedman, Steed, and Slater 2007). In MOOsburg, Blacksburg residents spatially organized water quality data, attended a virtual science fair, and distributed local museum exhibits throughout the town. In Second Life people meet and talk to other people and organize a variety of social activities, among them classes, spoken language practice, concerts and dances, and collaborative games. They also build houses, furniture, clothing, vehicles, toys and games, and other artifacts, which they then sell, trade, or give away. The Second Life scripting language allows one to specify actions for objects one has built, and people enjoy creating these interactions (Wagner 2007).

Community networks should be reconstructed to take advantage of Web 2.0 infrastructures (Carroll and Rosson 2003). The functionalities and community possibilities of our participatory design research projects can now be relatively easily incorporated, refined, and extended within contemporary web-based community systems. It is feasible today for community networks to support rich member interactions, such as multimedia forum discussions, collaborative document editing, and virtual integrations of community information and interaction with sacred spots and the social landscape of community groups and institutions. Today's community systems can also support specific community activities, such as collectively articulating and archiving community history and experiences, community mentoring and other participation in local schools, and cross-generational community projects. Of course, there is an even larger set of community interactions and activities that we did not directly investigate but that would also be much easier to implement and explore today, such as the many participatory roles that citizens can play with respect to local government.

An important lesson from participatory design research projects like MOOsburg is that such efforts can be important even if they do not directly and immediately transform their respective technology sectors and application contexts. With the benefit of hindsight, we see now that the user needs and interests to which we were orienting did in fact lead to paradigmatic change in the Internet. Moreover, we know that the mechanism for such transformations is rarely singular, direct, or simple, but instead involves gathering and developing a wide array of experience with existing approaches and ideas and prototypes for new approaches. We would have been delighted for MOOsburg to have directly transformed the BEV, and indeed to have transformed expectations about what Internet interactions could be like. That was always a long shot. However, projects like MOOsburg, across a wide variety of technology sectors and application contexts, together created the impulse that now has coalesced under the banner of Web 2.0. A lesson for community networks going forward is that this kind of innovation is important.

## Future community networks

The projects described in earlier chapters were undertaken in part to investigate new services and applications for community networks. We wanted to explore new possibilities enabled by the BEV's adoption of the World-Wide Web infrastructure, but we wanted also to push on the boundaries of what was possible within that infrastructure. As described just above, many of our system concepts can now be realized within the enhanced infrastructure of Web 2.0. However, Web 2.0 also presents challenges to community informatics. For example, the infrastructural affordances for interaction are considerable, but they cannot make the whole world into a comprehensive community network. Human capacity for sociality is quite limited (Dunbar 1996). Even if we are, in principle, able to interact with hundreds of Facebook friends and join dozens of online groups, most of those interactions will be quite superficial. One consequence of Web 2.0 sociality, already apparent, is the emergence of diffuse networks of looser and weaker ties (Resnick 2001; Wellman *et al.* 2001). We need to understand these emerging social paradigms; among many other issues, we need to understand their implications for community and community networks.

The challenge of exploiting and extended affordances of new socio-technical infrastructures in community networks is a vast project. Some directions for the development of future community networks are, however, obvious. One important direction for community systems is information aggregation. A key challenge for community networks throughout the decades has been the sheer effort required to maintain community information. As discussed in chapter 2, community networking depends on volunteers to identify, codify, publish, and discuss diverse and current community information. The ideal of community networking is that groups and individuals throughout the community contribute their proposals, events, and news, and also react to and improve the contributions of their neighbors. Adding information to information, ideas to ideas, excitement to excitement, has a cascading effect. The synergies among these discussions and reports enhance awareness and identity throughout the community, facilitate new social ties, and create further opportunities for participation. To some extent, this is just what happens.

However, it is also the case that community members and their groups are engaged in many other activities, including actually carrying out community work as opposed to communicating about it. A consequence is that the information posted on community websites is often out of date. This is not a circumstance unique to community websites; indeed, the Web is full of out-of-date web pages. However, out-of-date community information has a particularly depressive effect on the enthusiasm of volunteers, who, after all, are motivated by intrinsic values of community identity, participation, and social interaction. Community members who participate more passively, accessing information to stay informed and to plan occasional activities, will also visit less often or stop visiting a community site that is not current. This can cause a cascade of collapse in which members successively contribute less and visit less. Thus, an abiding challenge for community networks has been to develop methods and mechanisms to better ensure that information is always up to date.

A further factor in this challenge is the increasing disaggregation of community information. As observed in chapter 2, it is no longer the case that community information can be posted only on a single community website, as was the case in Blacksburg at the outset of the BEV project. Today, there are many community websites, and, moreover, individual community groups and community members maintain their own websites. Thus, if one wanted to know about current news and discussions, about events that are upcoming with regard to local sustainable development projects, about organic farming and gardening, and about water quality, this might involve finding and browsing half a dozen or more websites for even a modest-sized community. This disaggregation of information, as with any design, involves tradeoffs: The information at a particular organization's website may be more likely to be up to date and focused, but it is also likely to be quite sparse. Each individual group generates a relatively limited amount of news, organizes a relatively small number of events, and takes positions on relatively few community issues.

In our current work, Michael Horning, Harold Robinson, Blaine Hoffman, Craig Ganoe, Honglu Du, Mary Beth Rosson, and I are addressing the twin challenges of up-to-date content and sparse content by automatically aggregating feeds from a wide variety of community websites. Many users have experienced aggregation in the context of news feeds. For example, the Bookmarks toolbar in the Mozilla Firefox browser has the default item "Latest Headlines" and the Bookmarks menu of the Apple Safari browser has the default item "View All RSS Articles" (RSS stands for "real simple syndication," a standard web feed format). These operations subscribe the user's browser to information displayed at other sites – in this case, news sites. The owners of the various originating sites – for example, www.bbc.co.uk/news – have made their information available by providing a feed link. Users configure their newsreaders, also called feed aggregators, by adding various links to their feed list. When the user views latest headlines or all RSS articles, the browser's aggregator polls all the feeds on its list for new content, downloading titles, summaries, or entire articles, depending on how the feed source and the aggregator are configured.

The web feed paradigm has several advantages when contrasted with other ways of obtaining current web information. Most obviously, feed aggregation can be automated. Users can configure aggregators to poll feed lists at fixed intervals or when the feed is viewed, ensuring that current information is presented whenever it is available. Manually visiting web pages to check for current information is cumbersome and inefficient by comparison. A second advantage is that subscribing to a feed does not require users to disclose personal information, as they would if they were subscribing to an email list, for example. The aggregator is pulling information from the various feeds and disclosing no more identifying information that would be disclosed by manually visiting the feed source. A third advantage is that metadata can be added to feeds and feed items to automatically sort content – for example, by which feed or which category of feed provided the content. Finally, feeds are useful to the sources of the feeds, increasing their influence by making it easier for users to access their information.

We adapted and extended the mechanisms of feed aggregation to gather current information from a variety of community websites in State College, Pennsylvania, among them feeds from the local school district, the public library, the minor league baseball team, the public broadcasting system, the fire company, emergency medical services, the newspapers and television station, the county government, the regional parks and recreation authority, the Pennsylvania Organization for Women, and the area's congressional representative. We included feed from a variety of civic organizations, such as Our Children's Center, the YMCA, Meals-On-Wheels, Penn State 4-H, the State College Area Food Bank, the Nittany Valley Symphony, the State Theatre, Amnesty International at Penn State, Acoustic Brew concerts, and several church groups, as well as the personal blogs of local residents. Currently, we are continuing to work with community organizations to help them provide feed information so that we can assist in publicizing their information.

Our community feed aggregation project is called CiVicinity (www.civicinity.org; Hoffman *et al.*, submitted). It addresses the challenge of providing up-to-date community information by publishing feeds from local sources; it addresses the challenge of sparse information by aggregating the current information of many community sources in a single web page; and it helps to make community groups and their activity more visible to the community itself.

CiVicinity categorizes feed items in several ways. We separately aggregate news items, events posted in calendars, and tweets from a variety of Twitter sources. Among news items, we distinguish "breaking items," "community news," and "Penn State news." The breaking items category consists of the most recent three items from local news organizations; the Penn State news category consists of official Penn State news items (of which there are many; this is a special characteristic of the State College community); all other feed items are community news. Within these categories, we label items according to the type of the original feed source – an individual citizen, local government, a community organization, media, a local business, or an educational institution. Users can filter the current feed view to display only items from one of these types.

CiVicinity has a tabbed user interface design. The top-level tabs, as shown in Figure 8.1, are News, Events, Map, Pictures, Social, and Feeds. We currently aggregate event feeds from the State College Festival of the Arts, the First Night celebration, and the State College School District. This does not seem to be a large or active enough collection of community calendars, and we are seeking more calendar data to aggregate. Under the Map tab, users can access an interactive Google map displaying community landmarks, including open Wi-Fi hotspots. Under the Pictures tab, users can directly upload photographs of community places and events or view the current photo stream. Under Social, users can review most recently aggregated tweets. Under Feeds, they can configure their CiVicinity client with respect to which feeds are included.

Currently we are exploring further enhancements to our site. For example, we have recently added geo-tagging for news and event feed items; users can select "map it" for any item to display a Google map indicating (our best inference about) the location corresponding to that item. For example, an item from the public library about a local art exhibition has the library as its location. Map it can use the user's current location to provide a route to the location associated with a feed item. We have also implemented social media sharing capabilities in CiVicinity. Thus, in reading the art exhibition item, a user can notify friends

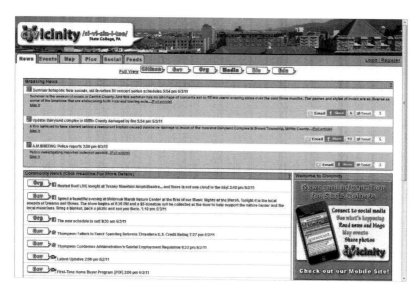

*Figure 8.1*  CiVicinity News tab displaying Breaking News items (upper panel) and several Community News items from local government and community organizations.

about the item using email, Facebook, or Twitter. We display a running count of the number of shares made using Facebook and Twitter as a way of indicating items of popular interest.

CiVicinity is an example of a new kind of community network site. In contrast to second-generation community networks like the BEV, CiVicinity aggregates activity and information distributed across the community, rather than itself seeking to be the focus for that online activity (Carroll, Horning *et al.* 2011). We have carried out preliminary studies of the concept, asking community members to react to scenarios illustrating various user interactions with Civicinity. In one study (Robinson *et al.*, submitted) we showed experimental subjects a video in which users gathered and integrated information from different websites. In one condition, they performed this task with a web browser and, in a second condition, they performed the task with CiVicinity. Subjects judged the aggregation task to be easier and more efficient with CiVicinity, and also felt it increased their interest in local news. In this study, we further contrasted a version of CiVicinity with labels for types of feeds (citizen, local government, community organization, mass media, local business, or educational institution) and a version of CiVicinity without such labeling. Subjects overwhelmingly felt that the labels were useful in guiding them to items they would like to read. Finally, we contrasted a version of CiVicinity with the three sharing buttons (for email, Facebook, and Twitter sharing) with a version not including this feature. Subjects felt they would be more likely to share items with friends using the interface that incorporated the buttons for sharing. (For an alternate approach that parses community web forums to create feeds, which are then aggregated, see De Cindio *et al.* 2006).

One very important direction for community systems, and for the Internet more generally, is mobility. Increasingly people are able to access Internet services and information as they move about the world through wireless local area networks, such as Wi-Fi, and mobile telecommunication networks, such as 3G. Mobile systems make the user's location an implicit resource for real-time interactions. Thus, one can query current traffic conditions, call for a taxi, get recommendations for nearby stores and restaurants, and even find out which friends are currently nearby; one's mobile device supplies location to these interactions. Services such as Facebook Places, Google Latitude, Foursquare, and Gowalla support such location-based interactions. Some of these services are available through ordinary cellular telephone; the United Nations' International Telecommunications Union (2011) predicts that there will be more than 5 billion cell phone subscriptions worldwide during 2011. More advanced location-based services are available through smartphones, such as Google's Android and Apple's iPhone; Berg Insight (2011), a Swedish business intelligence firm, predicts that 2.8 billion smartphones will be in use by 2015.

The possibility of mobile location-aware interactions, and the broad adoption of mobile Internet-capable devices and services, has many implications for community networks (Carroll and Ganoe 2008; Carroll and Rosson 2008; Hampton and Gupta 2008; Powell and Meinrath 2008). Community information systems always refer in some manner to locations in the community. This is one of their most distinctive properties. In desktop interactions, unless the community location is actually the same as that of the desktop, the relevant community location must be specified. For example, there must be a mouse click on the MOOsburg map, the user must scan a list of community groups and select the one desired, and so forth. In mobile location-aware interactions, the location of the interaction implicitly references a community location.

One example, discussed briefly in chapter 7, is a user interaction scenario in which one can access the history of a location in town while standing there. Thus, 301 South Main Street was the location of Annie Kay's Whole Foods, but in the 1960s it was the location of the Blacksburg station for the Huckleberry train, which ran between Blacksburg and the neighboring town of Christiansburg. A geographically oriented community system like MOOsburg could give users access to the history of places they visit in the system. But a mobile community system could give users access to the histories of locations in town when they are at those locations. The history of a place is often appreciated more vividly when one is there, which is presumably part of why people might prefer to visit Fort Ticonderoga rather than just read about it (or "Google" it). Hester's (1993) discussion of sacred spots in a community emphasizes how the meaning of such locations is evoked by moving through them and being in them (cf. Oldenburg 1989). This mobile approach to place in community systems also forces a unification of "where" one is in the town and in the community system, addressing the potential downside of the hall of mirrors issue as with respect to MOOsburg (Figure 7.9).

This scenario could be elaborated by allowing visitors to post place-based comments – that is, comments about a location that are accessed by being at the location. For example, in June 2011, Annie Kay's Whole Foods was vacant. A new store, Annie Kay's Main Street Market, had opened twelve blocks south. The old Annie Kay location is quite central to downtown. And, though the Huckleberry train is an even more storied bit of Blacksburg history, Annie Kay's Whole Foods was itself a landmark, albeit a more recent landmark. One wonders why Annie Kay moved and was renamed, and whether a new store will be opening at the old location any time soon. Such questions are indeed most likely to come to mind when one is at the old location.

There are many other mobile community network scenarios. Many of these involve coordinating community activity in real time (Rheingold 2002). A mobile community system would support reacting to opportunities that arise unexpectedly while one is in the town center. For example, it could be that another community member – not a close friend, but someone who has declared an interest in helping a local sustainable development group find office space in the downtown – is in a coffee shop. This could be the perfect time to have an unscheduled face-to-face chat about what can be done to help. This is a personal-level interaction scenario, but real-time coordination problems arise in many broader community contexts as well. Anchor community institutions like United Way sometimes organize an annual Day of Service in which teams of community members are dispatched to perhaps dozens of locations to carry out small projects, such as painting a fence or planting bulbs. A recurring issue for such large-scale and distributed community activities is that too many people show up for some projects, while not enough show up for others. Cellular telephones can be used to manage this, but not very efficiently, as they allow only one caller to exchange information with one other, or with a central coordinating office. A better solution is for all staff, indeed perhaps all participants, to be able to access a database and update their information, sharing it with everyone.

A particularly important category of larger-scale, distributed community activity is emergency management. In most communities in the United States, planning for and responding to emergencies, such as fires and floods, is primarily a local responsibility, and is addressed through the coordinated efforts of largely volunteer community groups, such as fire companies and emergency medical services (Schafer *et al.* 2008). The training and planning for, and the execution of, emergency operations are all strongly place based. They take place in the local community, and, sometimes, successful outcomes depend on local knowledge, such as knowledge about the layouts of particular buildings or about patterns of traffic congestion and potential shortcuts. A distinctive tension in emergency operations is the need for all responders to share a detailed and well-practiced plan, but also to be able to coordinate inevitable departures from the plan that arise through the course of the operation. Mobile community infrastructures can make a unique contribution by allowing all responders to share a dynamic representation of the original plan and the improvisations as the operation unfolds in real time.

Our studies of mobile community networking during the past several years have included direct prototyping and evaluation (Ganoe *et al.* 2010) as well as scenario-based investigations of the needs and interests of potential community users (Horning *et al.*, submitted). For example, during a series of community celebrations, each including many specific events distributed around State College, Pennsylvania, we made event information available and supported several activities, such as event blogging and photo sharing. People were able to use their own mobile devices to participate, and we loaned out a small number of additional devices. Of course, we identified many specific improvements for our software design. More generally, though, we found that, while they indeed used our prototype to guide themselves to events, people also blogged and commented on their experiences. We found that sharing photos was particularly popular in this context.

In our scenario-based study, we presented people with scenario descriptions of the use of a mobile community system involving a variety of cultural, economic, civic, social, and information-seeking behaviors and experiences. We asked them to rate how interested they would be to engage in the activities depicted in the scenarios. People were especially interested in mobile community network scenarios consistent with their current interests and practices. For example, those with existing civic Internet practices were more attracted to civic activity in mobile community network scenarios. More generally, people with a stronger sense of community, particularly those with stronger feelings of community identity, were more attracted to mobile community network scenarios. Finally, we

*Figure 8.2* Mobile client displaying the locations of First Night events in downtown State College, Pennsylvania.

found that those who already use wireless devices interstitially – that is, to fill time between larger daily activities – were more likely to be interested in our scenarios.

Feed aggregation and mobility are broad Web 2.0 opportunities for the future of community networking. The discussion above focused briefly on the particular examples our group is investigating. And of course there are many other trajectories for community networking, leveraging other sorts of information technology infrastructures. For example, my colleagues Victoria Bellotti and Janne Lindqvist and I are planning an investigation of a community task exchange, an active online bulletin board that would match neighbors and small tasks, such as getting a quart of milk for someone who is busy minding a child, or walking a dog for someone who has been delayed at work. Our idea is that such tasks often "cost" little or nothing to take on, but can be quite important to the person who needs them done. Many people are persistently connected to the Internet, and thus could post and accept such tasks within relatively short time scales. It seems that the amount of social capital generated by such interactions might be disproportionate to the costs of coordinating and doing them. The community task exchange concept leverages social media infrastructures and activities, but directs collective effort toward reciprocal and immediate action in the world to experience and build social capital, as opposed to worldwide message and photo exchanges and collaborative gaming, such as one see in Facebook, for example.

## Communities and technologies

Although people never did and never will need technology to create, experience, and sustain community, technology can play a role in facilitating community. Our studies emphasize that the relationship between communities and technologies should be understood as constituted by myriad socio-technical tradeoffs: Both desirable and undesirable outcomes are always possibilities in any technological innovation, and, most typically, some combination of upsides and downsides will in fact obtain. This does not mean that the relationship is too complex to fathom, that it can only be understood retrospectively, or that it is rational or moral to be conservative about technological innovation. Indeed, such positions most significantly resist engagement and responsibility; they do not minimize risks.

From the perspective of participatory design research it is rational and moral to become engaged and to take responsibility. The technologies of the early Internet were not created to facilitate community; they were appropriated to do so, as were the technologies of the early Web in the BEV and other projects. Web 2.0 was not created to facilitate community, but there is every reason to think that it can do so. Our study described specific ways in which community can thrive through appropriating information technology. The Blacksburg community was able to appropriate second-generation community networking to create and sustain a broad and innovative community-learning project. The BEV became a model for hundreds of such projects throughout North America and beyond in the latter 1990s. None of this was inevitable; it happened because community members made it happen – as the BEV Seniors did when they decided in 1995 to help the larger community make best use of the emerging World-Wide Web.

Participation in the BEV affected people – most strongly those who were most involved with the community and with the Internet. The BEV strengthened the Blacksburg community, elaborating and amplifying its identity, providing a wide array of new community-oriented activities and enhancing social ties and inter-personal support throughout the community. As socio-technical researchers, we found that the BEV helped to evoke a broad receptiveness to participatory design research investigating new concepts, applications, and infrastructures for community networking. The people with whom we worked were truly special people, but this was fundamentally because we had committed to participating with them for the long term. We asked a lot from our partners, as the BEV did more generally with respect to the Blacksburg community, and we got much more than we asked for. In participatory design research, partners become special when they are effectively facilitated in making their unique contributions.

Participation in design research projects in community informatics is a paradigm for community learning and community development. Lyon (1989: 240–51) distinguished between the "bare necessities" of public safety, strong economy, health care, education, clean environment, and optimum population and the "subjective components" of individual liberty, equality, fraternity, responsive government, local identification, and member diversity. He noted that, when basic needs are achieved, higher-order needs for belonging, for creative living, and for self-actualization are *just as keenly felt* (Maslow 1970). The people of Blacksburg were no longer worrying about conflicts with the Shawnee in the 1990s; they were a comfortable modern community attracted to the BEV as an opportunity to learn and to innovate, to work with their neighbors to proactively develop new community roles, resources, and activities. In the decades since, and as far as we can tell for the foreseeable future, information technology will continue to provide such opportunities. People will of course also learn about information technology in school and in the workplace, but community life – as it has been and continues to be reconstructed through conceptions of community networks – is a unique and generative area for innovation, collaboration, and learning.

In our participatory design research projects, we facilitated and investigated students, teachers, community mentors, and parents transforming a county school system into a distributed community collaboratory, elders creating online community history archives and joining forces with middle-school children on simulations depicting and analyzing community issues, and a variety of people and groups exploring the possibilities for a community network infrastructure emphasizing place-based interaction and awareness. We all learned a huge amount about one another's expertise and experience, about information technology possibilities and challenges, and about community and the Blacksburg community from these projects. And these various and otherwise disparate goals were nonetheless highly integrated and coherent in the context of these projects. Projects carried out with neighbors, embedded in one's own community, visible to and connected to all the people of daily life, are inherently intimate, unavoidably personal. These projects helped us to help one another develop as people, in Maslow's (1970) sense, to address higher-order human needs for belonging, for creative living, and for self-actualization.

Lyon (1989) also noted that the bare necessities of community must ultimately be addressed locally. In Warren's (1978) concept of vertical integration, critical spheres of community activity, such as schooling, commerce, government, and social services, are institutionally fragmented and constrained at the local level. They are codified and administered at higher levels, often nationally and even globally. Lyon observed that, to be effective, societal-level policies and programs must nevertheless be supported, implemented, localized, and sustained by the community. In other words, vertical integration, a fact of life in modern society, drives the level of activity and discourse in local communities to lower levels, but the mundane is neither amorphous nor predetermined. The same regional, national, or global policies can be – indeed, must be –implemented and enacted in varying ways across a spectrum of local contexts; this is the space for creativity and innovation at the local level.

Learning standards are an example. In the United States, higher levels of government dictate many curricular standards to local schools, as the Commonwealth of Virginia imposed its Standards of Learning (Virginia Department of Education 2005) on the Montgomery County schools. However, such standards do not dictate every classroom activity and discussion; they specify topics to be covered. Setting aside the quite substantive questions about standards-based education and particular standards, *all standards* leave a vast space of alternative pedagogical strategies and activities. Moreover, to have any chance of success, curricula must be appropriated by local teachers and parents. Vertical integration changes the scope and role of local institutions, but also depends fundamentally on their effectiveness.

Community in the twenty-first century is a different social structure than Tönnies's *Gemeinschaft* or the Lynds' Middletown. However, people yet reside in local contexts. Those contexts mediate the bare necessities of life for them and for their families, as well as higher-order needs for identity and belonging, for engagement and participation, and for association and awareness. The challenge for community informatics is to explore, cultivate, and disseminate creative and active roles for local communities in shaping the future of information technology *as community technology*. Broad participation is one key; it will always be easier to discourage than to nurture. Effectively including and engaging community members in participatory design research projects in community informatics will require a continuing commitment and ongoing effort. Optimistic but skeptical engagement with the possibilities and tradeoffs that inhere in potential community technologies is the second key; tradeoffs are numerous, varied, nuanced, and regularly misunderstood even by software technologists. Design research in community informatics provides a creative nexus for contemporary community activity. It allows people to materially construct their local community, and it helps to integrate situated learning and collaborative innovation into daily life, developing and enriching community in new ways.

# References

Abbate, J. (1999) *Inventing the Internet*. Cambridge, MA: MIT Press.

Abdelaal, A. and Ali, H. H. (2009) Community wireless networks: Emerging wireless commons for digital inclusion, in *Proceedings of the 2009 IEEE International Symposium on Technology and Society* (Tempe, AZ, May 18–20). Washington, DC: Computer Society, Institute of Electrical and Electronics Engineers, pp. 1–9.

Agostini, A., De Michelis, G., Divitini, M., Grasso, M. A. and Snowdon, D. (2002) Design and deployment of community systems: Reflections on the Campiello experience, *Interacting with Computers*, 14: 689–712.

Agre, P. and Schuler, D. (eds) (1996) *Reinventing technology, rediscovering community: Critical explorations of computing as a social practice*, Norwood, NJ: Ablex.

AlphaWorld (1995) Detritus accessible via http://www.archive.org/, with the URL http://www.worlds.net/alphaworld/; current AlphaWorld available at http://www.active-worlds.com/worlds/alphaworld/ (accessed June 24, 2011).

American Association for the Advancement of Science (1991) *Science assessment in the service of reform*. Washington, DC: American Association for the Advancement of Science.

American Association for the Advancement of Science (1993) *Benchmarks for science literacy*. New York: Oxford University Press.

Anderson, R. E., Crespo, C. J., Bartlett, S. J., Cheskin, L. J. and Pratt, M. (1998) Relationship of activity and television watching with body weight and level of fatness among children, *Journal of the American Medical Association*, 279: 938–42.

Anderson, R. H., Bikson, T. K., Law, S. A. and Mitchell, B. M. (1995) *Universal access to e-mail: Feasibility and societal implications*. Santa Monica, CA: RAND.

Anklesaria, F. and McCahill, M. (1993) The Internet gopher, in A. Heck and F. Murtagh (eds) *Intelligent information retrieval: The case of astronomy and related space sciences*. Dordrecht: Springer.

Archer, J. L. (1980) Self-disclosure, in D Wegner and R. Vallacher (eds) *The self in social psychology*. New York: Oxford University Press, pp. 183–204.

Arias, E., Eden, H., Fischer, G., Gorman, A. and Scharff, E. (2000) Transcending the individual human mind – creating shared understanding through collaborative design, *ACM Transactions on Computer–Human Interaction*, 7(1): 84–113.

Associated Press (1994) FCC says network is model system for communities, July.

Aurigi, A. (2000) Digital city or urban simulator?, in T. Ishida and K. Isbister (eds) *Digital cities: Technologies, experiences, and future perspectives*. New York: Springer, pp. 33–44.

Babchuk, N. and Booth, A. (1973) Voluntary association membership: A longitudinal analysis, in J. Edwards and A. Booth (eds) *Social participation in urban society*. Cambridge, MA: Schenkman, pp. 23–37.

Bandura, A. (1977) *Social learning theory*. Englewood Cliffs, NJ: Prentice-Hall.

Bandura, A. (1986) *Social foundations of thought and action: A social cognitive theory*. Englewood Cliffs, NJ: Prentice-Hall.

Bandura, A. (1997) *Self-efficacy: The exercise of control*. New York: W. H. Freeman.

Barab, S. A. and Squire, K. D. (2004) Design-based research: Putting our stake in the ground, *Journal of the Learning Sciences*, 13(1): 1–14.

Bartle, R. A. (2003) *Designing virtual worlds*. Indianapolis: New Riders.

Beamish, A. (1995) Communities on-line: Community-based computer networks. Masters thesis, Department of Urban Studies and Planning, Massachusetts Institute of Technology.

Bell, C. and Newby, H. (1971) *Community studies: An introduction to the sociology of the local community*. New York: Praeger.

Bellah, R., Madsen, R., Sullivan, W., Swindler, A. and Tipton, S. (1985) *Habits of the heart: Individualism and commitment in American life*. Berkeley: University of California Press.

Bem, D. J. (1967) Self-perception: An alternative interpretation of cognitive dissonance phenomena, *Psychological Review*, 74(3): 183–200.

Bendig, A. W. (1962) The Pittsburgh scales of social extroversion, introversion and emotionality, *Journal of Psychology*, 53: 199–209.

Benford, S., Brown, C., Reynard, G. and Greenhalgh, C. (1996) Shared spaces: Transportation, artificiality, and spatiality, *Proceedings of ACM Conference on Computer-Support Cooperative Work*. New York: Association for Computing Machinery, pp. 77–86.

Bennahum, D. S. (1996) City of bytes, *New York Magazine*, September 30: 22–3.

Bentley, R., Appelt, W., Busbach, U., Hinrichs, E., Kerr, D., Sikkel, S., Trevor, J. and Woetzel, G. (1997) Basic support for cooperative work on the World Wide Web, *International Journal of Human-Computer Studies*, 46(6): 827–46.

Berg Insight (2011) Available at http://www.berginsight.com/ (accessed June 17, 2011).

Berners-Lee, T. and Luotonen, A. (1994) *Web Interactive Talk, Dialectical collaboration system deployed on the Internet in June, 1994*. Geneva: World Wide Web Group, CERN (Conseil Européen pour la Recherche Nucléaire).

Berners-Lee, T., Cailliau, R., Groff, J.-F. and Pollermann, B. (1992) World-Wide Web: The information universe, *Internet Research*, 2(1): 52–8.

Berwick, R. C., Carroll, J. M., Connolly, C., Foley, J., Fox, E. A., Imielinski, T. and Subrahmanian, V. S. (1994) *Research priorities for the World-Wide Web: Report of the National Science Foundation Workshop*. Arlington, VA: US National Science Foundation.

Besselaar, P. van den and Koizumi, S. (eds) (2005) *Digital cities III – Information technologies for social capital: Cross-cultural perspectives. Third Annual Digital Cities Workshop* (Amsterdam, September 18–19, 2003). New York: Springer.

Bødker, S., Ehn, P., Kammersgaard, J., Kyng, M. and Sundblad, Y. (1987) A utopian experience, in G. Bjerknes, P. Ehn and M. Kyng (eds) *Computers and democracy: A Scandinavian challenge*. Brookfield, VT: Avebury, pp. 251–78.

Bowden, P. and Wiencko, J. (1993) *The Blacksburg Electronic Village partnership*, Virginia Tech Working Paper, October 1.

Bowles, S. (2009) Did warfare among ancestral hunter-gatherers affect the evolution of human social behaviors?, *Science*, 324 (June 5): 1293–8.

Brooks, F. P. (1975) *The mythical man-month: Essays on software engineering*. Reading, MA: Addison-Wesley.

Brown, A. L. and Campione, J. C. (1996) Psychological theory and the design of innovative learning environments: On procedures, principles, and systems, in L. Schauble and R. Glaser (eds) *Innovations in learning: New environments for education*. Mahwah, NJ: Lawrence Erlbaum, pp. 289–325.

Bruckman, A. (1998) Community support for constructionist learning, *Computer-Supported Cooperative Work*, 7: 47–86.

Bruckman, A. and Resnick, M. (1995) The MediaMOO project: Constructionism and professional community, *Convergence*, 1(1): 94–109.

Burt, R. S. (1992) *Structural holes*. Cambridge, MA: Harvard University Press.

Burt, R. S. (2002) Bridge decay, *Social Networks*, 24: 333–63.

Burt, R. S. (2004) Structural holes and good ideas, *American Journal of Sociology*, 110(2): 349–99.

Button, G. and Sharrock, W. (2009) *Studies of work and the workplace in HCI: Concepts and techniques*, Synthesis Lectures on Human-Centered Informatics. San Rafael, CA: Morgan & Claypool; available at http://www.morganclaypool.com/toc/hci/1/1 (accessed June 25, 2011).

Carroll, J. M. (1990) *The Nurnberg funnel: Designing minimalist instruction for practical computer skill*. Cambridge, MA: MIT Press.

Carroll, J. M. (ed.) (1995) *Scenario-based design: Envisioning work and technology in system development*. New York: John Wiley.

Carroll, J. M. (2000) *Making use: Scenario-based design of human–computer interactions*. Cambridge, MA: MIT Press.

Carroll, J. M. (2001) Community computing as human–computer interaction, *Behaviour and Information Technology*, 20(5): 307–14.

Carroll, J. M. (2005) The Blacksburg Electronic Village: A study in community computing, in P. van den Besselaar and S. Koizumi (eds) *Digital cities III – Information technologies for social capital: Cross-cultural perspectives. Third Annual Digital Cities Workshop* (Amsterdam, September 18–19, 2003). New York: Springer, pp. 43–65.

Carroll, J. M. and Campbell, R. L. (1989) Artifacts as psychological theories: The case of human–computer interaction, *Behaviour and Information Technology*, 8: 247–56.

Carroll, J. M. and Ganoe, C. H. (2008) Supporting community with location-sensitive mobile applications, in M. Foth (ed.) *Handbook of research on urban informatics: The practice and promise of the real-time city*. Hershey, PA: Information Science Reference, pp. 339–52.

Carroll, J. M. and Isenhour, P. L. (2011) Moving from MOOsburg, *International Journal of Web-Based Communities*, 7(1): 4–27.

Carroll, J. M. and Kellogg, W. A. (1989) Artifact as theory nexus: Hermeneutics meets theory-based design, *Proceedings of ACM Conference on Human Factors of Computing Systems* (Austin, Texas, April 30 – May 4). New York: Association for Computing Machinery, pp. 7–14.

Carroll, J. M. and Neale, D. C. (1998) Community mentoring relationships in middle school science, in A. S. Bruckman, M. Guzdial, J. L. Kolodner and A. Ram (eds) *Proceedings of ICLS 98: International Conference of the Learning Sciences* (Atlanta, December16–19). Charlottesville, VA: Association for the Advancement of Computing in Education, pp. 302–3.

Carroll, J. M. and Reese, D. D. (2003) Community collective efficacy: Structure and consequences of perceived capacities in the Blacksburg Electronic Village, in *Proceedings of Hawaii International Conference on System Sciences* (Kona, January 6–9), Washington, DC: Computer Society Press, Institute of Electrical and Electronics Engineers.

Carroll, J. M. and Rosson, M. B. (1991) Deliberated evolution: Stalking the view matcher in design space, *Human–Computer Interaction*, 6: 281–318.

Carroll, J. M. and Rosson, M. B. (1992) Getting around the task–artifact cycle: How to make claims and design by scenario, *ACM Transactions on Information Systems*, 10(2): 181–212.

Carroll, J. M. and Rosson, M. B. (1996) Developing the Blacksburg Electronic Village, *Communications of the ACM*, 39(12): 69–74.

Carroll, J. M. and Rosson, M. B. (1998) The neighborhood school in the global village, *IEEE Technology and Society*, 17(4): 4–9 and 44.

Carroll, J. M. and Rosson, M. B. (2001) Better home shopping or new democracy? Evaluating community network outcomes, *Proceedings of ACM Conference on Human Factors of Computing Systems* (Seattle, March 31–April 5). New York: Association for Computing Machinery, pp, 372–9.

Carroll, J. M. and Rosson, M. B. (2003) A trajectory for community networks, *Information Society*, 19(5): 381–93.

Carroll, J. M. and Rosson, M. B. (2007) Participatory design in community informatics, *Design Studies*, 28: 243–61.

Carroll, J. M. and Rosson, M. B. (2008) Theorizing mobility in community networks, *International Journal of Human-Computer Studies*, 66: 944–62.

Carroll, J. M., Kellogg, W. A. and Rosson, M. B. (1991) The task–artifact cycle, in J. M. Carroll (ed.) *Designing interaction: Psychology at the human–computer interface*. New York: Cambridge University Press, pp. 74–102.

Carroll, J. M., Singley, M. K. and Rosson, M. B. (1992) Integrating theory development with design evaluation, *Behaviour and Information Technology*, 11: 247–55.

Carroll, J. M., Rosson, M. B., Cohill, A. M. and Schorger, J. (1995) Building a history of the Blacksburg Electronic Village, *Proceedings of the ACM Symposium on Designing Interactive Systems* (Ann Arbor, August 23–5). New York: Association for Computing Machinery, pp. 1–6.

Carroll, J. M., Rosson, M. B., Chin, G. and Koenemann, J. (1998) Requirements development in scenario-based design, *IEEE Transactions on Software Engineering*, 24(12): 1–15.

Carroll, J. M., Rosson, M. B., VanMetre, C. A., Kengeri, R., Kelso, J. and Darshani, M. (1999) Blacksburg Nostalgia: A community history archive, in M. A. Sasse and C. Johnson (eds) *Proceedings of IFIP Conference on Human–Computer Interaction* (Edinburgh, August 30–September 3). Amsterdam: IOS Press/International Federation for Information Processing, pp. 637–47.

Carroll, J. M., Chin, G., Rosson, M. B. and Neale, D. C. (2000) The development of cooperation: Five years of participatory design in the virtual school, in D. Boyarski and W. Kellogg (eds) *DIS2000: Designing interactive systems* (Brooklyn, August 17–19). New York: Association for Computing Machinery, pp. 239–51.

Carroll, J. M., Rosson, M. B., Isenhour, P. L., Ganoe, C. H., Dunlap, D., Fogarty, J., Schafer, W. and Van Metre, C. (2001) Designing our town: MOOsburg, *International Journal of Human-Computer Studies*, 54: 725–51.

Carroll, J. M., Rosson, M. B., Isenhour, P. L., Van Metre, C., Schafer, W. A. and Ganoe, C. H. (2001) MOOsburg: Multi-user domain support for a community network, *Internet Research*, 11 (1): 65–73.

Carroll, J. M., Choo, C. W., Dunlap, D. R., Isenhour, P. L., Kerr, S. T., MacLean, A. and Rosson, M. B. (2003) Knowledge management support for teachers, *Educational Technology Research and Development*, 51(4): 42–64.

Carroll, J. M., Neale, D. C. and Isenhour, P. L. (2003) The collaborative critical incident tool: Supporting reflection and evaluation in a Web community, in C. Cavanaugh (ed.) *Development and management of virtual schools: Issues and trends*. Hershey, PA: Idea Group, pp. 192–219.

Carroll, J. M., Neale, D. C., Isenhour, P. L., Rosson, M. B. and McCrickard, D. S. (2003) Notification and awareness: Synchronizing task-oriented collaborative activity, *International Journal of Human-Computer Studies*, 58: 605–32.

Carroll, J. M., Neale, D. and Isenhour, P. I. (2005) The collaborative critical incident tool, in C. Howard, J. V. Boettecher, L. Justice, K. D. Schenk, P. L. Rogers and G. A. Berg (eds) *Encyclopedia of distance learning*, Vol. 4: *Online learning and technologies*. Hershey, PA: Idea Group Reference, pp. 233–9.

Carroll, J. M., Rosson, M. B., Dunlap, D. R. and Isenhour, P. L. (2005) Frameworks for sharing teaching practices, *Educational Technology & Society*, 8(3): 162–75.

Carroll, J. M., Rosson, M. B. and Zhou, J. (2005) Collective efficacy as a measure of community, *Proceedings of the ACM Conference on Human Factors in Computing Systems* (Portland, Oregon, April 2–7). New York: Association for Computing Machinery, pp. 1–10.

Carroll, J. M., Rosson, M. B., Convertino, G. and Ganoe, C. (2006) Awareness and teamwork in computer-supported collaborations, *Interacting with Computers*, 18: 21–46.

Carroll, J. M., Rosson, M. B., Kavanaugh, A., Dunlap, D., Schafer, W., Snook, J. and Isenhour, P. (2006) Social and civic participation in a community network, in R. Kraut, M. Brynin and S. Kiesler (eds) *Computers, phones, and the Internet: Domesticating information technology*. New York: Oxford University Press, pp. 168–81.

Carroll, J. M., Rosson, M. B., Farooq, U. and Xiao, L. (2009) Beyond being aware, *Information and Organizations*, 19(3): 162–85.

Carroll, J. M., Snook, J. and Isenhour, P. L. (2009) Logging home use of the Internet in the Blacksburg Electronic Village, *International Journal of Advanced Media and Communication*, 3 (3): 333–48.

Carroll, J. M., Convertino, G., Farooq, U. and Rosson, M. B. (2011) The firekeepers: Aging considered as a resource, *Universal Access in the Information Society*; available at http://www.springerlink.com/content/d4073w09388528x3/.

Carroll, J. M., Horning, M. A., Hoffman, B. E., Ganoe, C. H., Robinson, H. R. and Rosson, M. B. (2011) Community network 2.0: Visions, participation, and engagement in new information infrastructures, *Proceedings of 3rd International Symposium on End-User Development: IS-EUD* (Torre Canne, Brindisi, Italy, June 7–10). Berlin: Springer.

Cattagni, A. and Farris, E. (2001) Internet access in US public schools and classrooms: 1994–2000. Washington, DC: US Department of Education, National Center for Education Statistics.

Chandrasekaran, R. (1995) In Virginia, a virtual community tries plugging into itself, *Washington Post*, April 11, pp. A1, A12.

Cherny, L. (1995) The mud register: Conversational modes of action in a text-based virtual reality. PhD dissertation, Department of Linguistics, Stanford University.

Chin, G. (2004) A methodology for integrating ethnography, scenarios, and participatory design. PhD dissertation, Computer Science Department, Virginia Tech.

Chin, G. and Carroll, J. M. (2000) Articulating collaboration in a learning community, *Behaviour and Information Technology*, 19(4): 233–45.

Chin, G., Rosson, M. B. and Carroll, J. M. (1997) Participatory analysis: Shared development of requirements from scenarios, *Proceedings of ACM Conference on Human Factors in Computing Systems* (Atlanta, March 22–7). New York: Association for Computing Machinery, pp. 162–9.

Cisler, S. (ed.) (1995) *Ties that bind: Converging communities*. Cupertino, CA: Apple Computer Corporation Library.

Clifford J. (1986) Introduction: Partial truths, in J. Clifford and G. E. Marcus (eds) *Writing cultures: The poetics and politics of writing ethnography*. Berkeley: University of California Press, pp. 1–26.

Cohen, S., Mermelstein, R., Kamarck, T. and Hoberman, H. (1984) Measuring the functional components of social support, in I. G. Sarason and B. R. Sarason (eds) *Social support: Theory, research and applications*. The Hague: Martinus Nijhoff, pp. 73–94.

Cohill, A. and Kavanaugh, A. (eds) (2000) *Community networks: Lessons from Blacksburg, Virginia*. Norwood, MA: Artech House.

Coleman, J. S. (1957) *Community conflict*. New York: Free Press.

Coleman, J. S. (1988) Social capital in the creation of human capital, *American Journal of Sociology*, 94: S95–S120 [Supplement: Organizations and institutions: Sociological and economic approaches to the analysis of social structure].

Colstad, K. and Lipkin, E. (1975) Community memory: A public information network, *ACM Computers & Society*, 6(4): 6–7.

comScore (2008) Social networking explodes worldwide as sites increase their focus on cultural relevance, August 12. Available at http://www.comscore.com/Press_Events/Press_Releases/2008/08/Social_Networking_World_Wide (accessed June 21, 2011).

Convertino, G., Farooq, U., Rosson, M. B. and Carroll, J. M. (2005) Old is gold: Integrating older workers in CSCW, *Proceedings of Hawaii International Conference on Systems Science* (Waikoloa Village, January 3–6). Washington, DC: Computer Society Press, Institute of Electrical and Electronics Engineers.

Convertino, G., Ganoe, C. H., Schafer, W. A., Yost, B. and Carroll, J. M. (2005) A multiple view approach to support common ground in distributed and synchronous geo-collaboration, *Proceedings of the Third International Conference on Coordinated & Multiple Views in Exploratory Visualization* (London, July 5), pp. 121–32.

Convertino, G., Farooq, U., Rosson, M. B., Carroll, J. M. and Meyer, B. J. F. (2007) Supporting intergenerational groups in computer-supported cooperative work, *Behaviour and Information Technology*, 26(4): 275–85.

Cooperrider, D. and Avital, M. (eds) (2004) *Advances in appreciative inquiry: Constructive discourse and human organization*. New York: Elsevier.

Cuban, L. (1986) *Teachers and machines*. New York: Teachers College Press.

Cuban, L. (1993) *How teachers taught: Constancy and change in American classrooms 1890–1980*. New York: Longman.

Curtis, P. (1992) Mudding: Social phenomena in text-based virtual realities, *Proceedings of the 1992 Conference on the Directions and Implications of Advanced Computing*. Berkeley, CA: Computer Professionals for Social Responsibility.

Curtis, P. and Nichols, D. (1994) MUDs grow up: Social virtual reality in the real world, *Proceedings of the IEEE Computer Conference* (San Francisco, January 18–20). Los Alamitos, CA: Computer Society Press, Institute of Electrical and Electronics Engineers, pp. 193–200.

Czaja, S. J. and Lee, C. C. (2003) Designing computer systems for older adults, in J. Jacko and A. Sears (eds) *The Human–Computer Interaction Handbook*. Mahwah, NJ: Lawrence Erlbaum, pp. 413–27.

Dao, J. (2005) Philadelphia hopes to lead the charge to wireless future, *New York Times*, February 17, p. A18.

Darwin, C. ([1871] 1983) *The descent of man*. New York: D. Appleton.

Davies, D. (1991) Schools reaching out: Family, school, and community partnerships for student success, *Phi Delta Kappan*, 72 (January): 376–82.

De Cindio, F. and Ripamonti, L. A. (2010) Nature and roles for community networks in the information society, *AI & Society*, 25(3): 265–78.

De Cindio, F., Fiumara, G., Marchi, M., Provetti, A., Ripamonti, L. A. and Sonnante, L. (2006) Aggregating information and enforcing awareness across communities with the Dynamo RSS Feeds Creation Engine: Preliminary report, in R. Meersman, Z. Tari and P. Herrero (eds) *On the Move to Meaningful Internet Systems Workshop* (Montpellier, France, October 29 – November 3). Berlin: Springer, pp. 227–36.

Denning, P. J. and Kahn, R. E. (2010) The long quest for universal information access, *Communications of ACM*, 53(12): 34–6.

Dieberger, A. (1996) Browsing the WWW by interacting with a textual virtual environment, *Proceedings of ACM Hypertext Conference*. New York: Association for Computing Machinery, pp. 170–79.

Dieberger, A. and Frank, U. (1998) A city metaphor to support navigation in complex information spaces, *Journal of Visual Languages and Computing*, 9: 597–622.

Dunbar, R. I. M. (1996) *Grooming, gossip, and the evolution of language*. Cambridge, MA: Harvard University Press.

Dunlap, D. R., Neale, D. C. and Carroll, J. M. (2000) Teacher collaboration in a networked community, *Educational Technology and Society*, 3(3): 442–54.

Dunlap, D., Schafer, W., Carroll, J. M. and Reese, D. D. (2003) Delving deeper into access: Marginal Internet usage in a local community, in A. Venkatesh (ed.) *Proceedings of HOIT 2003: Home Oriented Informatics and Telematics, The Networked Home and the Home of the Future*, available at http://www.crito.uci.edu/noah/HOIT/2003papers.htm (accessed June 24, 2011).

Durkheim, E. ([1893] 1947) *The division of labor in society*, trans. G. Simpson. New York: Macmillan.

Durkheim, E. ([1897] 1952) *Suicide*. London: Routledge & Kegan Paul.

Edwards, J. and Booth, A. (1973) *Social participation in urban society*. Cambridge, MA: Schenkman.

Ellis, J. B. and Bruckman, A. S. (2001) Designing Palaver Tree Online: Supporting social roles in a community of oral history, *Proceedings of ACM Conference on Human Factors in Computing Systems* (Fort Lauderdale, Florida, April 5–10). New York: Association for Computing Machinery, pp. 474–81.

Erickson, T. (1993) From interface to interplace: The spatial environment as a medium for interaction, *Proceedings of the European Conference on Spatial Information Theory* (Elba Island, September 19–22). Berlin: Springer, pp. 391–405.

Ericsson, K. A. and Simon, H. A. (1984) *Protocol analysis: Verbal reports as data*. Cambridge, MA: MIT Press.

Erikson, K. T. (1966) *Wayward Puritans: A study in the sociology of deviance*. New York: Wiley.

Farooq, U., Rodi, C., Carroll, J. M. and Isenhour, P. L. (2003) Avatar proxies: Configurable informants of collaborative activities, *Proceedings of ACM Conference on Human Factors in Computing Systems* (Fort Lauderdale, Florida, April 5–10). New York: Association for Computing Machinery, pp. 792–3.

Farooq, U., Carroll, J. M. and Ganoe, C. H. (2005) Supporting creativity in distributed scientific communities, *Proceedings of ACM GROUP Conference* (Sanibel Island, November 6–9). New York: Association for Computing Machinery, pp. 217–26.

Farragher, T. (1995) In Blacksburg, Va., there's no wired place like home, *Philadelphia Inquirer*, May 14, pp. D1–D2.

Farrington, C. and Pine, E. (1997) Community memory: A case study in community communication, in P. Agre and D. Schuler (eds) *Reinventing technology, rediscovering community: Critical explorations of computing as a social practice*. Norwood, NJ: Ablex.

Festinger, L. (1957) *A theory of cognitive dissonance*. Stanford, CA: Stanford University Press.

Fetterman, D. (1989) *Ethnography: Step by step*. Newbury Park, CA: Sage.

Fischer, C. S. (1992) *America calling: A social history of the telephone to 1940*. Berkeley: University of California Press.

Flanagan, J. C. (1954) The Critical Incident technique, *Psychological Bulletin*, 51: 28–35.

Foot, H. C., Morgan, M. J. and Shute, R. H. (1990) *Children helping children*. New York: Wiley.

Foster, S. (1994) Road still a bit rough to info-land, *Roanoke Times and World News*, April 5.

Fox, S. and Vital, J. (2008) *Degrees of access (May 2008 data)*. Available at http://www.pewinternet.org/Presentations/2008/Degrees-of-Access-(May-2008-data).aspx (accessed June 21, 2011).

Frankenberg, R. (1966) *Communities in Britain: Social life in town and country*. London: Penguin.

Friedman, D., Steed, A. and Slater, M. (2007) Spatial social behavior in Second Life, in C. Pelachaud, J.-C. Martin, E. André, G. Chollet, K. Karpouzis and D. Pelé (eds) *Intelligent virtual agents*. New York: Springer, pp. 252–63.

Ganoe, C. H., Somervell, J. P., Neale, D. C., Isenhour, P. L., Carroll, J. M., Rosson, M. B. and McCrickard, D. S. (2003) Classroom BRIDGE: using collaborative public and desktop timelines to support activity awareness, *ACM Symposium on User Interface Software and Tools* (Vancouver, November 2–5). New York: Association for Computing Machinery, pp. 21–30.

Ganoe, C. H., Robinson, H. R., Horning, M. A., Xie, X. and Carroll, J. M. (2010) Mobile awareness and participation in community oriented activities, *Proceedings of the First International Conference and Exhibition on Computing for Geospatial Research and Application* (Washington, DC, June 21–3). New York: Association for Computing Machinery, pp. 1–8.

Gans, H. J. (1974a) Gans on Granovetter's "Strength of Weak Ties," *American Journal of Sociology*, 80: 524–7.

Gans, H. J. (1974b) Gans responds to Granovetter, *American Journal of Sociology*, 80: 529–31.

Gibson, S., Neale, D. C., Carroll, J. M., and VanMetre, C. A. (1999) Mentoring in a school environment, *Proceedings of Conference on Computer Supported Collaborative Learning* (Palo Alto, December 12–15). Mahwah, NJ: Lawrence Erlbaum, pp. 182–8.

Glasgow, N. A. (1996) *Taking the classroom into the community: A guidebook.* Thousand Oaks, CA: Corwin Press.

Glusman, G., Gore-Langton, R.E., Young, E. and Guellen, G. (1999) Internet training for biologists on BioMOO, *BioTechniques*, 27(4): 710–14.

Granovetter, M. (1973) The strength of weak ties, *American Journal of Sociology*, 78: 1360–80.

Guest, A. M., Lee, B. A. and Staeheli, L. (1982) Changing locality identification in the metropolis, *American Sociological Review*, 47(4): 543–9.

Gurstein, M. (2007) *What is community informatics (and why does it matter)?* Milan, Italy: Polimetrica.

Hampton, K. N. (2003) Grieving for a lost network: Collective action in a wired suburb, *The Information Society*, 19(5): 417–28.

Hampton, K. N. and Gupta, N. (2008) Community and social interaction in the wireless city: Wi-Fi use in public and semi-public spaces, *New Media & Society*, 10(6): 831–50.

Harary, F., Norman, R. Z. and Cartwright, D. (1965) *An introduction to the theory of directed graphs.* New York: Wiley.

Harrison, E. (1995) Virtual village opens up alternate reality for townspeople, *Los Angeles Times*, May 16, p. A4.

Harrison, S. and Dourish, P. (1996) Re-place-ing space: the roles of place and space in collaborative systems, *Proceedings of ACM Conference on Computer Supported Cooperative Work* (Boston, November 16–20). New York: Association for Computing Machinery, pp. 67–76.

Haynes, C. and Holmevik, J. R. (eds) (1998) *High wired: On the design, use, and theory of educational MOOs*, Ann Arbor: University of Michigan Press.

Henrich, J. (2004) Demography and cultural evolution: How adaptive cultural processes can produce maladaptive losses, *American Antiquity*, 69(2): 197–214.

Hester, R. T. (1993) Sacred structures and everyday life: A return to Manteo, NC, in D. Seamon (ed.) *Dwelling, seeing, and designing: Toward a phenomenological ecology.* Albany: State University of New York Press, pp. 271–97.

Hiltz, S. R. and Turoff, M. (1978) *Network nation: Human communication via computer.* New York: Addison-Wesley.

Hodas, S. (1993) Technology refusal and the organizational culture of schools, *Educational Policy Analysis Archives*, 1(10), September 14.

Hoffman, B. E., Ganoe, C. H., Horning, M. A., Robinson, H. R., Carroll, J. M. and Rosson, M. B. (submitted) CiVicinity: Feed aggregation to promote local civic awareness.

Hollan, J. and Stornetta, S. (1992) Beyond being there, *Proceedings of ACM Conference on Human Factors of Computing Systems* (Monterey, California, May 3–7). New York: Association for Computing Machinery, pp. 119–25.

Horning, M. A., Robinson, H. R., Ganoe, C. H., and Carroll, J. M. (submitted) Wireless proximal community networks: The importance of interstitial access.

Howe, J. (2009) *Crowdsourcing: Why the power of the crowd is driving the future of business.* New York: Crown.

Hunter, A. (1975) The loss of community, *American Sociological Review*, 40: 537–52.

Interactive Services Association (1995) *American Internet user survey.* Silver Spring, MD.

International Telecommunication Union (2011) Available at http://www.itu.int/ (accessed June 17, 2011).

Internet Systems Consortium (2009) *Internet domain survey.* Available at https://www.isc.org/solutions/survey/background (accessed May 29, 2011).

Isenhour, P. L. and Ganoe, C. H. (2004) *Bridgetools*, hosted at http://bridgetools.sourceforge.net/ (accessed June 28, 2011).

Isenhour, P. L., Carroll, J. M., Neale, D. C., Rosson, M. B. and Dunlap, D. R. (2000) The Virtual School: An integrated collaborative environment for the classroom, *Educational Technology and Society*, 3(3): 74–86.

Isenhour, P. L., Rosson, M. B. and Carroll, J. M. (2001) Supporting interactive collaboration on the Web with CORK, *Interacting with Computers*, 13: 655–76.

Ishida, T. (2005) Activities and technologies in Digital City Kyoto, in P. van den Besselaar and S. Koizumi (eds) *Digital cities III – Information technologies for social capital: Cross-cultural perspectives. Third Annual Digital Cities Workshop* (Amsterdam, September 18–19, 2003). New York: Springer, pp. 166–87.

Ishida, T. and Isbister, K. (eds) (2000) *Digital cities: Technologies, experiences, and future perspectives.* New York: Springer.

Jones, Q., Grandhi, S. A., Terveen, L. and Whittaker, S. (2004) People-to-people-to-geographical places: The P3 framework for location-based community, *Computer-Supported Coperative Work*, 13: 249–82.

Kanner, A. D., Coyne, J. C., Schaefer, C. and Lazarus, R. S. (1981) Comparisons of two modes of stress measurement: Daily hassles and uplifts versus major life events, *Journal of Behavioral Medicine*, 4: 1–39.

Kasarda, J. D. and Janowitz, M. (1974) Community attachment in mass society, *American Sociological Review*, 39(3): 328–39.

Katayama, L. (2007) 2-Channel gives Japan's famously quiet people a mighty voice, *Wired Magazine*, April 19. Available at http://www.wired.com/culture/lifestyle/news/2007/04/2channel (accessed June 27, 2011).

Kavanaugh, A. L. and Patterson, S. J. (2001) The impact of community computer networking on social capital and community involvement, *American Behavioral Scientist*, 45(3): 496–509.

Kavanaugh, A. L., Reese, D. D., Carroll, J. M. and Rosson, M. B. (2003) Weak ties in networked communities, in M. Huysman, E. Wenger and V. Wulf (eds) *Communities and Technologies*. Dordrecht: Kluwer Academic, pp. 265–86.

Kavanaugh, A. L., Carroll, J. M., Rosson, M. B., Reese, D. D. and Zin, T. T. (2005) Participating in civil society: The case of networked communities, *Interacting with computers*, 17(10): 9–33.

Kavanaugh, A. L., Carroll, J. M., Rosson, M. B., Zin, T. T. and Reese, D. D. (2005) Community networks: Where offline communities meet online, *Journal of Computer-Mediated Communication*, 10(4): Article 3.

Kavanaugh, A. L., Zin, T. T., Rosson, M. B., Carroll, J. M., Schmitz, J. and Kim, B. J. (2007) Local groups online: Political learning and participation, *Computer Supported Cooperative Work: The Journal of Collaborative Computing*, 16(4–5): 375–95.

Kies, J. K., Amento, B. S., Mellott, M. E. and Struble, C. A. (1996) *MOOsburg: Experiences with a community-based MOO.* Blacksburg: Center for Human–Computer Interaction, Virginia Tech.

Kim, A. J. (2000) *Community building on the Web: Secret strategies for successful online communities*. Berkeley, CA: Peachpit Press.

Kindon, S., Pain, R. and Kesby, M. (eds) (2007) *Participatory action research approaches and methods: Connecting people, participation and place*. London: Routledge.

Klaebe, H. and Foth, M. (2007) Connecting communities using new media: The sharing stories project, in L. Stillman and G. Johanson (eds) *Constructing and sharing memory: Community informatics, identity and empowerment*. Newcastle, UK: Cambridge Scholars, pp. 143–53.

Koenemann, J., Carroll, J. M., Shaffer, C. A., Rosson, M. B. and Abrams, M. (1999) Designing collaborative applications for classroom use: The LiNC project, in A. Druin (ed.) *The design of children's technology*. San Francisco: Morgan–Kaufmann, pp. 99–123.

Komito, L. (1998) The Net as a foraging society: Flexible communities. *The Information Society*, 14(2): 97–106.

Kouzes, R. T., Myers, J. D. and Wulf, W. A. (1996) Collaboratories: Doing science on the Internet, *Computer*, 29(8): 40–46.

Krasnow, J. (1990) Building new parent–teacher partnerships: Teacher researcher teams stimulate reflection, *Equity and Choice*, Spring: pp. 25–31.

Kraut, R., Patterson, M., Lundmark, V., Kiesler, S., Mukopadhyay, T. and Scherlis, W. (1998) Internet paradox: A social technology that reduces social involvement and psychological well-being?, *American Psychologist*, 53(9): 1017–31.

Kraut, R. E., Kiesler, S., Boneva, B., Cummings, J. N., Helgeson, V. and Crawford, A. M. (2002) Internet paradox revisited, *Journal of Social Issues*, 58(1): 49–74.

Kraut, R., Scherlis, W., Mukhopadhyay, T., Manning, J. and Kiesler, S. (1996) HomeNet: A field trial of residential Internet services, *Proceedings of Conference on Human Factors in Computing Systems* (Vancouver, April 13–18). New York: Association for Computing Machinery, pp. 284–91.

Kubey, R. and Csikszentmihalyi, M. (1990) *Television and the quality of life: How viewing shapes everyday experience*. Hillsdale, NJ: Lawrence Erlbaum.

Kubicek H. and Wagner R. M. (2002) Community networks in a generational perspective: The change of an electronic medium within three decades, *Information, Communication and Society*, 5 (3): 291–319.

Kuhn, T. S. (1962) *The structure of scientific revolutions*. Chicago: University of Chicago Press.

Laughton, S. (1996) The design and use of Internet-mediated communication applications in education: An ethnographic study. PhD dissertation, Computer Science Department, Virginia Tech.

Laumann, E. O., Galaskiewicz, J. and Marsden, P. V. (1978) Community structure as interorganizational linkages, *Annual Review of Sociology*, 4: 455–84.

Lave, J. and Wenger, E. (1991) *Situated learning: Legitimate peripheral participation*. Cambridge: Cambridge University Press.

Lee, R. B. and Daly, R. (eds) (2002) *The Cambridge encyclopedia of hunters and gatherers*. New York: Cambridge University Press.

Lenhart, A., Hitlin, P. and Madden, M. (2005) *Teens and technology*. Washington, DC: Pew Internet & American Life Project, July 27; available at http://www.pewinternet.org/Reports/2005/Teens-and-Technology.aspx (accessed June 26, 2011).

Lewis, T. L., Rosson, M. B., Carroll, J. M. and Seals, C. (2002) A community learns design: Towards a pattern language for novice visual programmers, *IEEE International Symposium on Human-Centric Computing Languages and Environments* (Arlington, Virginia, September 3–6). New York: Institute of Electrical and Electronics Engineers, pp. 168–76.

Lieberman, H., Paterno, F. and Wulf, V. (eds) (2006) *End user development*. Dordrecht: Springer.

Loomis, C. P. (1960) *Social systems: Essays on their persistence and change*. Princeton, NJ: D. Van Nostrand.

Lynd, R. S. and Lynd, H. M. (1929) *Middletown*. New York: Harcourt, Brace, Jovanovich.

Lyon, L. (1989) *The Community in Urban Society*. Long Grove, IL: Waveland Press.

McKeown, K. (1991) Social norms and implications of Santa Monica's PEN (Public Electronic Network), *presentation at the 99th Annual Convention of the American Psychological Association*, San Francisco, August; available at http://www.mckeown.net/PENaddress.html (accessed May 29, 2011).

McMillan, D. W. (1996) Sense of community, *Journal of Community Psychology*, 24 (4): 315–25.

McMillan, D. W. and Chavis, D. M. (1986) Sense of community: A definition and theory, *Journal of Community Psychology*, 14(1): 6–23.

Maslow, A. H. (1970) *Motivation and personality*. 2nd ed., New York: Harper & Row.

Mayer, R. E., Quilici, J., Moreno, R., Duran, R., Woodbridge, S., Simon, R., Sanchez, D. and Lavezzo, A. (1997) Cognitive consequences of participation in a "Fifth Dimension" after school computer club, *Journal of Educational Computing Research*, 16(4): 353–70.

Miller, B. D., Wood, B., Balkansky, A., Mercader, J. and Panger, M. (2006) *Anthropology: The study of humanity*. Boston: Allyn & Bacon.

Mitchell, A. (1997) Teacher identity: A key to increased collaboration, *Action in Teacher Education*, 19(3): 1–14.

Muller, M. J. (1992) Retrospective on a year of participatory design using the PICTIVE technique, *Proceedings of ACM Conference on Human Factors in Computing Systems* (Monterey, California, June 3–7). New York: Association for Computing Machinery, pp. 455–62.

Muller, M. J., Haslwanter, J. H. and Dayton, T. (1997) Participatory practices in the software lifecycle, in M. Helander, T. K. Landauer and P. Prabhu (eds) *Handbook of Human–Computer Interaction*. 2nd ed., Amsterdam: Elsevier, pp. 255–97.

National Research Council (1996) *National science education standards*. Washington, DC: National Academy Press.

National Science Teachers Association (1992) *Scope, sequence and coordination of secondary school science, Vol. 1: The content core*. Washington, DC: National Science Teachers Association.

Neuman, S. B. (1991) *Literacy in the television age: The myth of the TV effect*. Norwood, NJ: Ablex.

Nie, N. H. (2001) Sociability, interpersonal relations, and the Internet: Reconciling conflicting findings, *American Behavioral Scientist*, 45(3): 420–35.

Nisbet, R. (1976) *The quest for community*. New York: Oxford University Press.

O'Brien, C. and Bown, H. (1983) A perspective on the development of videotex in North America, *IEEE Journal on Selected Areas in Communications*, 1(2): 260–66.

Odasz, F. (1993) Big sky telegraph, *Bulletin of the American Society for Information Science*, December.

Oldenburg, R. (1989) *The great good place: Cafes, coffee shops, community centers, beauty parlors, general stores, bars, hangouts, and how they get you through the day*. New York: Paragon House.

Olson, G. M., Zimmerman, A. and Bos, N. (eds) (2008) *Scientific collaboration on the Internet*. Cambridge, MA: MIT Press.

O'Neill, D. K and Gomez, L. M. (1998). Sustaining mentoring relationships online, *Proceedings of ACM Conference on Computer-Supported Cooperative Work* (Seattle, November 14–18). New York: Association for Computing Machinery, pp. 325–34.

Osgood, C.E. (1980) *Lectures on language performance*, New York: Springer.

Park, J. (1995) Interviews with Ken Anderson, Andrew Cohill, Ron Secrist, and David Webster, for CS 6704 "Community Networks, Network Communities," Computer Science Department, Virginia Tech, November.

Perkins, D., Brown, B., and Taylor, R. (1996) The ecology of empowerment: Predicting participation in community organizations, *Journal of Social Issues*, 52(1): 85–110.

Piaget, J. and Inhelder, B. (1969) *The psychology of the child*. New York: Basic Books.

Pingdom (2010) Available at http://royal.pingdom.com/2011/01/12/internet-2010-in-numbers/ (accessed June 21, 2011).

Pitkow, J. E. and Kehoe, C. M. (1996) Emerging trends in the WWW user population, *Communications of the ACM*, 39(6): 106–8.

Porpora, D. V. (1989) Four concepts of social structure, *Journal for the Theory of Social Behavior*, 19(2): 195–211.

Powell, A. and Meinrath, S. D. (eds) (2008) Wireless networking for communities, citizens and the public interest, *Journal of Community Informatics*, 4(1) [special issue].

Powell, A., Shennan, S. and Thomas, M. G. (2009) Late Pleistocene demography and the appearance of modern human behavior, Science, 324: 1298–301.

Preece, J. (2000) *Online communities: Designing usability and supporting sociability*. New York: John Wiley.

Putnam, R. D. (1996) The strange disappearance of civic America, *The American Prospect*, 24 (Winter): 34–48.

Putnam, R. (2000) *Bowling alone: The collapse and revival of American community*. New York: Simon & Schuster.

Rafaeli, S. (1984) The electronic bulletin board: A computer-driven mass medium, *Social Science Computer Review*, 2: 123–36.

Resnick, P. (2001) Beyond bowling together: Sociotechnical capital, in J. M. Carroll (ed.) *Human–computer interaction in the new millennium*. Reading, MA: Addison-Wesley, pp. 247–72.

Rheingold, H. (2000) *The virtual community: Homesteading on the electronic frontier*. Cambridge, MA: MIT Press.

Rheingold, H. (2002) *Smart mobs: The next social revolution*. Cambridge, MA: Perseus.

Ritchie, S. M. and Rigano, D. L. (1996) Laboratory apprenticeship through a student research project, *Journal of Research in Science Teaching*, 33(7): 799–815.

Rittel, H. and Webber, M. (1973) Dilemmas in a general theory of planning, *Policy Sciences*, 4: 155–69.

Robinson, H. R., Horning, M. A., Hoffman, B. E., Ganoe, C. H., Rosson, M. B. and Carroll, J. M. (submitted) CiVicinity: Supporting aggregation, sharing and sorting of hyperlocal community content.

Rogers, E. M. (1983) *The diffusion of innovations*. 3rd ed., New York: Free Press.

Rogers, E. M., Collins-Jarvis, L. and Schmitz, J. (1994) The PEN project in Santa Monica: Interactive communication, equality, and political action, *Journal of the American Society for Information Science*, 45(6): 401–10.

Rosenberg, M. (1992) Blacksburg users anticipate linking as "computer village," *Roanoke Times and World News*, September 3.

Rosenholtz, S. J. (1989) *Teachers' workplace: The social organization of schools*. New York: Longman.

Rossman, M. (1975) Implications of community memory, *ACM Computers & Society*, 6(4): 7–10.

Rosson, M. B. (1999) I get by with a little help from my cyber-friends: Sharing stories of good and bad times on the Web, *Journal of Computer-Mediated Communication*, 4(4): Article 5.

Rosson, M. B. and Carroll, J. M. (2002) *Usability engineering: Scenario-based development of human–computer interaction*. San Francisco: Morgan-Kaufmann.

Rosson, M. B. and Carroll, J. M. (2003) Learning and collaboration across generations in a community, in M. Huysman, E. Wenger and V. Wulf (eds) *Communities and Technologies*. Dordrecht: Kluwer Academic, pp. 205–25.

Rosson, M. B. and Carroll, J. M. (2009) Developmental learning communities, in J. M. Carroll (ed.) *Learning in communities: Interdisciplinary perspectives on information technology and human development*. Dordrecht: Springer, pp. 29–34.

Rosson, M. B., Carroll, J. M. and Messner, D. (1996) A Web StoryBase, in M. A. Sasse, R. J. Cunningham and R. L. Winder (eds) *People and Computers XI: Proceedings of HCI '96* (London, August 20–23). London: Springer, pp. 369–82.

Rosson, M. B., Carroll, J. M., Seals, C. and Lewis, T. (2002) Community design of community simulations, *Proceedings of ACM Designing Interactive Systems* (London, June 25–8). New York: Association for Computing Machinery, pp. 74–83.

Rosson, M. B., Ballin, J. and Nash, H. (2004) Everyday programming: Challenges and opportunities for informal web development, *Proceedings of IEEE International Symposium on Visual Languages and Human-Centric Computing* (Rome, September 26–9). Washington, DC: Institute of Electrical and Electronic Engineers, pp. 123–30.

Rosson, M. B., Ballin, J. and Rode, J. (2005) Who, what and why? A survey of informal and professional web developers, *Proceedings of IEEE International Symposium on Visual Languages and Human-Centric Computing* (Dallas, Texas, September 21–4). New York: Institute of Electrical and Electronic Engineers, pp. 199–206.

Rosson, M. B., Dunlap, D. R., Isenhour, P. I. and Carroll, J. M. (2007) Teacher bridge: Creating a community of teacher developers, *Proceedings of Hawaii International Conference on System Sciences* (Waikoloa Village, January 3–6). Washington, DC: Computer Society Press, Institute of Electrical and Electronics Engineers.

Rothenbuhler, E. W. (1991) The process of community involvement, *Communication Monographs*, 58(1): 63–8.

Rubin, I. (1969) Function and structure of community: Conceptual and theoretical analysis, *International Review of Community Development*, 21–2: 111–19.

Sarason, S. B. (1974) *The psychological sense of community: Prospects for a community psychology*. San Francisco: Jossey-Bass.

Schafer, W. A. (2004) Supporting spatial collaboration: An investigation of viewpoint constraint and awareness techniques. PhD dissertation, Computer Science Department, Virginia Tech.

Schafer, W., Bowman, D., and Carroll, J. (2002) Map-based navigation in a graphical MOO, *ACM Crossroads*, 9(1): 8–15.

Schafer, W., Carroll, J. M., Haynes, S. and Abrams, S. (2008) Emergency management planning as collaborative community work, *Journal of Homeland Security and Emergency Management*, 5 (1): Article 10.

Schafer, W. A., Ganoe, C. H. and Carroll, J. M. (2009) Supporting community emergency management planning through a geo-collaboration software architecture, in J. M. Carroll (ed.) *Learning in communities: Interdisciplinary perspectives on information technology and human development*. Dordrecht: Springer, pp. 225–57.

Schön, D. A. (1983) *The reflective practitioner*. New York: Basic Books.

Schorger, J. R. (1995) Interview with Bob Heterick, January 13.

Schorger, J. R. (1997) A qualitative study of the development and first year of implementation of the Blacksburg Electronic Village. PhD dissertation, Curriculum and Instruction Department, Virginia Tech.

Schuler, D. (1996) *New community networks: Wired for change*. Reading, MA: Addison-Wesley.

Schuler, D. and Namioka, A. (eds) (1993) *Participatory design: Principles and practices*, Hillsdale, NJ: Lawrence Erlbaum.

Seals, C., Rosson, M. B., Carroll, J. M. and Lewis, T. L. (2002) Fun learning Stagecast Creator: An exercise in minimalism and collaboration, *IEEE International Symposium on Human-Centric Computing Languages and Environments* (Arlington, Virginia, September 3–6). New York: Institute of Electrical and Electronics Engineers, pp. 177–87.

Sears, C. (1996) (Re)visions of the village: Building and participating in the Blacksburg Electronic Village. Masters thesis, Science and Technology Studies, Virginia Tech.

Selznick, P. (1996) In search of community, in W. Vitek and W. Jackson (eds) *Rooted in the Land: Essays on community and place.* New Haven, CT: Yale University Press.

Serrano, N. and Torres, J. N. (2010) Web 2.0 for practitioners, *IEEE Software,* 27 (3): 11–15.

Shepherd, G. J. and Rothenbuhler, E. W. (eds) (2001) *Communication and community.* London: Routledge.

Shields, P. M. (1994) Bringing schools and communities together in preparation for the 21st century: Implications for the current educational reform movement for family and community involvement policies, in R. J. Anson (ed.) *Systemic reform: Perspectives on personalizing education.* US Department of Education; available at http://www2. ed.gov/pubs/EdReformStudies/SysReforms/ (accessed May 29, 2011)

Shirky, C. (1995) *Voices from the Net.* Emeryville, CA: Ziff-Davis Press.

Sidney, S., Sternfeld, B., Haskell, W. L., Jacobs, D. R., Chesney, M. A. and Hulley, S. B. (1998) Television viewing and cardiovascular risk factors in young adults: The CARDIA study, *Annals of Epidemiology,* 6(2): 154–9.

Siegler, M. G. (2011) Meet Duolingo, Google's next acquisition target: Learn a language, help the Web, *TechCrunch,* April 12; available at http://techcrunch.com/2011/04/12/ duolingo/ (accessed June 14, 2011).

Silver, D. (2004) The soil of cyberspace: Historical archaeologies of the Blacksburg Electronic Village and the Seattle Community Network, in D. Schuler and P. Day (eds) *Shaping the network society: The new role of civil society in cyberspace.* Cambridge, MA: MIT Press, pp. 301–24.

Simmel, G. (1972) Group expansion and the development of individuality, in D. Levine (ed.) *Georg Simmel on individuality and social forms.* Chicago: University of Chicago Press.

Siochrú, S. O. and Girard, B. (2005) *Community-based networks and innovative technologies: New models to serve and empower the poor.* New York: United Nations Development Programme; available at http://propoor-ict.net (accessed June 27, 2011).

Smith, A., Scholozman, K. L., Verba, S. and Brady, H. (2009) *The Internet and civic engagement.* Washington, DC: Pew Internet & American Life Project, September 1; available at http://www.pewinternet.org/Reports/2009/15-The-Internet-and-Civic-Engagement.aspx (accessed June 26, 2011).

Smith, D. (1992) Electronic village: Technology showcase, *Blue Ridge Business Journal,* February 15.

Smith, D. C. and Cypher, A. (1999) Making programming easier for children, in A. Druin (ed.) *The Design of Children's Technology.* San Francisco: Morgan Kaufmann.

Smith, M. and Kollock, P. (eds) (1999) *Communities in cyberspace.* London: Routledge.

Smith, R. B. (1987) Experiences with the Alternate Reality Kit: An example of the tension between literalism and magic, *IEEE Computer Graphics,* 7(9): 42–50.

Stefik, M., Bobrow, D. G., Foster, G., Lanning, S. and Tatar, D. (1987) WYSIWIS revised: Early experiences with multiuser interfaces, *ACM Transactions on Office Information Systems,* 5(2): 147–67.

Stephanidis, C. (ed.) (2009) *Universal access in human–computer interaction: Applications and services: Proceedings of 5th International Conference on Universal Access in Human–Computer Interaction* (San Diego, July 19–24). Berlin: Springer.

Sutcliffe, A. and Mehandjiev, N. (eds) (2004) Special section on "End-user development," *Communications of the ACM,* 47(9): 31–66.

Suthers, D. and Weiner, A. (1995) Groupware for developing critical discussion skills, *Proceedings of the International Conference on Computer Support for Collaborative Learning* (Bloomington, Indiana, October 17–20). Hillsdale, NJ: Lawrence Erlbaum, pp. 341–8.

Sutton, W. and Kolaja, J. (1960) Elements of community action, *Social Forces*, 38: 325–31.

Tocqueville, A. de ([1835] 2003) *Democracy in America*, trans. G. Bevan. New York: Penguin.

Tönnies, F. ([1887] 2002) *Community and society (Gemeinschaft und Gesellschaft)*, trans. and ed. C. P. Loomis. New York: Dover.

Trabasso, T. and Stein, N. (1997) Narrating, representing and remembering event sequences, in P. W. van den Broek, P. J. Bauer and T. Bourg (eds) *Developmental spans in event comprehension and representation*. Mahwah, NJ: Lawrence Erlbaum, pp. 237–70.

Tyack, D. and Cuban, L. (1995) *Tinkering toward utopia: A century of public school reform*. Cambridge, MA: Harvard University Press.

Uncapher, W. (1999) New communities/new communication: Big Sky Telegraph and its community, in M. Smith and P. Kollock (eds) *Communities in cyberspace*. London: Routledge, pp. 264–89.

US Catholic Bishops (1986) Economic justice for all: Pastoral letter on Catholic social teaching and the US economy, available at http://www.osjspm.org/economic_justice_for_all.aspx (accessed May 30, 2011).

US Census (2010) *Computer use and ownership*, available at http://www.census.gov/population/www/socdemo/computer.html (accessed May 30, 2011).

US Department of Education (1994) *Goals 2000: Educate America Act*, available at http://www2.ed.gov/legislation/GOALS2000/TheAct/ (accessed May 29, 2011).

Vetter, R. J., Spell, C. and Ward, C. (1994) Mosaic and the World Wide Web, *IEEE Computer*, 27 (10): 49–57.

Virginia Department of Education (2005) Nine out of 10 Virginia schools now fully accredited: Two percent of schools to 92 percent in 8 years, Press release, October 25; available at http://www.doe.virginia.gov/VDOE/NewHome/pressreleases/2005/oct25.html (accessed April 26, 2010).

von Ahn, L. and Dabbish, L. (2004) Labeling images with a computer game, *Proceedings of the ACM Conference on Human Factors in Computing Systems* (Vienna, Austria, April 24–9). New York: Association for Computing Machinery, pp. 319–26.

von Ahn, L., Maurer, B., McMillen, C., Abraham D. and Blum, M. (2008) reCAPTCHA: Human-based character recognition via Web security measure, *Science*, 321(5895): 1465–8.

Vygotsky, L. S. (1978) *Mind in society*. Cambridge, MA: Harvard University Press.

Wadsworth, D. (1997) Building a strategy for successful public engagement, *Phi Delta Kappan*, 78(10): 749–52.

Wagner, M. (2007) Twelve things to do in Second Life that aren't embarrassing if your priest or rabbi finds out, *Information Week's Digital Life Weblog*, April 10, http://www.informationweek.com/blog/229216325 (accessed June 14, 2011).

Warren, R. (1978) *The community in America*. Chicago: Rand McNally.

Webber, M. (1963) Order in diversity: Community without propinquity, in L. Wingo (ed.) *Cities and space: The future use of urban land*. Baltimore: Johns Hopkins University Press.

Weber, M. ([1921] 1968) *Economy and society*. New York: Bedminster Press.

Weiner, B. (1992) *Human motivation: Metaphors, theories and research*. Newbury Park, CA: Sage.

Wellman, B. (1988) The community question re-evaluated, in M. P. Smith (ed.) *Power, community and the city*. New Brunswick, NJ: Transaction Books, pp. 81–107.

Wellman, B., Haase, A. Q., Witte, J. and Hampton, K. (2001) Does the Internet increase, decrease, or supplement social capital? Social networks, participation, and community commitment, *American Behavioral Scientist*, 45(3): 437–56.

Wenger, E. (1998) *Communities of practice: Learning, meaning, and identity*. New York: Cambridge University Press.

Wenger, E., McDermott and Snyder, W. (2002) *Cultivating communities of practice: A guide to managing knowledge*. Cambridge, MA: Harvard Business School Press.

Wiencko, J. A. (1993) The Blacksburg Electronic Village, *Internet Research*, 3(2): 31–40.

Williams, K. (2005) Social networks, social capital, and the use of information and communications technology in socially excluded communities: A study of community groups in Manchester, England. PhD dissertation, School of Information, University of Michigan, Ann Arbor.

Williams, M. G. (1994) Enabling schoolteachers to participate in the design of educational software, *Proceedings of Participatory Design Conference* (Chapel Hill, NC, October 27–8), pp. 153–7.

Wissman, J. (2002) Examining minimalism in training older adults in a software environment. Masters thesis, Industrial and Systems Engineering Department, Virginia Tech.

Wolff, K. H. (trans. and ed.) (1964) *The sociology of Georg Simmel*. New York: Free Press.

Zablocki, B. D. (1978) Communes, encounter groups, and the search for community, in K. W. Back (ed.) *In search for community: Encounter groups and social change*. Boulder, CO: Westview Press.

# Index

Printed and bound by CPI Group (UK) Ltd, Croydon, CR0 4YY

18/10/2024

01776243-0005